Grounds for Difference

GROUNDS *for* DIFFERENCE

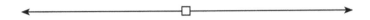

ROGERS BRUBAKER

Harvard University Press

Cambridge, Massachusetts
London, England

First Harvard University Press paperback edition, 2017
Second printing

Library of Congress Cataloging-in-Publication Data

Brubaker, Rogers, 1956–
    Grounds for difference / Rogers Brubaker.
        pages cm
    Includes bibliographical references and index.
    ISBN 978-0-674-74396-0 (cloth : alk. paper)
    ISBN 978-0-674-97545-3 (pbk.)
    1. Equality.   2. Ethnicity.   3. Race.   4. Religious tolerance.   5. Cultural
pluralism   6. Nationalism.   7. Transnationalism.   I. Title.
    HM821.B78 2015
    305.8—dc23

                                                              2014024298

For Susan

Contents

Acknowledgments

I am grateful to my students and colleagues for making UCLA so conge-
nial an intellectual home for nearly a quarter of a century. Special thanks go
to the students in my Comparative Ethnicity, Race, and Nationalism semi-
nar, where many of the ideas developed in this volume began to take shape;
to Andreas Wimmer, for his characteristically penetrating comments on
several chapters, and for his enlivening intellectual companionship and
friendship during his decade at UCLA; and to Roger Waldinger and Gail
Kligman, for long-standing friendship and colleagueship.

For exceptionally helpful critical comments on individual chapters, I
thank Mara Loveman, Jaeeun Kim, Peter Stamatov, Matthias Koenig, Rob
Mare, Matt Desmond, Mustafa Emirbayer, Sébastien Chauvin, Aaron Pan-
ofsky, Rick Biernacki, Richard Jenkins, Ann Swidler, Gil Eyal, John Bowen,
David Gellner, and Regina Bendix. Thanks also to Michael Banton, Abby
Day, Steven Mock, Trevor Stack, Maria Abascal, and Miguel Centeno, who
commented on an earlier version of Chapter 3 for a symposium in *Studies in
Ethnicity and Nationalism*. For arranging opportunities to present work
in progress, as well as for their comments on that work, I thank Michèle
Lamont, Kazuko Suzuki, Diego von Vacano, Nitsan Chorev, Sinisa Male-
sevic, Matthias Koenig, John Breuilly, Andrew Richards, Janine Dahinden,
Bernd Giesen, Phil Gorski, Natan Sznaider, Ulrike Ziemer, Donna Gabaccia,
and Consuelo Corradi. I am grateful to Kausar Mohammed for editorial
assistance and to Kristen Kao and Amy Zhou for research assistance.

Special thanks go to Susan Ossman, who provided crucial advice on the shape of the book as a whole and with whom I talked through much of the argument of the first three chapters, taking notes, one memorable spring afternoon, on the (paper) tablecloth at the River's End restaurant in Jenner, California, at the mouth of the Russian River. Those who know us know how much more I have to thank Susan for.

I would also like to express my gratitude to a set of remarkable teachers and scholars of the generation preceding my own, who have served as models of intellectual vocation: Allan Silver, my dissertation advisor at Columbia University, an exemplary thinker, writer, and teacher, and a model of intellectual civility, whose attunedness to religion, long before this became fashionable among political sociologists, encouraged me to think about religion in relation to ethnicity and nationalism; Gianfranco Poggi, whom I was fortunate to get to know long after reading his magnificently concise *The Development of the Modern State* as a graduate student; the late Aristide Zolberg, whose foundational work on international migration in historical and political perspective opened up new vistas for me as a graduate student and, a quarter century later, inspired Chapter 3 of this volume; the late Charles Tilly, whose powerful and restless mind and inexhaustible intellectual energy led in so many fruitful directions and whose *Durable Inequality,* which originated as a series of lectures at UCLA, provides the point of departure for Chapter 1; and the late Pierre Bourdieu, whose extraordinarily rich and generative oeuvre has served as a key point of reference since I immersed myself in it for an MA thesis thirty-five years ago.

EARLIER VERSIONS of Chapters 3–7 have been previously published (Chapter 7 only in Italian). I have taken the opportunity to make a number of minor (and, for Chapters 5 and 6, more substantial) changes for this volume and to incorporate some references to literature that has appeared since some chapters (notably Chapter 5) were first published. References have been consolidated into a single integrated bibliography.

Chapter 3, "Language, Religion, and the Politics of Difference," appeared in *Nations and Nationalism* 19 (2013):1–20, published by John Wiley & Sons. Chapter 4 appeared under a slightly different title as "Religion and Nationalism: Four Approaches" in *Nations and Nationalism* 18 (2012): 2–20, published by John Wiley & Sons. An earlier version of Chapter 5, "The 'Diaspora' Diaspora," appeared in *Ethnic and Racial Studies* 28.1 (2005): 1–19, published by Taylor & Francis. An earlier version of Chapter 6 appeared under a slightly different title as "Migration, Membership, and the Modern Nation-State: Internal and External Dimensions of the

Politics of Belonging" in *Journal of Interdisciplinary History* 41 (2010): 61–78. Chapter 7 was published in Italian as "Nazionalismo, etnicità et modernità," pp. 83–93 in *Dalla modernità alle modernità multiple,* edited by Consuelo Corradi and Donatella Pacelli (Soveria Mannelli, Italy: Rubbettino, 2011).

Grounds for Difference

Introduction

GROUNDS FOR DIFFERENCE is a sequel of sorts to my *Ethnicity without Groups*. Like that volume, this one seeks to develop fresh perspectives on the social organization and political expression of cultural difference. But it does so in quite different ways that reflect new directions in my work.

Ethnicity without Groups was written in analytical counterpoint to sustained ethnographic research. It was informed by a shift from the "big structures, large processes, [and] huge comparisons" (Tilly 1984) addressed in my two previous books (1992, 1996) to the smaller scale, more finely observed processes and dynamics that were the primary focus of *Nationalist Politics and Everyday Ethnicity in a Transylvanian Town* (Brubaker et al. 2006). *Ethnicity without Groups* was also informed by a twofold critical impulse, directed against prevailing "groupist" idioms in the study of ethnicity and against complacent and clichéd forms of constructivism, the most readily available alternative to such groupism. This critical engagement gave the book a rather programmatic cast, expressed in the proposal to analyze ethnicity "without groups," to go "beyond identity," and to conceive of ethnicity as a perspective on the world, rather than a thing in the world.

The present volume is less programmatic and more substantive, less focused on conceptual critique than on theoretical and empirical analysis, and less concerned with analytical disaggregation than with analytical synthesis. After the microanalytic turn of my recent books, the present volume also returns to meso- and macroanalytic levels of analysis.

Grounds for Difference emerged from three new lines of work, engaging three increasingly salient contexts for the contemporary politics of difference: the *return of inequality*, the *return of biology*, and the *return of the sacred*.[3]

The dramatic intensification of inequality in the United States and elsewhere in recent decades and, more recently still, the quiet devastation wreaked by the Great Recession have focused renewed public and academic attention on inequality. The Occupy movement galvanized and dramatized, if only briefly, concern with inequality. President Obama—quoting Pope Francis's denunciation of economic exclusion and inequality in his encyclical "Evangelii Gaudium"—called increasing economic inequality the "defining challenge of our time."[1] Serious journalistic analyses of inequality have proliferated in the past few years, along with books and papers written by scholars for broad public audiences, as well as more strictly scholarly research.[2] And Thomas Piketty's 685-page *Capital in the Twenty-First Century* (2014) became an unlikely best-seller.

Inequality has of course been a perennial theme in the social sciences; it never disappeared as an object of social theory and social research. But work influenced by the cultural and discursive turn focused more attention on identity and difference than on inequality, and more attention on inequalities in recognition than in resources. As students of race, ethnicity, and gender followed the cultural turn, they lost traction on structural forms of inequality grounded in the division of labor, the organization of production, or control over the means of coercion.[3]

In the past decade or so, the cultural and discursive turn in the study of difference seems to have run its course. In a context of economic crisis and exacerbated inequality, this has prompted efforts to reconnect structural sources of inequality with cultural dimensions of difference.[4] Chapter 1 contributes to this undertaking by analyzing how categories of difference are implicated in the production and reproduction of inequality. Taking as its point of departure a critical engagement with Charles Tilly's influential theory of categorical inequality, the chapter considers the very different ways in which citizenship, gender, and ethnicity (broadly understood to include race as well as certain forms of religion) work to generate and sustain inequality. It then goes on to outline—as an alternative to Tilly's exploitation and opportunity hoarding—three general processes through which categories of difference enter into the making and remaking of inequality: the allocation of persons to positions, the social production of persons, and the social definition of positions.

The second crucial context for the contemporary politics of difference is the *return of biology*. Of course biologically informed ways of construing sameness and difference did not disappear with the decline of scientific racism in the middle of the twentieth century. But biological (and notably genetic) discourse came to focus more on individuals and families than on group differences (Skinner 2006: 475; Condit 1999), while the social sciences came to construe diversity through the prism of culture rather than nature. A reflexive antibiologism became central to the disciplinary identity of sociologists in particular. Most sociologists have been uninterested in the interface between the social and the biological, and many have been hostile to any attempt to show the bearing of biology on social life, seeing "biology" and "the social" as "locked in an explanatory zero-sum game" (Freese et al. 2003: 234). Yet this has begun to change. In the past decade or so, a number of prominent sociologists (including Douglas Massey [2002] in his presidential address to the American Sociological Association) have argued that a principled antipathy to the biological is both intellectually narrow-minded and professionally self-defeating, threatening to make sociology irrelevant in an intellectual and social context in which the biological sciences are increasingly powerful and prestigious.

The return of biology has been particularly striking—but also particularly fraught, contested, and even paradoxical—in the study of race and ethnicity. Academic understandings of race and ethnicity—if not popular understandings—had moved decisively "beyond biology" in the final decades of the twentieth century. The triumph of constructivist understandings seemed to make biology irrelevant. While *myths* of descent were central to ethnicity, *actual* descent was irrelevant; and while the *classification* of bodies was central to race, the *bodies themselves* were not. Race was "only skin deep"; it had no deeper biological reality.

This has changed dramatically in the past fifteen years. The Human Genome Project was celebrated for highlighting species-wide genetic *commonality*, but the subsequent flood of relatively inexpensive genomic data has occasioned intensified exploration of between-group genetic *differences*. These differences have been explicitly linked to folk understandings of race, giving new respectability to the claim that social understandings of race have a biological foundation. The cultural authority of genomics has transformed understandings and practices of race and ethnicity in biomedical research, forensic investigation, and ancestry testing; it has informed new kinds of political claims; and it has challenged seemingly settled constructivist theories of race and ethnicity.

Genetically informed accounts of difference have deeply ambivalent implications for understandings of race and ethnicity. They risk reinforcing essentialist folk understandings of identity; yet they can also serve to undermine notions of "pure" or sharply bounded groups, highlighting instead the inextricable mixedness of all human populations and the genetic uniqueness of every individual. Chapter 2 explores the complex and ambivalent implications of the "return of biology" for the theory and practice of ethnicity, race, and nationhood. It surveys developments in biomedicine, forensics, genetic genealogy, and identity politics, and it concludes by outlining a constructivist response to the new objectivist and naturalist accounts of race and ethnicity.

The third undertheorized context for the contemporary politics of difference is the *return of the sacred*. The idea of secularization has figured centrally in accounts of modernity, and it has been the primary organizing paradigm of the sociology of religion. Developments of recent decades—the resurgence of political Islam, the spectacular global spread of Pentecostalism, and the renewed vitality of Christian, Jewish, Hindu, and Muslim fundamentalisms—have made simplistic versions of secularization theory ripe for criticism. Some theorists have spoken of "desecularization" (Berger 1999) or of "post-secular society" (Habermas 2008). But as other leading sociologists of religion have argued (Casanova 1994; Gorski and Altinordu 2008), secularization theory is more complex, interesting, and robust than many critics suggest.

Secularization has been understood in different ways by different theorists, but it generally designates one or more of three distinct processes: the *differentiation* of religion from other spheres of social life; the *decline* of religious belief or practice; or the *privatization* of religion. As José Casanova (1994) has argued, there is strong evidence for differentiation but only weak evidence (outside Europe) for decline. About the privatization thesis, the evidence is interestingly mixed. Religion (or its close cousin, spirituality) *has* become for many (especially but not exclusively in the West) an increasingly individual, subjective, and private matter—an affair of the heart, with little relevance for the public square. Yet recent decades have witnessed a striking resurgence of what Casanova calls "public religion." Against the expectations of the secularization theory of a generation ago, religion has refused to remain safely cantoned within a depoliticized private realm; it has insisted on entering the public sphere and making claims about the organization of public life.

The resurgence of public religion has major implications for how we understand diversity, multiculturalism, and the politics of difference. *That* societies worldwide are becoming more diverse and pluralistic is a truism, but *how* they are becoming more diverse is seldom examined. Discussions of diversity—academic debates as well as broader public discussions—often proceed in striking indifference to religion, as if the diversity that mattered were exhausted by race, ethnicity, gender, and sexuality. Yet the most vexed and contentious forms of diversity—what some political theorists have called "deep diversity"—are increasingly, and fundamentally, grounded in religious worldviews and ways of life.

The study of religion and the study of ethnicity, race, and nationalism have been largely separate domains of inquiry, with relatively little cross-fertilization between them. This mutual isolation has been detrimental to both fields. Two chapters in the present volume seek to remedy this by integrating religion more closely into the study of ethnicity and nationalism. Chapter 3 does so by way of a sustained comparison between religion and language as domains of group-forming cultural practice. Both religion and language are ways of identifying oneself and others, and of construing sameness and difference. In the language of Pierre Bourdieu, both are basic principles of vision and division of the social world. Both divide the world, in popular understandings, into bounded and largely self-reproducing communities. And claims are made in the name of both kinds of communities for recognition, resources, and reproduction. In all these respects, language and religion are both *similar* to ethnicity and nationalism and *similarly intertwined* with them. Language or religion or both together are central to most ethnic and national identifications, and they frequently serve as key emblems or symbols of such identifications.

Yet religion and language differ in key ways that have major implications for the political accommodation of cultural difference. Language is an inescapable medium of public as well as private life; religion is not. The state must privilege a particular language or set of languages, but it need not privilege a particular religion. The expansion of state employment, the introduction of universal schooling, and the increasingly "semantic" nature of work in an urban, mobile, and literate society have made language a crucial form of cultural capital. For all these reasons, language is chronically and pervasively politicized in the modern world, while much of religion has become privatized and depoliticized. On the other hand, religious pluralism tends to be more intergenerationally robust and more deeply institutionalized than linguistic pluralism in contemporary liberal societies. It also entails deeper and more divisive forms of diversity. Language is a medium of communication and a symbol of identity; it is not a structure of authority. But religion often involves an authoritative, binding, and comprehensive set of norms. These do not simply regulate private behavior; they reach into the public realm, addressing such matters as gender, sexuality, family life, education, and social policy. Conflicts over these matters often involve deep conflicts of principle and fundamental differences of worldview.

On a time scale of centuries, religion has become much *less* central to public life and political contestation in the West, while language—with the growth of democracy, mass education, urban commercial society, and the modern state—has become much *more* central. Yet in recent decades, conflicts over language have eased in liberal polities, while conflicts over religion have intensified, driven by the resurgence of public religion. The upshot is that religion has tended to displace language as the most heatedly contested terrain of the politics of cultural difference.

Chapter 4 addresses the relation between religion and nationalism. Two antithetical views have long structured discussions of this relation. One sees nationalism as intrinsically secular and links the rise of nationalism to the decline of religion. The other sees nationalism as intrinsically religious, as a "political religion" or a "cult of the nation" that sacralizes the collectivity and mobilizes religious emotion. While both views capture something important, neither is particularly nuanced, and a small but growing literature has begun to develop a variety of more complex accounts. Building on these accounts, this chapter identifies and critically analyzes four ways of studying the relation between religion and nationalism. The first is to treat religion and nationalism, along with ethnicity and race, as *analogous* phenomena. The second is to specify ways in which religion helps *explain* things about nationalism: its origin, its power, or its distinctive character in particular cases. The third is to treat religion as *part* of nationalism and to specify modes of interpenetration and intertwining. And the fourth is to posit a distinctively religious *form* of nationalism.

The chapter concludes by reconsidering—and, with qualifications, affirming—the much-criticized understanding of nationalism as a distinctively secular phenomenon. Nationalism and religion are often closely intertwined. But even when the idioms of religion and nation are intertwined, the fundamental ontologies and structures of justification differ. Nationalist politics presupposes and pivots on a shared public understanding of "the nation." On this understanding, nations are entitled to "their own" polities, and authority is legitimate only if it arises from "the nation." The development and diffusion of this structure of political argument and cultural understanding were made possible, in part, by a process of secularization. *Not*, to be sure, by the decline of religion: early forms of nationalist politics and national consciousness emerged in a period of intensified rather than declining religiosity. But another aspect of secularization—the emergence of understandings of economy, society, and polity as autonomous realms, differentiated from the religious sphere and governed by their own laws—did facilitate the development of the social and political imaginary that underwrites and informs modern nationalism.

The remaining three chapters address in different ways the *transnational and global dimensions* of ethnicity and nationalism. In the past two decades, a number of scholars have posited a fundamental shift toward a transnational or postnational world. They have argued that new communications and transportation infrastructures strengthen transborder ties and erode the capacities of nation-states to control cross-border flows of people, goods, messages, images, ideas, and cultural products. This, they suggest, has realigned the relation between politics and culture by detaching identities, loyalties, and subjectivities from the territorial and institutional frame of the nation-state.

The category *diaspora* figures centrally in attempts to theorize the social organization and political expression of cultural difference in this putatively postnational world. Diaspora-talk has exploded in recent decades, inside and outside the academy. But as the category has proliferated, its meaning has been stretched in various directions. Chapter 5 critically engages this burgeoning literature. It traces the dispersion of the term in semantic, conceptual, and disciplinary space; analyzes three core elements that continue to be understood as constitutive of diaspora; and proposes to treat diaspora not as a bounded entity but as an idiom, stance, and claim.

The chapter also skeptically assesses the claim that recent decades have witnessed an epochal shift in the organization of belonging. Notwithstanding repeated assertions of its obsolescence, the nation-state remains the decisive instance of belonging even in a rapidly globalizing world; and struggles over belonging *in* and *to* the nation-state remain the most consequential form of membership politics. The powers of the nation-state are in some respects increasing rather than declining. Far from escaping the control of the state, for example, migration is subjected to ever more sophisticated technologies of regulation and control. This does not mean, of course, that borders are hermetically sealed; but there is no indication that states (or the Schengen zone) have been losing their capacity to regulate the flow of persons across their borders.

The diaspora and transnationalism literatures are right to highlight the ways loyalties, identities, and subjectivities cut across territorial frontiers. But this does not entail a shift from a national to a postnational mode of membership politics or, still less, a shift from a state-centered to a nonstate mode of organizing migration and membership. States' ties to transborder populations—and transborder populations' claims on "homeland" states—are expanding and strengthening. But these new forms of external membership are neither trans-state nor transnational; they are forms of transborder nationalism. As such, they represent an extension and adaptation of the nation-state model, not its transcendence (Brubaker and Kim 2011: 21–22).

Chapter 6 places these new forms of transborder nationalism in the broader context of the politics of membership and belonging in the nation-state. It distinguishes internal and external dimensions of the politics of belonging. The internal dimension concerns people who are durably situated within the territorial ambit of the state but who are not—or not fully—members of that state. The external dimension concerns those who are durably situated outside the territorial ambit and jurisdiction of the state yet who claim—or are claimed—to belong, in some sense, to the state or to "its" nation. The chapter identifies four sources of the internal and external politics of belonging: the movement of people over borders, the movement of borders over people, deep and enduring inequalities between mainstream and minority populations, and the persisting legacies of empire.

The global diffusion and institutionalization of "diaspora" as a category of self-understanding and claims-making is one instance of a broader process of the diffusion and institutionalization of a set of basic categories of social and political understanding. The set includes nation, ethnicity, race, religion, indigeneity, and minorityhood, all of which have been institutionalized worldwide, in differing forms and to differing degrees, as ways of conceptualizing, organizing, and constituting diverse populations (Brubaker 2012). Together these comprise part of what might be called—at the risk of putting too grand a label on it—the "categorical infrastructure of modernity."

In recent decades, a vigorous literature on "multiple modernities" (Eisenstadt 2000; Spohn 2003) has challenged the idea of convergence around a single, originally Western pattern of institutions and cultural understandings; this literature has emphasized instead the irreducible multiplicity of institutional patterns and cultural and political programs and models. While fully acknowledging enduring institutional and cultural diversity, Chapter 7 makes the case for a "single modernity" perspective on ethnicity and nationalism. Such a perspective brings into focus the global, interconnected nature of the processes—socioeconomic, political, and cultural—that have generated and sustained nationalism, ethnicity, race, and related categories as basic forms of cultural understanding, social organization, and political claims-making. And it highlights the worldwide diffusion of a set of rhetorical idioms, organizational forms, and political templates that provide the cultural and institutional materials for various forms of nationalism and politicized ethnicity.

Nationalism, for example, was from the beginning an internationally circulating discourse. As it was taken up in new settings, it was of course adapted to local circumstances and blended with indigenous idioms. Yet the linked ideas and ideals of nation, state, citizenship, and popular sovereignty form a distinctive cultural, ideological, and organizational "package" that has diffused worldwide in the past two centuries.

The intertwined idioms of nationhood, peoplehood, and citizenship—like the idioms of race, religion, rights, and revolution—are eminently flexible and adaptable. They can be used to legitimize a polity but also to challenge its legitimacy, to demand a new polity, or to claim autonomy or resources within an existing polity. And the abstract category of nationhood or peoplehood can be imagined in a variety of ways: the nation can be understood to be grounded in citizenship, history, language, descent, race, religion, way of life, or shared political experience. A "single modernity" perspective can make sense of both the core elements of the "package" and the flexible adaptability and chronic contestation of its component ideas and organizational forms.

CHAPTER ONE

Difference and Inequality

W HAT IS THE RELATION between difference and inequality? I want to approach this deceptively simple yet formidably abstract question by way of a thought experiment. Consider a world characterized—like our own—by both horizontal and vertical social divisions (Blau 1977: 8–9). On a horizontal plane, people categorize themselves and others according to a *logic of significant similarity and difference.* They identify with others whom they see as similar in some meaningful way, and they distinguish themselves from others whom they see as significantly different—in ethnicity, nationality, citizenship, language, religion, gender, sexuality, taste, temperament, or the like. On a vertical plane, people can be ranked according to whether they have *more or less* of some generally desired good: more or less wealth, income, education, respect, health, occupational prestige, legal rights, basic existential security, or the like.

Now imagine—and here's where the thought experiment comes in—that horizontal categories and vertical rankings were entirely independent of one another. The horizontal categories into which people sort themselves and others—groupings based on ethnicity, religion, or musical taste, for example—would not differ systematically by income, wealth, education, and so on. Differences of income, wealth, and education would be differences *within* social categories, not *between* them. Members of different categories would have the same chances of being ranked high or low on any vertical dimension.

In this hypothetical world, difference would have no bearing on inequality. People would be different, and they would be unequal; but the mechanisms that generate inequalities would be unconnected with the processes through which people sort themselves and others into categories based on similarity and difference. The mechanisms that generate inequalities would be difference-blind: who *is* what would be independent of who *gets* what.

This is evidently not the world we inhabit. In our world, differences of race, ethnicity, language, religion, gender, sexuality, citizenship, and so on *do* have a systematic bearing on inequality. But how? This is the question I address in this chapter, focusing on the ways *categorical* differences—differences that are organized, experienced, and represented in terms of discrete, bounded, and relatively stable categories (such as black and white, Sunni and Shiite, male and female, citizen and foreigner)—are implicated in the production and reproduction of inequality.

These and other ascribed categorical differences are not *intrinsically* linked to inequality; *different* does not necessarily imply *unequal*. The relation between difference and inequality is contingent, not necessary; it is empirical, not conceptual. And the degree to which and manner in which inequality is structured along categorical lines vary widely over time and context. Certain categorical differences that were once pervasively implicated in regimes of inequality—such as distinctions among Protestants, Catholics, and Jews and among certain ethnic categories in the United States—are no longer so implicated today. And a wide range of legally mandated forms of categorically unequal treatment has been delegitimized throughout the developed world in a remarkably short span of time. To study the relation between difference and inequality is to study historically situated social processes; it is not to identify timeless truths.

I begin by critically engaging Charles Tilly's influential account of how categories of difference are implicated in the generation and maintenance of inequality. Taking issue with Tilly's claim that major categories of difference work in fundamentally similar ways, I consider in subsequent sections how citizenship, gender, and ethnicity—broadly understood as including race as well as ethnicity-like forms of religion—contribute to the production and reproduction of inequality in quite differing ways. I return in the penultimate section to a more general level of analysis and outline three general processes through which categories of difference work to produce and sustain position-mediated inequalities: the allocation of persons to reward-bearing positions; the social production of unequally equipped categories of persons; and the social definition of positions and their rewards. In the final section, I discuss ways in which inequalities not only are mediated by reward-bearing positions but also—notably in the case of the social distribution of honor—attach directly to categories of persons, independently of the positions they occupy. I suggest in closing that even as inequality has increased dramatically in certain respects in recent decades, it has assumed forms that are less strictly categorical.

Tilly on Categorical Inequality

The theory of categorical inequality Tilly developed in *Durable Inequality* (1998) focuses on organizations—firms, hospitals, universities, and states, for example—as key sites of inequality. Organizations are key because inequalities of wealth, income, prestige, and even health and basic physical security are increasingly mediated by positions in formal organizations. Jobs are the obvious example of such positions. Income inequality in the United States depends primarily on unequal rewards from jobs rather than unequal holdings of capital assets. Today's rich are not rentiers; they are the "working rich" (Saez 2013; Godechot 2007): highly paid employees and entrepreneurs.[1] Tilly's account focuses primarily on how inequality is generated through linked and bounded clusters of jobs to which sharply differing rewards are attached. But positions in organizations structure inequality in other ways as well. Citizenship, for example, is a position in an organization (the modern state); as I show below, it profoundly shapes life chances on a global scale, structuring access to vastly different rewards and opportunities.

Durable inequality, on this account, turns on the matching or pairing of *internal* organizational categories with pervasively available *external* categories. Internal categories designate unequal positions (or clusters of positions) within an organization, differentiated by some combination of remuneration, authority, working conditions, and mobility opportunities. Examples include enlisted soldier and officer, doctor and nurse, executive and secretary, and the like. External categories are those that serve as major axes of distinction and inequality in the wider social environment, around which cluster scripts and stories that explain and justify the inequalities. Examples include gender, race, ethnicity, citizenship, religion, and education.[2]

Tilly shows how external categories are "imported" into organizations along with scripts and local knowledge—shared understandings (or stereotypes) about the incumbents of those categories. He gives particular attention to the "matching" of internal and external categories: the processes through which positions in organizations are allocated such that major internal categorical divisions (between executive and secretary, for example) coincide with major external categorical divisions (between men and women, for example).

This is an original and fertile way of thinking about the organizational dimension of durable inequality. But while Tilly's account of the mechanisms that sustain durable inequality is richly suggestive, it is also elusive. Probing the ambiguities in Tilly's account can bring into sharper focus the social processes through which categorical differences are implicated in the production and reproduction of inequality.

Categorical inequality, for Tilly, is generated in the first instance by two mechanisms: exploitation and opportunity hoarding.[3] Exploitation "operates when powerful, connected people command resources from which they draw significantly increased returns by coordinating the effort of outsiders whom they exclude from the full value added by that effort" (1998: 10). As the last clause of the definition suggests, this notion of exploitation—like the Marxist notion—would seem to depend on a theory of value. But Tilly neither endorses the notoriously problematic Marxian labor theory of value nor proposes an alternative. His notion of exploitation remains informal, resting on a commonsense understanding of powerful people coordinating the labor of outsiders and reaping the benefits of that labor.

The reference to "outsiders" suggests that categories of difference are implicated in processes of exploitation. Tilly illustrates this by analyzing the exploitation of Africans in South Africa under apartheid and of women in capitalist labor markets. While duly noting the evidently sharp differences, he argues that exploitation works through analogous causal processes in the two cases (1998: 136). The key in both cases is matching between major organizational divisions and external categorical pairs (White/African and male/female).[4] Such matching is said to facilitate exploitation. The reasons for this are not fully spelled out, but the argument seems to be that matching stabilizes regimes of inequality and lowers the cost of maintaining them.

The matching processes that implicate race in South Africa under apartheid and gender in capitalist labor markets may be analogous at a certain level of abstraction. But they differ sharply in both degree and kind. Racial categories in South Africa under apartheid were constructed from above, legally defined, formally administered, and coercively enforced. They are not easily subsumed under Tilly's notion of "external categories"—categories that are pervasively available in the wider environment and "imported" into organizations along with scripts and stories. Racial categories were of course pervasively available in South Africa prior to the construction of the system of apartheid. But the available categories were radically reconstructed, codified, and formalized by the state in a gigantic top-down exercise in authoritative categorization. The processes through which racial categories were matched with economic position were directly political, legal, administrative, coercive, and formalized. The processes through which gender is matched with positions in capitalist firms, by contrast, are loose, informal, probabilistic, decentralized, and mediated through individual-level self-understandings, occupational aspirations, and human capital endowments; and the *degree* of matching is also much lower.

Tilly identifies "categorical exclusion" as a key element of his general analytical model of exploitation (1998: 128–132). This might seem to imply exclusion on the basis of categories of difference like race, gender, or citizenship, as in the examples he discusses at length. But there is an equivocation here. Categorical exclusion involves "boundaries between unequal and paired categories in which members of one category benefit from control of sequestered resources and receive returns from the other's output" (1998: 131). But what are the "unequal and paired categories"? They may simply be *internal* categories, defining unequally rewarded clusters of positions within an organization (manager and worker, doctor and nurse, or officer and enlisted soldier). Or they may be *external* categories (such as race, gender, or citizenship) that are matched (to differing degrees and through differing processes) to the internal categories. Tilly highlights the latter configuration in his theoretical argument, but exploitation requires only the former. And his most powerful and compelling empirical analyses of "unequal and paired categories" that generate clearly categorical forms of exclusion in contemporary liberal democratic capitalist contexts concern internal organizational categories, not external categories.

In Marx's account, from which Tilly claims to draw inspiration, exploitation requires only what Tilly would call internal categories: owners of the means of production, on the one hand, and workers who have been separated from the means of production, on the other. It does not require the matching of internal and external categories. And in Tilly's own account, exploitation requires only that some—those who control valuable yet labor-demanding resources—enlist and coordinate the labor of others, while reaping for themselves (at least part of) the value added by that labor. These others need not differ by race, gender, citizenship, or the like; they may simply occupy subordinate organizationally defined positions (casual in relation to career employees; adjuncts in relation to tenured professors; or nurses in relation to physicians). These organizational distinctions may—and of course often do—map onto external categories (such that nurses are overwhelmingly women, and physicians, as was the case not so very long ago, overwhelmingly men); and Tilly calls attention to such cases. But the phenomenon of exploitation—and, more generally, the dynamics of capitalism—does not *pivot* or *depend* on this mapping.[5] And while the matching of internal and external categories may stabilize regimes of categorical inequality (1998: 76, 78, 81), it may also have the opposite effect: in a world in which formal categorical inequality has been powerfully delegitimized, the tight matching of internal and external categories may *destabilize* regimes of inequality, while the *loosening* of connections between internal and external categories may help legitimize and stabilize massive inequalities in control over organizational resources.

By identifying the processes and mechanisms through which external categories of difference can be linked to internal organizational categories, Tilly shows *how inequality can be categorical,* but he does not show *how categorical* the generation of inequality really is: how centrally implicated are categories of difference like race, ethnicity, gender, and citizenship in the processes that generate inequality. I shall argue in the conclusion to the chapter that even as "the intensity of capitalist inequality" (Tilly 1998: 38) has increased substantially in recent decades, categories of difference—with some exceptions—figure in the production and reproduction of inequality in an increasingly gradational and distributional manner rather than in the more strictly categorical manner suggested by Tilly's notion of the matching of internal and external categories.

The second mechanism generating categorical inequality is what Tilly, building on Weber's discussion of social closure, calls opportunity hoarding. This occurs when members of a "categorically bounded network" (1998: 91) reserve for themselves access to some valuable resource, such as job opportunities, clients, information, marriage partners, credit, patronage, or the right to practice a profession or trade. Like exploitation, opportunity hoarding depends on a boundary between insiders who control a valuable resource and outsiders who do not. But while exploitation requires insiders to mobilize the labor of outsiders, and then to exclude them from the full value added by that labor, opportunity hoarding is conceptually simpler: it does not require the coordination of the labor of outsiders, just their exclusion from access to the resource (1998: 91).[6] Tilly gives many examples in passing but focuses on immigrant ethnic niches and, more briefly, licensed trades and professions.

"Categorically bounded networks" is a suggestive phrase, though an elusive one that Tilly does not seek to clarify. It usefully evokes three ways in which categories may enter into the workings of networks. First, networks may take root in categorically organized institutions (such as ethnic churches or associations). Second, network members may account for their connectedness in categorical terms (for example, through stories about common origins or common attributes). This self-understanding may lead them to exclude entire categories of outsiders from their networks and to limit new ties to categorical insiders. Recognized category membership may thus offer a point of entry into a network, even if it does not guarantee acceptance in the network; categorical outsiders, on the other hand, may have no chance of acceptance. A common language or religion, finally, may lower transaction costs, foster trust and accountability, promote the formation of social capital, and facilitate the development of networks of cooperative action (Landa 1981).

Its suggestiveness notwithstanding, the notion of "categorically bounded networks" conceals a tension, joining elements with quite different logics that may work separately in practice. Categories are defined by commonality, networks by connectedness. Categories are classes of equivalent elements; networks are sets of relationships. Category members are not necessarily connected to one another, and relationally connected people need not belong to the same category. Definitionally positing "categorically bounded networks" as the agents of opportunity hoarding elides the difference between *network-based* and *category-based* modes of social closure and forecloses the question of whether, when, and how categories of difference are involved in insiders' efforts to monopolize goods and opportunities.[7]

Keeping in mind the distinct logics of networks and categories makes it clear that networks—of friends, kin, or collaborators, for example—can hoard opportunities, regardless of whether their members belong to the same category. Even when their members do belong to the same category, the boundary between insiders (who can benefit from the monopolized opportunities) and outsiders is often determined by relational connectedness, not mere categorical commonality: what matters is *whom you know,* not just *who you are.* All network members may belong to the same ethnic category, for example, but not all members of the ethnic category belong to the network. To outsiders who belong to other ethnic categories, such opportunity hoarding may *appear* categorical; but those who belong to the same ethnic category, yet not to the relevant network, will be just as effectively excluded. The boundaries of networks, then—even ethnically organized networks—seldom correspond to the boundaries of categories; the line between insiders and outsiders depends on connectedness, not mere categorical commonality. Still, it's clear that network-based opportunity hoarding can and does contribute to categorical inequality, as African Americans, for example, get shut out of jobs in immigrant-dominated niches (Waldinger 1997).

While some forms of opportunity hoarding turn on informal relational connectedness, others turn on formal category membership. This is notably the case for licensed trades and professions. Here the boundary between insiders and outsiders—between those permitted to practice the profession or trade and others—is rigorously categorical. At the categorical boundary, networks are irrelevant: what matters is not whom you know but simply whether or not you are a member of the licensed category. (Inside the categorical boundary, to be sure, networks are once again relevant: particular networks of practitioners may hoard clients, for example.) Other examples of formal category-based opportunity hoarding—not mentioned by Tilly—include contracts that restrict jobs to union members; clubs that restrict the use of facilities to members; systems of quotas that reserve positions for members of particular social categories; and, with some stretching, legislation that reserves certain benefits for members of certain categories.

Does this kind of category-based opportunity hoarding contribute to categorical inequality? In one sense, of course, it does: by definition, it reserves certain goods and opportunities for category members and excludes nonmembers. But occupational licensing—Tilly's main example of category-based occupational hoarding—does not necessarily contribute to categorical inequality in the larger sense that is the main focus of *Durable Inequality*. It does not necessarily contribute, that is, to inequality based on race, gender, or other major categories of difference. The operative categorical boundary is drawn between the licensed and the unlicensed, not, for example, between blacks and whites, or between men and women.

When opportunities are reserved for members of some internal, organizationally defined category (holders of an occupational license, for example, or members of a union, church, or club), this in itself does not contribute to categorical inequality in the broader sense. Category-based opportunity hoarding does, however, contribute to broader categorical inequality when admission to the *organizational* category depends on one's *social* category membership. Clubs that reserve facilities for members contribute to categorical inequality, for example, when they exclude women or blacks from membership. The same holds for churches or associations that exclude homosexuals, for legislation that bars same-sex marriage, and for labor unions that have historically excluded African Americans.

Yet contemporary occupational licensing regimes do not ordinarily involve this kind of two-stage category-based closure. Access to professional and occupational licenses—though it may in some cases require prolonged and expensive training—is in principle open to all, regardless of their social category membership. Licensing regimes constitute opportunity hoarding or social closure because they restrict competition by limiting the supply of practitioners, not because they exclude certain social categories from practicing. Where licensed occupations and social categories coincide—as in the case of nursing, for example, which remains overwhelmingly female, or manicurists, which is a Vietnamese ethnic niche—this is *not* because the licensing regime itself excludes persons belonging to other categories. The concentrations of women in nursing and Vietnamese among manicurists reflect other social processes, notably the sex-typing of jobs and workplaces in the former case, and ethnic niche formation in the latter (Snyder and Greene 2008; Eckstein and Nguyen 2011).

Tilly's pursuit of parsimony and penchant for abstraction lead him to argue that "gender, class, ethnicity, race, citizenship, and other pervasive categorical systems do not each operate sui generis but instead share many causal properties" (1998: 82). These shared causal properties make it possible to specify "how categories work" across domains of categorization and how categorical inequality is generated through cross-domain mechanisms of exploitation and opportunity hoarding. So much is subsumed under these headings, however, that the outlines begin to blur. Exploitation and opportunity hoarding are not clearly delineated analytical categories; they are loose collections of processes with different proximate causal logics. Tilly's notion of exploitation bundles together the legally formalized and directly coercive bureaucratic processes through which racial categories were matched with economic position in South Africa under apartheid and the informal, decentralized allocative and self-sorting processes through which gender is matched—much more loosely—with economic position in the ordinary workings of contemporary capitalism. Similarly, the notion of opportunity hoarding by categorically bounded networks conflates network-based and category-based processes.

In subsequent sections, I adopt a more differentiated and disaggregated strategy. Rather than assuming for the sake of theory-building that the major categories of difference are implicated in the production and reproduction of inequality in fundamentally *similar* ways, I begin with the assumption that citizenship, gender, and ethnicity contribute to regimes of durable inequality in interestingly *different* ways. These differences can help bring into focus—at a somewhat lower level of abstraction and in less parsimonious but more clearly delineated and analytically tractable manner—the specific ways in which categories of difference help to generate and maintain inequality. To understand the relation between difference and inequality, in other words, it is helpful to begin with *different kinds of difference.*[8]

Different Differences: Citizenship,
Gender, Ethnicity

Citizenship

I begin with citizenship because it contributes to the production and re-production of inequality in particularly clear, straightforward, analytically tractable, profound, pervasive, and yet inadequately theorized ways.

Students of inequality have paid little attention to citizenship, while students of citizenship long paid little attention to inequality. The influential line of work inaugurated by T. H. Marshall (1950), long dominant in the sociology of citizenship, highlighted the egalitarian dynamics of citizenship, seen as counteracting the inequality-generating logic of capitalism. In recent decades, to be sure, the duality of citizenship—internally inclusive but externally exclusive—has been widely recognized, and citizenship has been analyzed as an "instrument and object of social closure" (Brubaker 1992: chapter 1). Yet the exclusionary workings of citizenship have been studied in severely truncated perspective. The *visible* workings of citizenship (and related categories) within the territory of the state are well studied, but the more profound and consequential *invisible* workings of citizenship outside the territory of the state have been neglected.

In all modern states, conceived as the states of and for their citizens, citizenship and related categories of membership (like permanent resident status) function transparently as instruments of social closure. In the United States today, this is most salient at the boundary between citizens and permanent residents on the one hand and the roughly 11 million undocumented immigrants on the other, who are excluded from a vast range of rights, benefits, and opportunities, above all, the right to work and the right to secure residence in the territory.[9]

On a global scale, however, the visible exclusion of tens of millions of undocumented residents from a range of benefits *within* the territories of prosperous and peaceful states is dwarfed by the invisible exclusion of *billions* of noncitizens *from* the territories of such states. The categorical distinction between citizens and foreigners is not only built into the basic structure of the modern state; it is built into the basic structure of the modern state *system*—a system of bounded and exclusive citizenries, matched with bounded and exclusive territorial polities. By assigning every person at birth, in principle, to one and only one territorial state, the institution of citizenship is central to the fundamentally segmentary organization of the state system (Joppke 2003: 441).[10] The segmentary logic of citizenship binds the vast majority of the world's population to the state to which they have been assigned by the accident of birth. Given the immense economic, political, demographic, health, and environmental disparities among states, this segmentary system of forced immobility contributes decisively to perpetuating vast global inequalities in life chances.

"Forced immobility" might seem an odd or even perverse expression given the magnitude of international migration flows. Yet only about 3 percent of the world's people live outside the country of their birth, and fewer than half of these represent south-north migrants (International Organization for Migration 2013: 55). This amounts to a very large number in absolute terms, estimated at between 75 and 95 million in 2010, but it remains a small number in relation to the many hundreds of millions of people who would seek work, welfare, or security in prosperous and peaceful countries if they were free to do so, yet who can be routinely, legitimately, and invisibly excluded, simply by virtue of their citizenship (Brubaker 1992: ix).[11]

There is a circular quality to citizenship-based territorial closure. Only citizens enjoy free access to the territory, yet only (legal) residents have access to citizenship. This circularity permits nation-states to remain relatively closed and self-perpetuating communities, open only at the margins to the exogenous recruitment of new members (Brubaker 1992: 34).

The routine territorial excludability of noncitizens permits citizens of prosperous and peaceful countries to reserve (largely) for themselves a wide range of economic, political, social, and cultural goods, opportunities, and freedoms, not to mention such basic goods as relatively clean air and water, a functioning public health infrastructure, and public order and security. In Tilly's terminology, this amounts to opportunity hoarding on a colossal scale. Yet the contribution of citizenship to global inequality has been largely untheorized until recently—including by Tilly himself, who (like others) considers only the within-state workings of citizenship.[12] And apart from a few academic discussions, it remains legally, politically, and morally largely unchallenged. Those excluded *from* the territory—unlike those excluded *within* the territory of a liberal democratic state—have neither the legal standing nor the political and organizational resources to challenge their exclusion.[13] And unlike legally codified and administratively enforced exclusion on the basis of gender, race, or religion, exclusion on the basis of citizenship—an ascribed status like the others—continues to be taken for granted as natural and understood as morally and politically legitimate (Pritchett 2006: 77–92).

Citizenship-based territorial closure did not *produce* the vast between-country inequalities, but it does serve to *perpetuate* them. It does so by locking (most) people into the countries to which they were assigned at birth. These assigned positions carry over to subsequent generations. Citizenship is not just a privilege (or for those with a "bad" citizenship, a disability); it is an *inherited* privilege (or disability), and one that is transmitted, in turn, to one's descendants. As legal theorist Ayelet Shachar has argued in her aptly titled book *The Birthright Lottery* (2009), this makes citizenship (for people with the right kind of citizenship) a form of inherited property.[14] As for those with the wrong kind of citizenship, they and their descendants are bound to a subordinate position in a powerful and consequential global structure of unequal positions, constituted by nation-states with vastly unequal public and private goods and opportunities.

Citizenship is a unique category by virtue of its pivotal place in the overall segmentary architecture of the nation-state system. But in other respects it works just like other state-created or state-sanctioned categories whose workings are governed by administrative practice and dictated by law. Citizenship thus provides an occasion to note the distinctive dynamics of law—and, more broadly, formal rules—as a medium of categorical inequality. Law can be understood as a *disembedding* technology. It makes certain facts legally relevant, regardless of their social context, and defines all other considerations as irrelevant. When certain benefits are reserved by law for citizens—or for men, for whites, or for any other social category—all that matters, in principle, is one's category membership; other considerations are irrelevant. Legalization—or, more broadly, formalization—makes categorical exclusion more systematic, consistent, and rigorous: formally defined and administered categories like citizenship leave relatively little room for ambiguity and reduce the scope for negotiation. The administration of such formally mandated categorical inequality is thus relatively uniform across time and space. And formal exclusion tends to work in a more *categorical* way than informal exclusion; it creates and enforces sharper and more consistent boundaries between insiders and outsiders.

Of course the law on the books should not be conflated with the law in practice. Law is never fully disembedded, and laws—when enforced at all—are often not enforced uniformly.[15] The analytical point I want to underscore here is a comparative one. Formal categorization, coupled with formally mandated differential treatment, contributes to categorical inequality in a very different way from informal social categorization and informally practiced differential treatment. The antiformalism that has been central to sociology—the commitment to going behind formal, official structures and institutions in order to discover the real workings of things—should not blind us to the fact that formalization, codification, and legalization are themselves interesting and socially consequential social phenomena (Bourdieu 1987).

Gender

Like citizenship-based categorical inequality, gender-based categorical inequality can work through the medium of law (or, more broadly, formal
rules). The multiple legal disabilities long suffered by women are well
known. In the United States, for example, married women could not own
property or exercise independent legal agency until the second half of the
nineteenth century. Women were formally barred from a range of occupations, and they were not permitted to vote, hold elective office, or serve on
juries. Over the course of the past century and a half, however, the legal
disabilities have been abolished, and the law now serves to protect and
promote women's rights in a variety of domains. In contemporary liberal
democratic contexts, gender has ceased to work as a legally or otherwise
formally codified basis of exclusion.[16]

The elimination of *formal* gender-based inequalities, of course, has left
wide-ranging *substantive* inequalities in place, and these (unlike citizenship-
based inequalities) have been the subject of a very large literature. I limit
myself here—as in the subsequent discussion of ethnicity—to some highly
selective observations, with empirical evidence drawn from the United
States, in an effort to highlight the different ways in which major categories of difference are implicated in the production and reproduction of
inequality.

In my discussion of citizenship, I highlighted the segmentary organization of the nation-state system. Ethnicity too is sometimes organized in
segmentary fashion, as a set of relatively self-enclosed and endogenously
self-reproducing communities. (This is characteristic of "thick" forms of
ethnicity, marked by high degrees of "institutional completeness.") The social organization of gender is radically different. Men and women do not
constitute self-enclosed, self-sufficient, self-reproducing communities.[17]
They are profoundly interdependent and closely connected with one another as parents, partners, friends, lovers, neighbors, colleagues, and kin
(Tilly 1998: 240–241; Ridgeway 2011: 46). This complicates the analysis
of gender inequality, since men and women form supra-individual units of
procreation, socialization, labor, consumption, and identification.[18]

The interdependence of men and women and the accompanying ideologies of essential difference and complementarity are powerfully concretized
in the profoundly gendered division of labor in heterosexual households.
The division of household labor and child care has changed substantially
in recent decades in the United States, but women still spend about twice
as many hours on both housework and child care as men do (Bianchi et al.
2006: 62–67, 116–117). This is both a crucial form of inequality in its

own right and a key contribution to inequality in the workplace (Ridgeway 2011: chapter 5).

Earnings differences between men and women in the United States have narrowed substantially in recent decades: women's median weekly earnings have increased from 62 percent of men's in 1979 to 82 percent in 2011 (Bureau of Labor Statistics 2012), though convergence has slowed since the early 1990s (Blau and Kahn 2007). The earnings gap could result from one or more of three processes: (1) the differential allocation of men and women to different sorts of jobs; (2) the differential assignment of rewards to male- and female-dominated jobs; or (3) differential pay for the same jobs (Petersen and Morgan 1995). The detailed workplace-level data examined by Petersen and Morgan suggest that the last factor—within-job wage discrimination—accounts for very little. The importance of the second factor—what Petersen and Morgan call "valuational discrimination," by which female-dominated jobs pay less than male-dominated jobs, after controlling for skills and working conditions—is the subject of considerable controversy (Tam 1997; England et al. 2000), as well as the focus of political and legal struggles over "comparable worth" (England 1992). But it is widely agreed that the first factor—occupational sex segregation—is the main source of earnings disparities.

In line with these findings—and to keep the discussion manageable—I focus here on inequalities that are mediated by occupational sex segregation. Despite the entry of large numbers of women into previously male-dominated professional and managerial fields, overall levels of occupational sex segregation remain strikingly high; after declining substantially in the 1970s and 1980s, they have held stable in the United States since the mid-1990s. In 2009, 40 percent of women in the United States (but only 5 percent of men) worked in occupations that were at least 75 percent female, while 44 percent of men (and only 5 percent of women) worked in occupations that were at least 75 percent male (Hegewisch et al. 2010). Many of these occupations are characterized by extreme levels of segregation. In 1999, more than 90 percent of preschool and kindergarten teachers, dental assistants and hygienists, secretaries and administrative assistants, child care workers, receptionists, tellers, and registered as well as licensed practical and licensed vocational nurses were women, while more than 97 percent of automotive and other vehicle mechanics, masons, carpenters, plumbers, construction equipment operators, roofers, electricians, and construction workers were men.[19]

What generates such high levels of occupational sex segregation? In the most systematic recent treatment of the subject, Charles and Grusky (2004: chapter 1) distinguish between mechanisms that further "horizontal"

segregation by channeling men and women disproportionately into manual and nonmanual sectors, respectively, and those that further "vertical"
segregation by channeling men disproportionately into positions of greater
authority and rewards within both manual and nonmanual sectors.[20] Both
horizontal and vertical segregation are sustained by deeply rooted and widely
shared understandings of differences between men and women. Horizontal segregation is sustained by "gender essentialism"—by understandings
of women as more skilled in service, nurturing, and interaction, and of men
as more competent in the manipulation of things and more capable of stren-
uous physical labor. Vertical segregation is sustained by "male primacy"—
by understandings of men as generally more status-worthy and as better
suited for positions of authority and power.

Gender essentialism and male primacy work to sustain occupational sex
segregation through a series of intermediary processes. These operate on
both the "demand side" (by shaping employers' preferences, perceptions,
and practices) and the "supply side" (by shaping prospective employees'
preferences, informing—and possibly biasing—their self-evaluations, and
channeling their educational investments). The supply-side processes are
especially complex—and especially robust—because of the feedback loops
involved. Occupational aspirations and educational investments, for example, are shaped not only (and not always) by the internalization of beliefs about the distinctive natures of men and women, but also—even for
those who do *not* internalize and indeed expressly reject such beliefs—by
an awareness of the prevalence of gender-essentialist beliefs in the wider
society and consequently of the costs and sanctions likely to be incurred
by pursuing a gender-atypical line of work. Occupational aspirations and
educational investments are also shaped by awareness of the prevailing
gender-differentiated division of domestic labor and of prevailing normative expectations about women's primary and overriding commitment to
family (Ridgeway 2011: 128ff; Blair-Loy 2003). Awareness of these expectations and anticipation of the likely unequal burdens of household labor
and child care may shape occupational choices and educational investments even on the part of those who reject prevailing cultural constructions of motherhood and who would prefer an equal division of domestic
labor. Such considerations may lead career-minded women, for example,
to pursue occupations (or specializations within broader occupations) that
are more hospitable to combining family and work obligations.

Home and work are thus complexly intertwined as sites of gender inequality. The domestic division of labor affects workplace gender inequality
through a linked series of temporal modalities. The anticipated *future* gendered division of household labor shapes women's occupational aspira-

tions and educational investments; the *current* gendered division of household labor limits the time and energy they have for paid work;[21] while the *past* gendered division of household labor affects earnings by virtue of having limited the continuity and duration of women's work experience.

The persistence of high levels of occupational sex segregation in the United States and other wealthy liberal democratic countries—notwithstanding the diffusion of egalitarian gender attitudes, the closing and indeed reversing of the gender gap in higher education, and steadily increasing female labor force participation rates—reflects the deeply rooted nature of gender essentialism (Charles and Grusky 2004: 3, 23–28, 306–310). The diffusion of egalitarian attitudes and changes in women's educational and occupational profiles appear to be undermining, at least in part, understandings of male primacy, and specifically assumptions of generally superior male cognitive competence (Ridgeway 2011: 169). But prevailing understandings of essentially different male and female natures seem robustly entrenched. Their staying power may reflect their compatibility with prevailing liberal forms of gender egalitarianism, focused on notions of equal opportunity and free choice, and with the prevailing cultural emphasis on self-expression, which can legitimate the pursuit of gender-differentiated courses of study or lines of work, understood as expressions of one's identity (Charles and Bradley 2009: 925–930, 960–961). Deprived of its cultural and ideological support, vertical sex segregation is becoming more attenuated, especially in the nonmanual sector, where hiring procedures are more universalistic and bureaucratic. But horizontal sex segregation shows no sign of weakening (Charles and Grusky 2004: 23–28).

I want to conclude this section by returning to broader questions about the distinctive ways in which gender as a category of difference is implicated in the production and reproduction of inequality. As a primary frame of sense-making, sex categorization and the rich understandings of gender that it primes are chronically and pervasively available in interaction (Ridgeway 2011: chapter 2). Unlike citizenship, sex categorization and gender understandings are implicated not only in gatekeeping encounters and organizational routines—not only at points of decision about access to resources—but in the entire range of processes through which selves and subjectivities are formed, re-formed, and performed. They are implicated not only in the allocation of goods to different categories of persons but in the production and reproduction of deeply gendered selves. Sex categorization and gender understandings are also chronically implicated—in diffuse, decentralized, distributed, and interactionally embedded ways—in the myriad interpersonal encounters (and sometimes struggles) in families, workplaces, and other private and public arenas. It is in and through these everyday encounters that respect, recognition, and status are distributed in iterative and cumulatively consequential ways, and understandings of gender inequality (or equality) and gender difference (or sameness) are negotiated, reproduced, and transformed.

Two moments of categorization are intertwined in all processes of social categorization: self-identification and categorization by others (Jenkins 1996). But the relative weight of the internal and external moments varies widely. Citizenship and citizenship-like immigration statuses stand at one extreme: the external moment is overwhelmingly dominant. In determining access to the territory, the right to vote, and eligibility for certain social benefits, what matters is the categorical identity imposed or bestowed by the state and certified by official documents. How people identify themselves is irrelevant. The dominance of external categorization is characteristic of all forms of exclusion that work through legal or otherwise formal categories. External categorization is also dominant in certain informal regimes of exclusion. It is central by definition to discrimination on the basis of sex, race, religion, or any other category.

Yet while categorization by others is crucial to the dynamics of gender inequality, so too is self-identification. (Of course one can distinguish the two only analytically; self-identification and categorization by others are intricately, and dialectically, related in practice.) Unlike citizenship (for most people, most of the time), gender is not just an externally defined but a *deeply inhabited* category of difference, at the core of most people's understanding of who they are. The internal moment—the moment of self-identification and self-understanding—is therefore vital to the workings of gender.[22]

The distinction between self-identification and categorization by others points to two very different sorts of social psychology, both relevant to understanding how gender is implicated in the production and reproduction of inequality. One focuses on social cognition, specifically on the ways social categories are implicated in stereotypes, schemas, and cognitive biases (Fiske 1998; Reskin 2000). The other addresses the full range of processes involved in the social production of persons with pervasively gendered aspirations and self-understandings. The former might seem to be most relevant to gatekeeping processes, though it also specifies the mechanisms by which persons may develop biased self-assessments. The latter adds a richer and more thoroughly social dimension to our understanding of the full range of continuous, lifelong processes through which persons develop gendered self-understandings that lead them to form gendered occupational aspirations at a young age, pursue gendered courses of study and human capital investments, participate in the gendered division of household labor, and seek out gender-differentiated forms of employment.

There are limits to both social psychologies. Cognitive research on gender stereotypes can't necessarily be directly applied to organizational decision-making contexts. Research on gender (and racial) stereotypes focuses on unconscious and automatic modes of cognition.[23] But decisions on hiring, promotion, and firing, especially in large organizations, are generally made in a deliberative manner, with attention to the potential costs of discriminating (or even of appearing to discriminate [Petersen 2006]).[24] The cognitive biases that inform automatic categorization may therefore be more relevant to informal gatekeeping processes and everyday interaction than to bureaucratic decision making.

The notion of deeply gendered selves also has its limitations. It risks contributing to an oversocialized understanding of gender—or perhaps to an overgendered understanding of socialization (Lovell 2000). Processes of gender socialization may be ubiquitous and lifelong, but they are uneven and contradictory, not uniform and consistent. And the contradictions are found within as well as between persons. Selves are not so deeply or tightly constituted by gender (or any other social identity) as to preclude distance, self-reflection, change, or struggle. Gender is *both* a set of deeply taken-for-granted and widely shared background expectancies *and* a terrain of improvisatory interaction and performance and chronic micro- and macropolitical struggle.

The implication of citizenship and gender—as categories of difference—in the production and reproduction of inequality can be summarized schematically as follows. Citizenship is externally defined, formally codified, socially disembedded, intermittently relevant, and bureaucratically enforced; its workings are concentrated at a few key thresholds. Gender—in contemporary liberal contexts—is internally as well as externally defined, deeply internalized and embodied, primarily informal and uncodified, socially embedded, and interactionally ubiquitous; its workings are diffuse and distributed rather than concentrated. Citizenship contributes to inequality by directly and categorically excluding noncitizens at certain key points of access. Gender contributes to inequality through more complex, subtle, and intertwined pathways, operative not only, or even especially, in gatekeeping encounters but also in the shaping of selves, subjectivities, and ways of making sense of the world.

Ethnicity

Ethnicity—which I interpret broadly to include race as well as ethnicity-like forms of religion[25]—is implicated in the production and reproduction of inequality in some ways that are analogous to the workings of gender. But in other respects the inequality-generating processes and mechanisms are quite different. To bring these differences into focus, I begin with a stylized and deliberately oversimplified comparison of the processes underlying structures of gender and racial (specifically black-white) inequality in the United States. I then broaden the discussion to highlight other ways in which ethnicity, race, and ethnicity-like forms of religion are drawn into processes and structures of categorical inequality.

Like gender inequality, racial inequality was long legally mandated and enforced. Quite apart from legal support for slavery, free blacks in northern as well as southern states suffered a variety of legal disabilities before the Civil War (Hiers 2013: chapter 2). They were barred in most northern states from voting and in some from testifying against whites, holding real estate or even settling in the territory. These state-level provisions were supplemented by exclusionary municipal ordinances. And while legal exclusions were dismantled in the postbellum North, a comprehensive system of legally mandated segregation was instituted in the post-Reconstruction South, where it endured for three quarters of a century.

These formal legal exclusions, like those based on gender, have been fully abolished. But as in the case of gender—only to a greater extent—the elimination of formal inequalities has left massive substantive inequalities in place. Some of these, and the processes that generate them, are analogous to those in the domain of gender. Racial earnings differentials, for example, have been studied in the same way as gender earnings differentials: through individualist approaches that focus on human capital differences or employer discrimination and through structural approaches that focus on labor market characteristics such as occupational segregation and the devaluation of jobs dominated by women and minorities. Racial and gender discrimination have also been studied in similar ways: through cognitively oriented research aimed at uncovering the properties stereotypically associated, consciously or unconsciously, with social categories; through attempts to estimate discrimination indirectly as the unexplained residual that remains after controlling for other explanatory factors; and, increasingly, through efforts to measure discriminatory behavior directly through experimental audit studies.

The analogies might seem to go deeper. Four massive and deeply institutionalized facts profoundly shape gender inequality: sex categorization as a primary and ubiquitous means of sense-making, deeply rooted and widely shared essentialist understandings of male-female differences, high levels of occupational sex segregation, and the unequal division of domestic labor.[26] With the exception of the last, all of these have analogues in the domain of race. But they work in very different ways. Occupational sex segregation emerges in large part from sex-typed occupational aspirations and educational choices, which are themselves legitimated as the expressions of authentic and deeply gendered selves. It is also driven by the unequal household division of labor, which draws women disproportionately into relatively family-friendly service sector occupations. Occupational segregation by race reflects neither self-expressive supply-side sorting nor the constraints of an unequal domestic division of labor; it is driven more by employer discrimination and human capital differences. There are of course entrenched forms of racial as well as gender essentialism, but the former do not afford the robust and widely shared understandings of *complementary* difference that enable the latter to generate and legitimize gender-differentiated educational paths and occupational choices. And while occupational sex segregation is offset by interdependence and dense relational connectedness between men and women in other domains, occupational segregation by race is just one aspect of a much larger pattern of segregation. So while certain proximate mechanisms work in similar ways to sustain racial and gender inequality, the underlying structures and processes differ sharply.

Racial inequality in the post–Jim Crow era has been profoundly shaped by two massive institutional complexes with no analogue in the domain of gender. The first is segregation; the second (which in a sense is just an extreme form of the first [Wacquant 2010: 81]) is incarceration. Residential segregation has been the "structural linchpin" of racial inequality.[27] Segregated neighborhoods have entailed not just segregated schools, churches, associations, and networks but also segregated experiences. And since this segregation has been imposed rather than chosen, and produced in tandem with a process of "sociospatial relegation" (Wacquant 2008: 2) to systematically disfavored spaces, it has generated and perpetuated massive, cumulative, and mutually reinforcing inequalities in housing, education, amenities, public safety, municipal services, trust, social capital, job opportunities, and exposure to environmental hazards, crime, delinquency, and stress.

Residential clustering and associated forms of institutional duplication are of course characteristic of many ethnic groups. In the United States, however, black-white segregation has been unique in both degree and kind. At its peak in the 1960s, it had reached levels far higher than those experienced by any other ethnic group, prompting Massey and Denton (1993: 74–78) to speak of "hypersegregation." And it has been generated and sustained by different mechanisms: initially by residential segregation ordinances and—when these were invalidated by the Supreme Court—by violence against blacks seeking to move into white neighborhoods, subsequently by massive white flight from integrating neighborhoods and a variety of institutional mechanisms, including restrictive covenants barring the sale of properties to blacks; government-sanctioned redlining that made entire neighborhoods ineligible for government-insured mortgages; subtle and not so subtle steering practices by the real estate industry; and racially targeted urban renewal programs (Massey 2007: 58–65; Wacquant 2008: 75–80). Although restrictive covenants, redlining, and housing discrimination on the basis of race have been illegal for nearly half a century, audit studies have documented substantial continuing discrimination against blacks in the rental, sale, and financing of housing (Massey 2007: 76–84).[28]

Since 1970, aggregate measures of black-white residential segregation have slowly but steadily declined (Logan and Stults 2011).[29] During the same period, however, the social, economic, cultural, and political isolation of poor inner-city blacks has intensified, accentuating the nexus of cumulative, concentrated, and heritable forms of disadvantage (Wilson 1987; Sampson et al. 2008; Wacquant 2008; Sharkey 2013). Incarceration has been increasingly central to the production and reproduction of this landscape of concentrated disadvantage. The hypertrophy of the carceral complex is often described as involving the "mass incarceration" of African Americans. But as Wacquant argues, "mass" suggests a broad and indiscriminate process, while the spectacular growth in incarceration has in fact been narrowly targeted not only by race but also by class and space, amounting to the "*hyper*incarceration of (sub)proletarian African-American men from the imploding ghetto" (2010: 74). Public attention has focused on the shockingly large racial discrepancies in incarceration rates, and for good reason, but class differentials *within* racial categories are even larger than differentials *between* racial categories.[30] The melding of class and race follows from the spatial focus of the carceral revolution, concentrated on the infrastructurally crumbling, economically subproletarianized, and territorially stigmatized space of the ghetto. The triple targeting by race, class, and space highlights the connection between prison and ghetto as "institutions of forced confinement": "As the ghetto lost its economic function of labor extraction and proved unable to ensure ethnoracial closure, the prison was called on to help contain a dishonored population widely viewed as deviant, destitute, and dangerous" (Wacquant 2010: 81).

For young, poorly educated African American men, incarceration has become a modal experience, a "normal" part of the life course. By 1999 black high school dropouts had a 60 percent chance of going to prison by their mid-thirties, while the larger category of black men without any college had a 30 percent chance (Pettit and Western 2004).[31] Incarceration is not only a key dimension of inequality in its own right; it is a cause of further inequalities, with widely ramifying and long-lasting consequences for employment prospects, the kinds of jobs held, earnings, the likelihood of marriage and divorce, and the chances for the formation of stable families (Western 2006; Pager 2008). Moreover, the regime of hyperincarceration masks the full extent of racial inequality since the incarcerated population is not included in the surveys from which data on unemployment, poverty, wage levels, and a variety of other social conditions are derived (Western 2006: chapter 4; Pettit 2012). Including the incarcerated population (and other institutionalized populations, notably military personnel) dramatically increases rates of black joblessness and substantially increases black-white differences in such rates. It reveals that the narrowing black-white wage gap observed for young men in the late 1980s and 1990s was largely a statistical illusion, the result of massively increased joblessness (much of it due to soaring incarceration rates) among young black men with low education and little earning power (Western 2006: chapter 4). And it leads to much higher estimates of black high school dropout rates (and a much higher black-white gap in such rates [Pettit 2012: 57–61]).

HAVING CONSIDERED—in schematic and grossly oversimplified fashion— some of the major structures underlying racial (specifically black-white) inequality and how these differ from the main structures underlying gender inequality, I turn now to a broader (and no longer exclusively U.S.-focused) consideration of the ways ethnicity (including ethnicity-like forms of religion) is implicated in the production and reproduction of inequality. Here again I must be ruthlessly selective.

Like gender and other categories of difference, ethnicity is constituted by the interplay of internal and external moments of identification and categorization (Jenkins 1997: 53ff). External categorization has been decisive in shaping racial inequality, from slavery and Jim Crow through contemporary residential segregation, hyperincarceration, marital segregation, and discrimination in its manifold forms. It is sometimes argued that external categorization is constitutive of race, and internal self-identification of ethnicity. But this view does not stand up to scrutiny: self-identification is central to many forms of "racial" identity, while external categorization is equally central to innumerable "ethnic" configurations.[32]

External categorization shapes ethnic inequality in many ways.[33] It works—just to note a few recurring patterns—through the authoritative allocation of persons to positions (as, for example, in many colonial and postcolonial settings); through the matching of ethnic categories with specific territories (as, for example, in Soviet and Chinese nationality policy and in the construction of tribal ethnic homelands in Africa); through the exclusion, restriction, expropriation, or expulsion of ethnic outsiders or the privileging of ethnic insiders in such matters as employment, university admission, and business opportunities; through the allocation of public resources via systems of ethnic patronage; through public policies that lead (as with race in the United States) to residential concentrations in disfavored neighborhoods, disproportionate incarceration, and the de facto if not de jure segregation of schools; and through informal practices of exclusion, discrimination, and stigmatization. Besides shaping *socioeconomic* inequality in these and other ways, external categorization may profoundly shape specifically *political* inequalities. In a world of nation-states, often understood as the states *of* and *for* particular ethnoculturally defined nations, those identified as ethnocultural outsiders may be excluded from equal citizenship, and they may be targeted for forced assimilation, forced emigration, or even genocide. Even where ethnic fragmentation prevents the identification of the state with a single ethnocultural nation, as in many postcolonial states, certain groups may be defined as outsiders.

The literature on ethnic inequality has focused on the external moment in categorization and on the power to make such external categorization matter. There are good reasons for this emphasis on authoritative external categorization. But the internal moment matters as well. The internal moment in gender refers to the workings of gender as a deeply embodied and inhabited identity that shapes and channels action from within by way of deeply gendered desires, aspirations, and self-understandings. I take the internal moment in ethnicity and religion in a broader sense, referring not only to internalized identifications but also to forms of cultural practice and social organization that are understood and experienced as self-generated and self-organized expressions of a collective way of life, emerging from within, not simply constrained from without (Cornell and Hartmann 1998: 77–81).

In modern economic and political contexts, where education requires mastery of standard idioms and work is increasingly semantic rather than physical (Gellner 1997: 85), language repertoires and linguistically embedded forms of cultural capital are central to the determination of life chances.

Some forms of linguistically mediated inequality are externally driven, involving diverse forms of discrimination, stigmatization, and social closure. But differing linguistic repertoires also contribute to inequality through a *self-enforcing* dynamic that does not require any active exclusion or closure. Opportunities—not just for education and employment but also, even more fundamentally, for the formation of broad and strong social ties and for full participation in a broad spectrum of collective activities—are systematically limited for those who lack proficiency in the prevailing language. This systematic constriction of opportunities works largely through self-exclusion from the pursuit of opportunities that require forms and degrees of linguistic competence beyond those possessed; it therefore holds even for those who experience no discrimination, stigmatization, or active exclusion. It is a kind of agentless exclusion, an exclusion without excluders, but it is no less powerful for that. The distinction between externally driven and self-enforcing modes of linguistically mediated inequality, to be sure, applies only to inequality-generating processes *within* particular sociolinguistic environments, not to the larger-scale processes that have *shaped* those environments. The large-scale transformations involved in colonialism, nation-state building, and the spread of global capitalism, for example, have created vast inequalities among languages, raising the economic, political, and social value of some and devaluing others (Gal 1989: 356–357).

Religiously mediated inequality, like linguistically mediated inequality, may be externally driven by the systematic privileging or disprivileging, formal or informal, of certain religious categories.[34] Formal discrimination on religious grounds has been sharply curtailed in liberal polities, but it has not been and cannot be eliminated; it is now widely recognized that states can never be entirely neutral in matters of religion (Bader 2007: 82ff), even though they can make, and have made, substantial moves in the direction of a more even-handed treatment of different religions.[35] Informal discrimination and stigmatization remain important as well, notably toward Muslims in European countries of immigration.

Religious beliefs and practices can also generate inequality from within. The traditional gender norms promoted by various (often ethnoculturally inflected) forms of conservative religion, for example, may generate gender inequalities in educational attainment, labor force participation, and earnings, while also disadvantaging the larger ethnoreligious categories in which such traditional gender norms are prevalent. Ultra-Orthodox Jewish families may be similarly disadvantaged by the religious premium placed on large families and full-time Torah study for ultra-Orthodox men.

Distinctive forms of religious belief and practice may confer advantages as well as disadvantages. These may be mediated by the social forms of participation in religious institutions or by the cultural content of religious beliefs and practices. Participation in religious institutions can generate social capital and network-linked advantages, as well as a wide range of physical and mental health benefits. Distinctive religious beliefs and practices may confer economic advantages indirectly (for example, by curbing drinking, drug abuse, and other risky behavior) or more directly (for example, by sanctioning the pursuit of worldly success, as in "prosperity theology").

Inequality along ethnic or religious lines can be generated by social separation as well as cultural difference. By social separation I mean concentration in residential, occupational, institutional, social-relational, marital, consumption, media, and recreational space. Such social separation regularly arises in postmigration contexts as an incidental byproduct of scarce resources, limited information, language constraints, and, above all, the network-mediated dynamics of migration and settlement, which can lead to the formation of ethnically organized business niches, churches, and other institutions. But social separation can also be pursued as a *deliberate strategy of insulation* from surroundings that are perceived as physically dangerous, economically disadvantaging, morally compromising, or culturally threatening. Whether arising as an incidental byproduct or pursued as a deliberate strategy (and of course these are not mutually exclusive alternatives), such self-organized (though resource-constrained) *separation* differs sharply from externally imposed *segregation,* formal or informal. While imposed ethnoracial segregation is massively and cumulatively, albeit unevenly, disadvantaging, uniting cultural stigmatization and material deprivation, self-organized social separation is more ambivalent in its implications for inequality.

The flip side of the incidental social separation characteristic of almost all immigrant communities is the social-relational and institutional density of the ethnic enclave, which can provide resources and opportunities for those without the contacts, resources, or language skills to flourish in the wider society. Yet many second-generation immigrants experience enclosure within ethnically organized institutions as constraining rather than enabling and as limiting the range of opportunities and the reach of networks. A similar ambivalence characterizes strategies of deliberate insulation. Some ethnoreligious communities—or more specifically, some husbands and fathers in such communities—may seek to isolate and thereby insulate their wives and daughters from what is regarded as an (ethno)religiously unsuitable, morally dangerous, and potentially dishonoring public realm. Such enclosure can generate and reproduce not only gender inequality but broader forms of ethnoreligious inequality. On the other hand, poor immigrants, constrained to live in neighborhoods they see as undesirable, often enlist a strategy of insulation in the service of social mobility (as well as cultural reproduction).[36] Such strategies of insulation can be employed in an attempt to prevent the behavioral or attitudinal assimilation of their children to peers in the immediate environment, as a means of enhancing their longer term educational and occupational chances. Dissimilation and social encapsulation in the short term (in relation to a disfavored immediate urban milieu) may facilitate long-term assimilation and integration (in relation to a wider middle-class national environment).

What can be said in summary about the distinctive ways in which ethnicity—as a category of difference—is implicated in the production and reproduction of inequality? The broad understanding of ethnicity adopted here, embracing race as well as ethnicity-like forms of religion, complicates matters. Still, this much can be said: Like gender, and unlike citizenship, ethnicity (in contemporary liberal contexts) is internally as well as externally defined, primarily informal and uncodified, and socially embedded; its workings are diffuse and distributed rather than concentrated at a few key thresholds. Yet there are key differences between ethnicity and gender. Social separation—whether externally driven (as in the residential, educational, and network segregation of African Americans) or self-organized (as in ethnic niches and neighborhoods and ethnic or religious strategies of insulation)—is central to the inegalitarian workings of ethnicity, while social interdependence, as concretized in the household division of labor, is central to the inegalitarian workings of gender. Essentialist understandings of self and other are central to both ethnicity and gender, but while gender essentialism features widely shared understandings of complementary difference that generate and legitimize gender-differentiated educational paths and occupational choices, ethnic essentialism can constitute ethnic, racial, or religious others as stigmatized, despised, or feared outsiders.

General Processes

I have argued in the preceding sections, contra Tilly, that citizenship, gender, and ethnicity are implicated in very different ways in the production and reproduction of inequality. Having analyzed these differing forms of difference, I return now to a more general level of analysis. I identify three general processes—alternatives, in a sense, to Tilly's proposed general mechanisms of exploitation and opportunity hoarding—by which categories of difference generate and sustain inequality. I consider first the *allocation of persons to positions*; next *the social production of persons* with different self-understandings, dispositions, aspirations, and skills; and finally the *structuring of positions* themselves and the rewards that are attached to them.

Allocation and Exclusion

The channeling of persons to positions, broadly understood, begins at birth, or in fact before birth, with the social and even biological (genetic and epigenetic) inheritance of the persons concerned. Here, however, I focus on the proximate dynamics of allocation and exclusion: on gatekeeping processes at points of access to desirable positions. I consider in the next section the anterior processes that endow people with different dispositions and resources and channel them differentially toward (and away from) such points of access.

Four types of processes can produce categorical exclusion from or unequal representation in desirable social positions: formal categorical exclusion; informal yet strictly or largely categorical exclusion; categorically inflected selection; and category-neutral screening on category-correlated, position-relevant characteristics.

Formal categorical exclusion—with the conspicuous exception of exclusion based on citizenship—is now vestigial in liberal democracies. In a remarkably short time, the "minority rights revolution" (Skrentny 2002) has transformed law from an instrument that permitted and even mandated categorical exclusion to one that forbids such exclusion and may even mandate preferential treatment for formerly disadvantaged categories. I noted this in my discussion of gender and race, but the transformation extends to other ascriptive categories, including ethnicity, national origin, religion, and, increasingly, sexual orientation.

By informal yet strictly or strongly categorical exclusion, I have in mind processes such as the exclusion of blacks from white neighborhoods; the exclusion of Jews from WASP-dominated law firms (and restrictions on the admission of Jews to elite colleges [Karabel 2005]); the exclusion of religious or racial outsiders from clubs; and the exclusion of women and minorities from a wide range of jobs, both by discrimination at the point of hiring and by the exclusionary practices of self-consciously macho or white occupational or workplace cultures. Processes like these could and often did result in wholesale categorical exclusion—in the exclusion of all or almost all members of certain categories—despite their informal nature. Yet these too have been massively delegitimated and legally prohibited in the past half-century—except in the increasingly narrowly defined sphere of private association such as marriage and friendship choices.[37]

Despite the elimination of most formal categorical exclusion and the erosion—as a result of legal prohibitions and changing cultural understandings—of strictly categorical informal regimes of exclusion, substantial between-category inequalities continue to result from point-of-allocation processes. They do so in part through what I call *categorically inflected* selection processes. These are processes in which category membership matters but is not the only thing that matters. This can happen in two ways. First, gatekeepers may hold conscious beliefs—correct or incorrect—about average group differences in position-relevant characteristics. Selection processes are categorically inflected to the extent that gatekeepers' decisions are based not only on their assessments of observed *individual* characteristics but also on their beliefs about average *group* characteristics, taken as a proxy for unobserved individual characteristics.[38] Second, unconscious category-linked associations may bias gatekeepers' assessments of individual characteristics. Categorically inflected selection processes are not *strictly* categorical: they do not select solely on the basis of category membership. But they contribute to categorical inequality by skewing selection processes—to varying degrees—to the advantage of members of some categories and the disadvantage of others.[39]

Finally, even selection processes that are scrupulously category-neutral at the point of selection may generate between-category inequalities. This can happen when skills, experience, or other qualifications are unequally distributed across categories or when supply-side processes generate categorically skewed applicant pools.

The first two processes involve unambiguous and wholesale categorical exclusion, formal and informal. The third—categorically inflected selection—involves differential treatment but not wholesale exclusion. The fourth generates a disparate impact but without differential treatment or direct discrimination. This last process highlights the limits of analyses that focus on allocation and exclusion at the point of selection (or on formal or informal categorical exclusion from selection processes). A broader view of the processes through which categories of difference are implicated in the production and reproduction of inequality must encompass the social production of persons and the social structuring of positions.

The Social Production of Persons

The social production of persons includes the full range of processes that generate agents endowed with particular self-understandings, dispositions, aspirations, skills, experience, human or cultural capital, and ways of thinking and acting. The persons so produced subsequently present themselves at points of selection—or refrain from presenting themselves—as differently qualified candidates. The processes involved in the social production of persons generate both *difference* and *inequality*. On the one hand, they generate forms of difference—in self-understandings, aspirations, and commitments—that channel different categories of people (men and women, most obviously, but also members of different racial, ethnic, or religious groups) in different directions (toward different educational choices and occupational aspirations, for example, or into different networks). This differential channeling and social separation may then generate inequality as a secondary result, even in the absence of initial inequalities in skills or levels of education. On the other hand, the social production of persons directly generates between-group inequalities in skills, education, and other aspects of human capital.[40] These in turn generate inequalities in access to positions, even in the absence of any categorical exclusion or discrimination.

Between-group differences in skills, education, and other qualifications figure both as an *explanation* of inequality (in individualist accounts that focus narrowly on the point of selection) and as a *dimension* of inequality that requires explanation in its own right (in structural accounts that are more broadly concerned with the social production of persons and the social structuring of positions). As a dimension of inequality, such between-group differences emerge from differences—at once social structural and cultural—in the key environments (families, schools, neighborhoods, and peer groups) in which dispositions, skills, and aspirations are formed, insofar as these environments are differentiated and stratified not only by class but also by sex, race and ethnicity, or religion.[41]

In Bourdieusian perspective, dispositions more or less conducive to achieving or maintaining a privileged position in social space are formed through a twofold process of internalization. On the one hand, the social structure is internalized: the constraints, opportunities, and resources inscribed in the social structure—which vary by sex, race and ethnicity, religion, and so on as well as by class—are translated into the dispositions, skills, and aspirations that constitute the habitus and embodied forms of cultural capital. Aspirations are adjusted to opportunities through what Bourdieu calls the "causality of the probable," which is "no doubt one of the most powerful factors of conservation of the established order" (2000: 231; 1974).

On the other hand, the symbolic structures of domination are also internalized: the prevailing schemas of classification, perception, and evaluation, which systematically valorize dominant positions, dispositions, and forms of cultural capital while devalorizing and sometimes stigmatizing others.[42] The internalization of such self-devaluing schemas of classification and appraisal allows the dominated to collude, if only unconsciously, in their own domination, for example by way of downwardly biased self-assessments, depressed aspirations, self-hatred, or self-destructive behavior.[43] Symbolic violence becomes thereby a key mechanism linking difference and inequality.

Positions and Their Rewards

Accounts of inequality that focus narrowly on the allocation of persons to positions neglect the social processes that form the persons and structure the positions, generating (1) persons unequally disposed and equipped to pursue desirable positions and (2) the structure of unequally rewarded positions itself. Having addressed, all too briefly, the former, I turn now to the latter.

Sociologists and anthropologists have long distinguished between positions in the social structure and the persons who occupy them. Corresponding to this is a distinction between two forms of inequality: inequality between *categories of positions* and inequality between *categories of persons*.[44] The relation between difference and inequality depends in obvious ways on the latter. But it depends on the former as well, insofar as inequality between categories of persons is mediated by unequal access to categories of positions. If women and minorities are disproportionately represented in low-status positions, for example, then the magnitude of male-female or majority-minority inequality depends not only on the degree of disproportional representation but also on the degree of inequality inscribed in the structure of positions itself. If occupations, social classes, neighborhoods, and schools differ relatively little in the rewards attached to them, then the disproportionate representation of minorities in less desirable occupational, class, residential, or school positions matters less for the overall structure and experience of between-group inequality than it does when positional inequality is greater. In a more egalitarian social structure, questions of what categories of people live in which neighborhoods, attend which schools, and work at which jobs are much less consequential.

As this suggests, the connection between difference and inequality can be attenuated in two ways. If one takes positional inequality as given, the connection can be attenuated only by changing the allocation of persons to positions (which may in turn depend, in the longer run, on changing the social production of persons). But the connection between difference and inequality can also be attenuated by reducing positional inequality: by shrinking the gap in rewards between more and less desirable positions. This could be done, for example, by raising the minimum wage, strengthening labor unions, or instituting more progressive taxation of income. Formally, these measures are difference-blind, concerned only with categories of positions; substantively, however, they would reduce inequalities between categories of persons.

This raises the questions of how rewards get assigned to positions, how particular degrees and forms of inequality get built into structures of positions, and how patterns of positional inequality change over time. These large and complex questions, which engage broad macroeconomic debates about technology and labor market structure as well as sociological debates about positional inequality, are beyond the scope of this chapter. But one issue requires brief discussion here: How do categories of difference figure in the structuring of positions? More specifically: In what ways, and to what degree, is the structure of positions—especially the assignment of different rewards to different positions—affected by the categorical identities of their incumbents?

According to the devaluation hypothesis, female- and minority-dominated jobs suffer a wage penalty, net of skills, experience, onerousness, and other factors that affect pay levels (England et al. 1988; Tomaskovic-Devey 1993; Petersen and Morgan 1995). The hypothesis remains controversial (on gender, see Tam 1997, 2000; England et al. 2000). But it illustrates an important general mechanism through which the categorical composition of incumbents can affect the rewards assigned to a position or, more abstractly, the "quality" or "value" of a position.

One can see this by broadening the conception of "position" beyond jobs to include neighborhoods as positions in residential space, schools as positions in educational space, and class positions. The literature on racial residential segregation, discussed earlier, makes clear that the categorical composition of a neighborhood's residents can affect the services provided to the neighborhood, the willingness to invest in the neighborhood, and the image or discursive representation of the neighborhood, generating in some cases a mutually reinforcing nexus of confinement, neglect, abandonment, and territorial stigmatization (Wacquant 2008). A similar point can be made about the categorical composition of public schools or other public institutions. And the changing racial, ethnic, or religious composition of the working poor and subproletarian population, who can easily be represented as "them" rather than "us," may have contributed to diminishing support for redistributive policies in contemporary liberal democratic settings (Larsen 2011). In other contexts, the ethnoracial or ethnoreligious composition of economically privileged commercial or landowning strata has rendered them vulnerable to expropriation, expulsion, or worse, particularly at moments of economic or political crisis (Brubaker 2011a).

Obviously the processes that shape and reshape positional inequalities are enormously complex, and I have not been able to provide even the briefest account of them here. I have sought rather to highlight the social definition of positions and their rewards as a distinct inequality-generating mechanism that interacts with the allocation of persons to positions and with the social production of persons endowed with different and unequal dispositions and resources. And I have noted some ways in which categories of difference—specifically the categorical identities of incumbents—may shape the social definition of positions and the rewards that are attached to them. Positions and their rewards are the objects of chronic struggles, and these struggles (for improved pay or working conditions, for a wider jurisdiction, or for recognition as a licensed trade or profession, for example) are driven in the first instance by the *positional* identities and interests of the incumbents, not by their ascriptive *categorical* identities and interests. As these struggles alter the social definition and rewards of positions, making them more or less attractive, the categorical composition of their incumbents may change. But as I have suggested here, the reverse causal process may also occur: exogenously driven changes in the categorical composition of incumbents can lead to a social redefinition and revaluation of positions and their rewards.

Conclusion

What is the relation between difference and inequality? Tilly's influential account of categorical inequality focused on processes of exploitation and opportunity hoarding through which internal organizational divisions—the boundaries between clusters of similarly rewarded positions—are matched or aligned with major axes of categorical division in the wider social environment, such as gender, race, ethnicity, religion, or citizenship. Probing the ambiguities in Tilly's discussion of exploitation and opportunity hoarding, however, cast doubt on his claim that the major categories of difference are implicated in the production and reproduction of inequality in fundamentally similar ways. This led me to adopt a more differentiated and disaggregated analytical strategy and to consider separately the relation between difference and inequality in the domains of citizenship, gender, and ethnicity. In the penultimate section, I returned to a more general level of analysis and specified—as an alternative to Tilly's exploitation and opportunity hoarding—three general processes through which categories of difference enter into the production and reproduction of inequality: the allocation of persons to (or their exclusion from) reward-bearing positions; the social production of persons unequally disposed and equipped to pursue desirable positions; and the structuring of positions and their rewards.

Position-Mediated and Category-Mediated Inequality: The Social Distribution of Honor

I have focused my analysis on inequalities that are mediated by reward-bearing positions. Jobs are the paradigmatic example of such positions; other examples include neighborhoods, schools, clubs, and nation-states. There are good reasons for focusing on position-mediated inequalities. Not only inequalities in income and wealth but also inequalities in basic physical security and in mental and physical health are increasingly mediated in the contemporary world by such positions. Even the social distribution of honor is mediated by positions. Incumbents of different positions enjoy differing degrees of respect, prestige, and deference (Goffman 1956; Shils 1968; Goldthorpe and Hope 1972). Stigma too attaches not only to categories of persons but to categories of positions: there are stigmatized jobs (Hughes 1958: chapter 3; Ashforth and Kreiner 1999; Drew et al. 2007), stigmatized neighborhoods (Wacquant 2007), even stigmatized countries.

Yet inequality is not only mediated by positions; it also attaches directly to categories of persons. I therefore wish to supplement my position-focused analysis with some brief comments on forms of inequality that are mediated by category membership per se. Exposure to violence, for example, is crucially mediated by country, region, class, and neighborhood. But some forms of violence specifically target categories of persons, notably women, gays, and members of ethnoracial or ethnoreligious minorities. Unequal exposure to such targeted forms of violence thus attaches directly to categories of persons.

The distribution of honor, respect, and esteem, too, is only partly mediated by positions.[45] Some forms of disrespect, dishonor, or symbolic aggression, like some forms of physical violence, target particular categories of persons. Apart from such deliberate, consciously targeted acts of disrespect, members of subordinate categories may be exposed to chronic and routine affronts to dignity.[46] Even in a context in which overt racism is marginal and thoroughly delegitimated, for example, African Americans—independently of the positions they occupy—risk being stopped for "driving while black." And apart from such specific instances of disrespect, whether or not deliberately intended as such, people may enjoy more or less honor, respect, and esteem simply by virtue of their category membership, again independently of the positions they occupy.[47]

The categorically unequal distribution of honor, respect, and esteem is in the first instance a form of *symbolic* inequality, that is, of inequality in the distribution of symbolic goods. But such inequality is not *merely* symbolic. Insofar as it operates through the internalization of dominant self-devaluing schemes of classification and appraisal, it has material effects. In this way, the social distribution of honor can be incorporated and embodied in individual persons: in bodily hexis, ingrained ways of thinking and feeling, and other somatic manifestations such as susceptibility to stress and disease. These incorporated *dispositional* inequalities can contribute, in turn, to *positional* inequalities by downwardly biasing self-assessments, depressing occupational aspirations and educational investments, and channeling members of subordinate categories away from the pursuit of highly rewarded positions.[48] There is thus a reciprocal relation between positional inequality and the social distribution of honor. On the one hand, positional inequality shapes the distribution of honor through the positive and negative honor attached to positions. On the other hand, the directly category-mediated distribution of honor shapes positional inequality through the internalization of self-devaluing schemas of classification and appraisal and the effects of this internalization on self-assessments, aspirations, dispositions, and behavior.

There is of course a risk in overstating the power of this circular dynamic of incorporation and externalization that leads from positions to dispositions and then back to positions. It's worth underscoring in this connection that inequality in the distribution of honor exists quite apart from such deep, self-devaluing incorporation. "Shallower" forms of symbolic inequality—the unequal enjoyment of honor, respect, and esteem that supervenes on membership in valued and devalued, marked and unmarked categories—can be significant in their own right, even if members of subordinate categories do *not* internalize dominant schemas of evaluation and appraisal but instead challenge and contest those schemas through strategies of transvaluation (Wimmer 2013: 57–58) or de-stigmatization (Warren 1980; Lamont 2009; Lamont and Mizrachi 2012).

Categorical Inequality Revisited

"Categorical inequality" is a leitmotif of Tilly's book, and the phrase has appeared many times in these pages. But the term is elusive and ambiguous. Weak and strong meanings can be distinguished. The weak meaning is purely descriptive: it designates *any* significant between-category inequality, irrespective of how that inequality is generated. Differences in average earnings between women and men are an instance of categorical inequality in this sense, simply because average earnings are lower for women than for men. We would continue to speak of categorical inequality in this weak sense even if there were no evidence of discrimination in hiring or promotion and no evidence of the devaluation of female-dominated occupations. Categorical inequality in this sense refers solely to the *fact* of between-category inequality; it says nothing about the *processes* through which such inequality arises. Such inequality is *measured* by the analytic use of *statistical categories* for which data are available, but it need not be *produced* by the exclusionary workings of *social categories*.

The strong meaning turns on the contrast between *categorical* and *gradational* forms of inequality. This contrast applies both to inequality between *positions* and to inequality between *persons*. With respect to the former, positions in large organizations tend to be organized in bounded clusters, separated by large gaps in rewards and virtually insurmountable mobility barriers (between workers and upper managers in firms, for example, or between enlisted soldiers and officers in the military). Inequality tends to be gradational *within* clusters of positions but categorical *between* clusters.

With respect to inequality between persons, the contrast between categorical and gradational inequality has both a *global* meaning, referring to the basic structure of the social order as a whole, and a more *local* and restricted meaning, referring to different modes of allocating particular rewards and opportunities. The global contrast distinguishes social orders stratified on the basis of ascriptive and morally incommensurable categories of personhood to which radically different rights and obligations are attached (nobles and commoners, landowners and serfs, men and women, upper and lower castes, free and slave) from social orders like our own in which the dominant principle of differentiation is functional, and basic categories of persons are assumed to enjoy equal moral status and legal rights (Schmidt 2013). The local contrast distinguishes two ways in which specific rewards and opportunities can be allocated: on the basis of ascribed categorical identities or on the basis of individual qualifications and performances.[49]

Combining this local idea of categorical allocation with the notion of categorically distinct clusters of positions yields a strong local meaning of categorical inequality: *positions defined by discontinuous bundles of rewards and opportunities* are *assigned or allocated on the basis of ascribed categorical identity.* Strong forms of categorical identity in this sense have persisted well into the modern era. But they have eroded dramatically over the course of the past two centuries, especially during the "minority rights revolution" of the past half-century (Skrentny 2002). Legally mandated categorical exclusions—as well as strongly categorical informal regimes of exclusion—have been massively delegitimized; the law now mandates equal treatment on the basis of sex, race, ethnicity, religion, and (to a lesser extent) sexual orientation, and it may even mandate preferential treatment for members of previously excluded categories. This has undermined and illegalized informal as well as formal regimes of categorical exclusion, insofar as these go beyond a narrowly defined sphere of private association. Although this development has proceeded furthest in the West, it is a global phenomenon, evident in a series of striking changes at the level of the world polity (Koenig 2008; Schmidt 2013).

There is one conspicuous yet seldom noticed exception to this precipitous decline in legally mandated or sanctioned categorical inequality. While discrimination on the basis of other ascribed identities has been massively delegitimated, discrimination on the basis of citizenship has been largely unchallenged. Countries—or more precisely, clusters of countries—can be seen as positions in the global nation-state system, to which discontinuous bundles of rewards and opportunities are attached; and access to these positions is assigned on the basis of a categorical identity that is assigned at birth. Citizenship is the great remaining bastion of strong categorical inequality in the modern world; this inherited status continues to underwrite and legitimate immense structures of between-country inequality on a global scale.

Other ascribed categories of difference continue, of course, to enter into the production and reproduction of inequality in important ways that I have sought to clarify in this chapter. But they do so, on the whole, in ways that have become less strictly categorical. Categorical inequality in the weak, statistical sense is ubiquitous; but categorical inequality in the strong, processual sense—referring to the allocation of categorically distinct bundles of rewards and opportunities on the basis of ascribed categorical identities—is increasingly vestigial in liberal democratic contexts.

A great strength of Tilly's *Durable Inequality* is its sustained attention to the categorical nature of inequality between clusters of organizational positions. Yet Tilly does not consistently distinguish this kind of intra-organizational categorical inequality from categorical inequality in the allocation of persons to positions or in the social production of persons. Categorical inequality among *organizational positions* and categorical inequality among *persons* have quite distinct causes and need not go hand in hand. Strictly categorical inequality between clusters of positions is the rule in contemporary large organizations; strictly categorical inequality in the allocation of persons to positions, or in the social production of persons, is the exception.

Of course, this does not mean that the mechanisms that generate and sustain inequality are difference-blind. But even when the mechanisms are not difference-blind, they no longer turn centrally on strictly categorical forms of exclusion, formal or informal. They turn instead on categorically inflected selection processes, which—without being strictly categorical—may skew selection processes to the advantage of some categories and the disadvantage of others. They turn on the social production of categories of persons unequally disposed and equipped to pursue desirable positions. They turn on the social definition and valuation of positions in ways that reflect, in part, the categorical identities of their incumbents. And they turn on the ways honor, esteem, and respect—and their opposites—attach not only to categories of positions but also, if in diminishing measure, to categories of persons.

Inequality has increased dramatically in recent decades. But it has not become more categorical. Changes in the *degree* of inequality and changes in the *mode* of inequality result from different processes. Though it is beyond the scope of this chapter, I would speculate in closing that inequality has become less categorical in recent decades, while categorical differences have become less inegalitarian.[50] The dynamics of unbridled capitalism that are primarily responsible for intensifying systemic inequalities do not turn, in the first instance, on ascribed categories of difference. Financialization, for example, has contributed in a major way to increasing inequality (Lin and Tomaskovic-Devey 2013); but ascribed categories of difference have been largely irrelevant to the dynamics of financialization. At the same time, the differentialist turn of recent decades in liberal democratic polities has eroded some of the symbolic harms and inequalities associated with categories of difference. The social distribution of honor remains far from category-neutral, and some categories of difference—notably "Gypsy" in east central Europe and "Muslim" in northern and western Europe—have become more rather than less stigmatized in recent decades. But many forms of difference are much more likely to be publicly ratified and privately accepted today than, say, a half-century ago, and the social distribution of honor and esteem has become much less glaringly category-based.

Categories of difference figure in the production and reproduction of inequality, arguably, in a decreasingly categorical manner. This does not make them any less important. But it does highlight the limits of the closure paradigm in the analysis of inequality: an overextended notion of categorical exclusion obscures more than it reveals about the dynamics of inequality (Brubaker 2014). And it suggests that Tilly's account of categorical inequality, paradoxically, may be overly categorical. In his concern to distinguish his approach as sharply as possible from prevailing gradational and individualist modes of analysis, he insists too much on the strictly categorical nature of durable inequality. I have tried to outline a more differentiated account of the relation between difference and inequality, sensitive both to strictly categorical and to a variety of other processes and dynamics.

CHAPTER TWO

The Return of Biology

THE LAST DECADES of the twentieth century witnessed a striking change in prevailing understandings of race and ethnicity in the social sciences. This can be described most concisely as a shift from *objectivist* to *subjectivist* understandings. For the former, race and ethnicity exist independently of people's beliefs and practices; for the latter, they are *generated* by such beliefs and practices. For the former, racial and ethnic divisions are prior to the classification practices through which they are subsequently recognized (or misrecognized); for the latter, racial and ethnic divisions are *constituted by* classification practices. For the former, in short, race and ethnicity are *things in the world;* for the latter, they are *perspectives on* and *constructions of the world.*[1]

This gloss requires further unpacking to avoid misunderstanding. On the subjectivist account, race and ethnicity are not *experienced* as subjective. To any given individual, race and ethnicity may have a massive and refractory facticity, a thing-like externality and constraint. This is a result of the collective work of objectification and reification involved in all processes of institutionalization.[2] Race and ethnicity are indeed independent of any *particular* person's beliefs, practices, representations, or classifications; but they exist and persist only insofar as they are institutionalized, recognized, and reified in and through ongoing, chronically reproduced beliefs, practices, representations, and classifications. The resultant "objectivity of the subjective" (Bourdieu 1990) accounts for the paradox of the simultaneous obdurate facticity and evanescent insubstantiality of race and ethnicity.

A small but telling indicator of the subjectivist turn is the shift in the way basic definitional questions are posed. By the last decades of the twentieth century, discussions of race in the social sciences would seldom begin by asking "What is a race?" To pose the question this way—and to provide a straightforward answer of the form "A race is . . ."—would presuppose that races exist as objective entities. Instead discussions would begin by asking "What is race?" The difference might seem inconsequential; after all, the latter question also presumes the reality of race. But the two questions point to very different ways of construing the reality of race. On one approach, the reality of race follows from the objective existence of races. On the other, it follows from the pervasiveness and power of racial ideologies, discourses, and systems of classification. An influential text, for example, defines race as "a concept which signifies and symbolizes social conflicts and interests by referring to different types of human bodies." Although the concept has "no biological basis," it "continues to play a fundamental role in structuring and representing the social world" (Omi and Winant 1994: 54–55).[3] The reality of *race,* then, does not depend on the reality of *races.* Indeed it has become conventional to highlight one's denial of the objective existence of "races" through the use of quotation marks as a distancing device.[4]

As this example suggests, subjectivist accounts of what race *is* are often built on an assertion of what race *is not.* This negative thesis—that race has no biological foundation—is often supported by an appeal to the authority of biology (Gannett 2004: 325). At the turn of the century, this appeal seemed unproblematic. Biological thinking about human differences had changed radically over the course of the twentieth century, as typological thinking gave way to populationist and statistical thinking (Mayr 1970: 4–5; 1982: 45–47). If racialism, and even racism, could claim the mantle of science at the beginning of the century, antiracialism—the denial of the biological reality of race—could plausibly claim that mantle by the century's end.

The shift from typological to populationist understandings of difference in biology disrupted the congruence between scientific and folk understandings of race that had been characteristic of the late nineteenth and early twentieth century. Typological understandings of race in biology, like commonsense understandings, were essentialist and often hierarchical. Racial differences were understood as differences between types, not as differences between individuals. Differences between types were real and fundamental; differences between individuals—who were but imperfect expressions or impure mixtures of the underlying types—were accidental and theoretically uninteresting. Differences between types could be construed as sharp and discontinuous, even if differences between individuals—relegated to the realm of the accidental—were gradual and continuous. Typological understandings of difference could thus underwrite essentialist and hierarchical social thinking on race.

The populationist understanding of difference that emerged from the "evolutionary synthesis" of the 1930s and 1940s could not underwrite essentialist social understandings of race in the same way. Populationist understandings of difference were fundamentally statistical. Differences between individuals were real and fundamental. There was no underlying type: population-level characteristics existed only as statistical abstractions. Population thinking was incompatible with the notion of pure, unchanging types separated from one another by sharp discontinuities (Mayr 1970: 4).

Accounts of the shift between typological and populationist thinking have been justly criticized for obscuring the continuities in biological understandings of human difference (Provine 1986; Proctor 1988: 174–175; Gannett 2001; Reardon 2005; Gissis 2008; Yudell 2008; El-Haj 2007). Biologists did not simply abandon objectivist understandings of race when they embraced population-centered ways of thinking. Some biologists, to be sure, did assert categorically that races did not exist. In a classic 1962 article, for example, Frank Livingstone argued that "there are no races, only clines," that is, continuous geographic gradients. Many geneticists and physical anthropologists, however, continued to work with objectivist understandings of race, now reformulated in populationist terms.

Yet by the final decades of the twentieth century, the appeals of social scientists to the authority of biology to validate their assertion that race has no biological foundation were seldom contradicted, and they were often expressly endorsed.[5] Biology, to be sure, did not and does not speak with a single voice; and appeals of social scientists to the authority of biology to validate their subjectivist and constructivist understandings of race glossed over ongoing disagreements among biologists. Yet few biologists found it opportune to contest, directly and publicly, social scientists' claims to exclusive jurisdiction over the phenomenon of race.

There were two reasons for this stance. One was the gap between biological and folk understandings of race. The same term may have been used, but it often referenced very different concepts. Genetic definitions of races as populations differing in the frequency of one or more genetic variants (Dunn and Dobzhansky 1952: 118) meant that race (unlike, say, species) could not serve as a stable principle of taxonomy, since what counted as a race depended on the interests of a particular investigator. Races identified on the basis of one genetic variant or set of variants (the genes governing skin color, for example) would differ, sometimes radically, from races identified on the basis of another set (the genes controlling, say, blood type). Patterns of genetic variation would thus pick out "races" that did not correspond to folk understandings of race. The claim that race has no biological foundation—understood as the claim that prevailing *folk* understandings of race have no biological foundation—could thus be accepted even by biologists who held objectivist understandings of race.

The second reason for biologists' acquiescing in and sometimes expressly endorsing social scientists' denial of the biological reality of race involved political and moral sensibilities (Skinner 2006: 464–466). Objectivist understandings of race, already on the defensive in the United States in the 1920s and 1930s as anthropologists, sociologists, and psychologists came to construe diversity through the analytical prism of culture rather than nature (Degler 1991),[6] had been massively discredited by their centrality to Nazi theory and practice. This was strikingly expressed in the "Statement on Race" drafted by UNESCO in 1950, which declared inter alia that "for all practical social purposes, 'race' is not so much a biological phenomenon as a social myth."[7] This formulation was decades ahead of its time; sharp criticism from geneticists and physical anthropologists led to a revised, more cautiously formulated statement in 1951 (Provine 1986: 873–877). But the formulation would have been utterly unremarkable by the last decades of the century. The liberal antiracist ethos that was shared by most postwar natural as well as social scientists was not logically incompatible with objectivist understandings of racial and ethnic differences, but it contributed substantially to a general uneasiness with such understandings and to fears that they might be misused. Even if biologists themselves were comfortable with objectivist understandings, they were aware that others were not. Political and moral sensibilities—their own sensibilities and their awareness of prevailing public sensibilities—led many biologists to drop *race* in favor of the less fraught and more neutral and technical *population* (Banton 1998: 111–112; Gannett 2001: S486). These sensibilities led others to place a rhetorical emphasis on commonality to legitimate their own research on human differences. And they kept biologists from publicly challenging social scientists' claims that race was biologically meaningless, even when they continued to use objectivist understandings of race (or substantively equivalent objectivist understandings of population) in their own work.

The upshot was a tacit and largely uncontested division of jurisdiction between social scientists and biologists.[8] Social scientists, in effect, claimed exclusive jurisdiction over the phenomenon of race as it was experienced and enacted in social, cultural, economic, and political life. They grounded this jurisdictional claim—and their subjectivist accounts of race—on the assertion that race had no objective foundation: race was a social and cultural fact but a biological fiction. For both intellectual and political reasons, biologists did not contest this claim; they tacitly ceded jurisdiction over race to social scientists. Biologists could best ensure the legitimacy of their own—objectivist—studies of difference and variation by emphasizing that they were not challenging social scientists' exclusive jurisdiction over race.[9] They were studying populations; social scientists could study race. (Those biologists who continued—in dwindling numbers—to use the language of race made it clear that their technical use of *race* had little to do with ordinary uses of the term.) Biologists and social scientists alike found it convenient to treat the objectivist study of populations and the subjectivist study of race as independent orders of inquiry.[10]

The announcement of the completion of the "rough draft" of the human genome in June 2000 marked both the symbolic culmination of this division of jurisdiction and the beginning of its erosion. At the White House press conference heralding the event, the three speakers went out of their way in their brief remarks to emphasize that the Human Genome Project was *not* about race. President Clinton underscored "one of the great truths" to emerge from the project: "that in genetic terms, all human beings, regardless of race, are more than 99.9 percent the same." Francis Collins, director of the National Human Genome Research Institute, was "happy that today, the only race we are talking about is the human race." Craig Venter, head of Celera Genomics Corporation, was more categorical: the project showed that "the concept of race has no genetic or scientific basis."[11]

The celebration of commonality, however, soon yielded to the renewed exploration of difference.[12] Two randomly chosen humans might share 99.9 percent of their genome (though this figure has been challenged [Pearson 2006]). But the roughly 3 billion base pairs of the human genome left a lot of room for variation. And while most genetic variation is found *within* rather than *between* groups,[13] there was still plenty of between-group variation to explore. As the cost of sequencing plummeted, these differences could be explored with dazzlingly powerful and increasingly affordable tools.

In the biomedical field—the major driver of genomic research—these differences have been increasingly and explicitly linked to folk understandings of race. This has made it newly respectable to claim biological reality and scientific legitimacy for commonsense racial categories, and it has contributed to bridging the gap between biological and folk understandings of difference that opened up in the second half of the twentieth century. On the terrain of biomedicine, genomics has come to be understood, at least in the public eye, less as a *post*racial than a *neo*racial science.

Emblematic of the scientific rehabilitation of commonsense racial categories—and contributing significantly to that rehabilitation—is the work of leading genetic epidemiologist Neil Risch (Braun 2006). In a widely discussed opinion piece in *Genome Biology* (Risch et al. 2002), Risch directly challenged the claim—which had been endorsed, most recently, by editorials in both the *New England Journal of Medicine* (Schwartz 2001) and *Nature Genetics* (2001)—that race has no biological foundation. That claim, Risch suggested, rested on political sensitivities, not on scientific evidence. He argued that population genetic studies have validated traditional understandings of race, based on continental ancestry; that differences between continental races are not "merely cosmetic" but medically significant; and that standard measures underestimate genetic differences between races since rare disease-predisposing alleles, not captured in standard measures, are more likely than common alleles to be specific to a single race.

Risch claimed not only the mantle of scientific objectivity but also the moral and political high ground. To ignore race in biomedical research would not only be scientifically unwarranted; it would also be morally and politically problematic, hampering efforts to reduce health disparities between races. This exemplifies the emergence of what Catherine Bliss has called an "anti-racist racialism," a "race-positive" yet politically progressive stance among geneticists, as part and parcel of a broader political and cultural shift from color-blind (and more generally difference-blind) liberalism to an inclusive differentialism (Bliss 2012: 5, 15–17, 74ff; Fullwiley 2008). For decades, political and moral sensibilities had delegitimized objectivist understandings of race; now—at least in the domain of biomedicine—they could relegitimize such understandings. This antiracist racialism is of course not uncontroversial, but it cannot be ignored.

The new objectivism and naturalism present a challenge to subjectivist and constructivist accounts of race and ethnicity. The foundational assertion of such accounts—that race is a social fact but a biological myth—can no longer be supported by a straightforward appeal to the authority of biology, as if that appeal could settle the matter. Though some biologists continue to endorse this claim, others no longer hesitate to challenge it. These challenges come not from the fringe, not from "ogre naturalists" (Hacking 2005), not even necessarily from conservatives eager to deflect responsibility for racial inequality from social to natural causes. The assertion of the biological reality of race comes from the mainstream, in significant part from scientists who consider themselves progressives or liberals and who enlist racial objectivism in the service of reducing health disparities (Bliss 2012). This has helped to "redeem" (Morning 2011: 226–235) objectivist understandings of race, to cleanse them of their stain of association with early twentieth-century eugenics and Nazi atrocities.

The newly respectable biological objectivism about race—the claim that social understandings of race *do* have a biological foundation—has undermined the largely uncontested jurisdictional monopoly over race that the social sciences enjoyed in the last decades of the twentieth century. Biologists had tacitly ceded to social scientists the authority to speak about race, but they are now reclaiming that authority. Their claims have been powerfully supported by the media, which represents genomics as an "authoritative source of racial expertise" (Bliss 2012: 3; Braun 2006).

The cultural authority of genomics in matters of race, grounded in the ever-expanding world of biomedicine, extends to other domains as well, notably forensics, genealogy, and identity politics. In all these domains, as Ian Hacking (2005: 109) has observed with specific reference to biomedicine, "naturalism about race, far from being an atavistic throwback to an era well left behind, is a topic for today." This poses a challenge to constructivist theories of race and ethnicity, but it also creates new data for such theories. The return of biology is not just an intellectual challenge; it is an increasingly consequential cultural and social fact. The validity of biological accounts of race can be contested, but their cultural and social significance is beyond dispute.

The authority of genomics has made it respectable, even routine, to appeal to biology to underwrite and validate folk understandings of race and ethnicity. But the contemporary appeal to biology does not simply *reauthorize* commonsense understandings and practices; it *transforms* them (Gilroy 2000; Nash 2004; Skinner 2006; El-Haj 2007; Nelson 2008a). It does so in a complex and ambivalent way. By providing a natural foundation for social identities, geneticization can essentialize, even absolutize understandings of difference. Yet by highlighting the genetic heterogeneity within any collectivity, the dominance of within-group over between-group variation, and the histories—ancient and modern—of migration, gene flow, and admixture, geneticization can undermine understandings of pure, internally homogeneous, externally bounded groups. And by highlighting the uniqueness of every person's genetic makeup, genomics can ultimately dissolve collective into individual identities—which is precisely the ideal of "personalized genomic medicine." Race is not simply reauthorized by the return of biology; it is reconstructed. The nominal continuity of the word *race* masks significant shifts in its meaning.

The return of biology presents both a challenge and an opportunity for social scientists who write about race and ethnicity in a subjectivist and constructivist idiom. The challenge is to respond to the neo-objectivist, neonaturalist accounts without simply reasserting the usual mantra that there are no biologically significant differences between socially defined racial categories. The opportunity is to explore the ways in which ideas about the genetic foundations of race and ethnicity—regardless of their validity—have informed and transformed vernacular and organizational understandings and practices.

Social scientists—sociologists and anthropologists in particular—have begun to take up both the challenge and the opportunity. But this work—and the scientific and broader public debates about genetics in relation to race and ethnicity—has yet to be integrated into mainstream scholarship on race and ethnicity.[14] I seek in this chapter to provide a synoptic overview of these lines of work, to clarify the key issues at stake, and to bring these developments and debates to the attention of wider social science audiences. I proceed by reviewing transformations in the fields of biomedicine, forensics, genealogy, and identity politics. I conclude by outlining a subjectivist and constructivist response to the neo-objectivist, neonaturalist challenge.

Biomedicine

By far the most powerful engine driving the renewed salience of objectivist understandings of race and ethnicity is the vast juggernaut of biomedical research. Medicine has long been a privileged terrain of racial objectivism, a prime site for the constitution of putatively scientific understandings of racially differentiated human bodies (Wolff 2006). But the more proximate context for the return of racial objectivism is the distinctive system of ethnoracial counting and accounting that has come to be pervasively institutionalized in biomedical research in the United States in the past two decades.

Since 1995, researchers supported by the National Institutes of Health (NIH)—the overwhelmingly dominant funder of biomedical research—have been required to include racial and ethnic minorities as well as women as research subjects in clinical trials and to report any differences in results by race, ethnicity, or sex. This is the basic pillar of what Steven Epstein (2007) has called the "inclusion-and-difference paradigm" in biomedical research. That paradigm was subsequently "thickened" and extended in various ways, notably by Food and Drug Administration (FDA) rules requiring data from drug testing to be broken down by "important demographic subgroups," namely race, sex, and age (Epstein 2007: 117, 123).[15] These reforms, to be sure, built on existing traditions of counting and categorizing by race and ethnicity in epidemiology and public health. In particular, they built on a tradition of "health disparities" research that quantifies the massive inequalities between blacks and whites in nearly every measurable aspect of health. What was new in the 1990s was how the longstanding concern with *racial disparities in health outcomes* legitimized a newly respectable concern with possible *racial differences in disease processes.*

The institutionalization of this scheme of ethnoracial counting and accounting has been laced with ironies. In the first place, race and ethnicity were added as an afterthought to a legislative proposal that had been driven by concerns with women's health (Epstein 2007: 79). That biological differences between men and women might warrant the inclusion of women in at least some clinical trials (and the breakdown of results by sex) seemed self-evident; the much more controversial and problematic assumption that possible biological differences between racial or ethnic groups warranted the inclusion of minorities in clinical trials (and the breakdown of results by race and ethnicity) escaped serious critical examination. Race and ethnicity were smuggled in, without serious scrutiny, on the back of a sex-driven initiative.

Second, the requirements *for* the use of racial and ethnic categories were implemented just as subjectivist and constructivist arguments *against* the routine and uncritical use of such categories in biomedical research began to be taken seriously by public health and biomedical researchers and journal editors. The 1997 revision of the "Uniform Requirements for Manuscripts Submitted to Biomedical Journals" cautioned authors about using racial and ethnic categories and underscored their ambiguity (Epstein 2007: 207). Some journals went further. A *Nature Genetics* (2000) editorial criticized the use of race and ethnicity as "pseudo-biological variables" and announced that it would henceforth "require that authors explain why they make use of particular ethnic groups or populations, and how classification was achieved"; the *Archives of Pediatrics and Adolescent Medicine* announced in 2001 that authors should "not use race and ethnicity when there is no biological, scientific, or sociological reason for doing so" (Epstein 2007: 208); and a 2004 editorial in the *Journal of the American Medical Association* emphasized that the collection of data on race "is not sufficient reason to analyze outcomes by racial categories" (Winker 2004: 1614).

Third, the inclusion-and-difference paradigm has been *self-validating.* By mandating not only the recruitment of subjects but also the analysis and reporting of results by race and ethnicity, the paradigm was bound to generate just the sort of "difference findings" that were used to justify its introduction (Lee et al. 2001: 23; Epstein 2007: 109, 220–221). The avalanche of ethnoracially organized data generated by the subgroup comparison mandate has guaranteed that many statistically significant findings would be generated by chance alone.

Fourth, and most important, the requirement to recruit research subjects and report results by race and ethnicity was justified by the growing salience of racial and ethnic health disparities and the intensifying political commitment to reducing or eliminating them. Yet while the health disparities framework in epidemiology and public health highlights the *social* causes of disparities, the routine use of ethnoracial categories in biomedical research highlights putative *biological* causes of health disparities and contributes thereby to the naturalization of social categories (Kahn 2005; Shields et al. 2005; Epstein 2007: 296ff).

One key to this slippage between the social and the biological is the ambiguity of race as a variable in biomedical research. This is not simply a problem of how race is *measured;* it is a problem of what race *means* in a biomedical context. Self-identified race is taken by many biomedical researchers as a proxy for geographic ancestry, which is taken as a proxy for the probability of possessing certain medically relevant genetic variants.[16] But self-identified race is also a proxy for a wide array of social and environmental factors that are associated both with race and with medical outcomes. Researchers are of course aware of the potential for confounding, and they routinely seek—if only in a perfunctory way—to control for confounding factors. But since self-identified race is associated with so wide a range of social and environmental factors with a known or plausible connection to health outcomes, and because these are so difficult to measure, controlling for confounding factors is notoriously difficult (Kaufman et al. 1997).[17] Yet notwithstanding this difficulty, residual racial differences in medically significant outcomes—differences that remain after controlling for other factors—are routinely taken as suggesting genetic rather than social causes (Kahn 2013: 160–161).

A second key to the slippage between the social and the biological is the bureaucratic logic of what Epstein (2007: 90–93, 147–151) calls "categorical alignment." In operationalizing the mandate to recruit subjects and report results by race and ethnicity, the NIH and FDA adopted the standard set of census-based categories that was originally codified by the Office of Management and Budget (OMB) in its Directive 15 of 1977. Originally issued to ensure consistency in the gathering and reporting of data relevant to the enforcement of civil rights legislation, the unsung yet astonishingly influential Directive 15 governs the collection of racial and ethnic data at all levels and in all branches of government, and in the private and non-profit sectors as well. From the point of view of bureaucratic consistency and comparability, it made sense to import these ubiquitous administratively mandated categories—already used to organize a vast amount of data, including epidemiological and public health data—into biomedical research, despite the lack of any biomedical rationale for using what OMB itself underscored was a "socio-political construct" that was "not anthropologically or scientifically based."[18] But this alignment of ethnoracial categories across very different institutional domains—administrative practice, identity politics, and biomedical research—has facilitated the grafting of biological meanings onto social, political, and administrative categories. As biomedical "difference findings" have accumulated and have been organized and filtered through familiar racial and ethnic categories, these categories have come to be seen, once again, as grounded in biological differences. The upshot of this categorical alignment has been a deepening naturalization of social categories through the conflation of the social and biological meanings of race (Lee et al. 2001: 55; Shields et al. 2005; Epstein 2007: 91–92; Kahn 2006: 1966; Fujimura et al. 2008).

Categorical alignment operates not only between domains but within the domain of health research. The same ethnoracial categories are used in both *epidemiological* and *etiological* research. Epidemiological research uses racial categories to monitor health outcomes at the *population* level; etiological research uses the same categories to explain disease processes at the *cellular* level. Epidemiological research has documented massive health disparities along racial lines; the use of the same racial categories in etiological research makes it easy to suggest that these disparities are grounded in racially differentiated disease processes, and ultimately in racially differentiated genetic makeup (Kaufman and Cooper 2001; Shields et al. 2005: 89).[19]

The case of BiDil, the first race-specific drug to be approved by the FDA, shows how this slippage can occur in practice.[20] BiDil was not originally targeted by race; nor was it a new drug. It originated as a combination of two generic vasodilators, then known (by the initials of the generic drugs) as H/I, whose effectiveness in treating heart failure was suggested by a clinical trial in the early 1980s. A follow-up study in the late 1980s showed that ACE inhibitors, a different category of drug, were even more effective in treating heart failure, and these became part of the standard therapy. But H/I remained of medical interest since roughly a quarter of all patients do not respond well to ACE inhibitors (Kahn 2004: 12–13), and a single-dose version of the combination was patented in 1989 under the name BiDil. In 1997, however, the FDA declined to approve BiDil, on the grounds that the clinical data from the 1980s trials, which had not been designed as new drug trials, failed to satisfy criteria for new drug approval.

Only at this stage did race enter the picture. Having discovered racial differentials in a reanalysis of the data from the 1980s trials, cardiologists Jay Cohn and Peter Carson were able to secure a new patent for BiDil as a drug specifically tailored to African Americans. This new racial spin earned them an additional thirteen years of patent protection. After a clinical trial exclusively for African Americans (known as A-HeFT) showed a dramatic decrease in mortality for patients taking BiDil in addition to standard therapy (including ACE inhibitors), the FDA approved BiDil in 2005 for the treatment of heart failure in African American patients.

FDA approval made BiDil a media sensation as the first "race drug," and the impressive results of A-HeFT seemed to some commentators to validate the argument that heart disease is a "different disease" for blacks and whites (Kahn 2004: 9–11, 18–20). But in fact A-HeFT showed nothing of the kind. It showed conclusively that BiDil (in conjunction with standard therapies) was very effective for some patients. But since A-HeFT was limited to African Americans, the study did not and could not show that BiDil was more effective for African Americans than for others. The differential response by race that emerged in post hoc subgroup analysis of the 1980s trials, which served as the basis for the race-specific patent, did *not* pertain to the use of BiDil in addition to now-standard ACE inhibitors. Treatment of heart failure was quite different in the 1980s, and mortality rates from heart failure have subsequently declined dramatically across the board. Post hoc racial subgroup analysis, moreover, is problematic in any case (Ellison et al. 2008: 2–3); given the association of race with exposure to a variety of health risks, measured racial differentials are open to a variety of interpretations and provide at best equivocal evidence of biologically based racial differences in response to treatment.[21]

The racialization of an originally nonracial drug and the suggestion of a genetic basis for possible racial differences in drug response illustrate the importance, underscored earlier, of the ambiguity of race as a variable in biomedical research and of the alignment of categories across institutional domains. Because self-identified race encodes both biogenetic and socioenvironmental factors, the racial differences that appeared in the retrospective analysis of the 1980s clinical trials could be interpreted as suggesting an underlying genetic cause and as warranting the conversion of BiDil into a race-targeted drug. And categorical alignment—the employment of the same ethnoracial categories, operationalized in the same way, in sociopolitical and biomedical contexts—facilitated the racialization of

BiDil by enabling its backers to cast the drug as a response to the morally and politically urgent need to address the apparently dramatic (though in fact often grossly exaggerated [Kahn 2004: 18ff]) racial disparities in heart disease.

The evidence for differential response by race to BiDil was outdated and at best ambiguous. But it is of course possible that BiDil *is* more effective in treating African Americans and that this greater effectiveness has some basis in biology, and ultimately in genetics. Pharmacogenetic research has identified certain genetic variants that affect drug response, notably by influencing the behavior of drug-metabolizing enzymes. Such variants can make a difference both in the effectiveness of a drug and in its side effects. And some of these variants exhibit nontrivial differences in frequency across socially defined racial categories (Tate and Goldstein 2004; Goldstein et al. 2003).[22] It's possible that some such genetic variants make BiDil more effective, on average, for African Americans.

The irony is that if this were to prove true, race might become *less* rather than *more* relevant. BiDil has been marketed exclusively to African Americans and represented as a race-specific drug. Yet if genetic variants affecting the drug's workings become known, race would lose its clinical significance. Instead of prescribing the drug on the basis of a patient's race, one could directly test all patients for the relevant genetic variants and adjust drug choice or dosage accordingly. BiDil might be indicated for a higher fraction of black than white patients, but it might cease to be a "race drug." The assertion of a *potential* genetic basis for health disparities deepens the racialization of medicine, but the discovery of an *actual* genetic basis for differential disease susceptibility or drug response could work in an individualizing and deracializing direction.[23]

Just this is the goal of personalized medicine, which seeks to tailor treatment to the unique circumstances, and the unique genome, of every individual, and thereby to render race clinically irrelevant (Ng et al. 2008; Ginsburg and Willard 2009; Personalized Medicine Coalition 2014). Yet in a further irony, this vision of an eventually personalized, individualized, and therefore postracial medicine licenses the continued use of race as a provisional and temporary practice. The rhetoric of eventual personalization legitimizes the reality of continued—and even expanded—racialization (Kahn 2013: 157–165).[24] Defenders of the use of racial categories often concede that race per se is not a biologically meaningful category, that it is at best a crude surrogate for currently unknown genetic differences, and that advances in genetic knowledge will eventually obviate the use of this surrogate. But they argue that it would be irresponsible not to use race as a serviceable proxy in the meantime.

The "meantime," however, stretches indefinitely into the future.[25] Hopes for an imminent genomically driven revolution in medical care have proved to be unfounded, and the hype that surrounded personalized medicine in the early 2000s in connection with the completion of the Human Genome Project has yielded to more sober and realistic assessments (Burke and Psaty 2007; Kraft and Hunter 2009; Li 2011; Brunham and Hayden 2012).[26] Increased awareness of the limitations and complexities of genetically based predictions of disease susceptibility and drug response has made personalized medicine a more distant prospect today than it appeared to be a decade and a half ago. In the long run, research may indeed dissolve the biological correlates of race into genetic and epigenetic individuality. Yet for the foreseeable future, race is likely to become more rather than less central to biomedical research, drug development, and clinical practice.

Forensics

Biomedical research is a vast cosmos unto itself. Even as it points to clinical applications as its raison d'être, it operates at a considerable remove from clinical practice. Forensic DNA analysis, by contrast, is directly driven by practical applications. The dominant application seeks to match DNA profiles obtained from crime scene samples to profiles obtained from known individuals. A second, still emerging application seeks to predict the phenotype of an unknown perpetrator from crime scene DNA. These two applications engage issues of race and biology in very different ways.

At present, DNA analysis is used overwhelmingly in an *individualizing* mode. What matters is the DNA signature or "fingerprint" that identifies a unique individual (except in the case of identical twins). An interlocking series of technical, political, and cultural developments has made DNA a core forensic technology of identification: (1) the refinement of techniques for extracting, manipulating, and storing DNA from even minute and degraded crime scene samples (Williams and Johnson 2008: 59–67); (2) the reduction of the staggering complexity of genetic information to a standardized, tractable, easily comparable, and virtually unique digital DNA profile through the sampling of an astonishingly small number of highly variable genetic loci (Kahn 2008); (3) the rapid accumulation of such digital profiles—drawn from crime scene samples and from persons convicted of (and in some cases merely arrested for) an increasingly wide range of offenses—in government-mandated, easily searchable databases (Roberts 2011); and (4) the legal, political, and broader cultural construction of DNA evidence as authoritative (Lynch et al. 2008).

Controversy has focused on the establishment and expansion of DNA databases. Originally populated with profiles drawn from those convicted of the most serious and violent crimes, the databases have expanded dramatically in the past two decades. The U.S. database, CODIS, now contains over 12 million profiles (Federal Bureau of Investigation 2013); the UK database, NDNAD, is even more comprehensive, containing profiles of 6 million individuals (or 10 percent of the population, vs. less than 4 percent in the United States [National DNA Strategy Board n.d.]).[27] The databases have grown as the range of offenses has broadened and as some jurisdictions have begun to take (and retain) samples from all persons arrested for certain offenses, regardless of whether a conviction ensues. In California, for example, a strongly supported 2004 ballot initiative mandated the collection of DNA samples from all adults arrested for any felony charge, as well as all adults and juveniles convicted of any felony. About 13 percent of the profiles in CODIS and 20 percent of those in NDNAD are from persons arrested but not convicted (Federal Bureau of Investigation 2013; National DNA Strategy Board n.d.).[28]

The databases permit three kinds of matching: (1) the matching of one crime scene profile to another, indicating that two crimes may have been committed by the same person; (2) the matching of a crime scene profile to the DNA profile obtained from a suspect identified through some other, nongenetic means; and (3) the matching of a crime scene profile to a DNA profile stored in the database.

Race enters the picture in connection with this last kind of matching: the "cold hits" that identify suspects whose profiles are stored in a database.[29] But it does so in a very different way in database-driven DNA profiling than in biomedical research. The routine use of social race categories in biomedical research facilitates the grafting of biological meaning onto social categories. Database-driven DNA profiling does not promote the same conflation of social and biological processes. DNA data banks are not intrinsically racialized systems of knowledge. The DNA profiles they contain comprise strings of numbers representing the number of times short sequences of DNA are repeated at thirteen highly variable genetic loci; they do not contain racial identifiers or labels, and the DNA at these noncoding loci contain no information about phenotype. The DNA profiles are analogous to fingerprints: they index unique individuals, not racial or other categories. These DNA fingerprints have been used to exonerate more than three hundred wrongly convicted criminals, 70 percent of them non-white.[30]

Yet while the DNA profiles stored in data banks are not themselves racially encoded, they are generated by massively racialized social processes. A large literature has explored the ways in which race—as a practically

salient social category—is implicated in the workings of the criminal justice system, inter alia through racial profiling by the police, racial differentials in sentencing practices, and, most consequentially, the targeting of the
"war on drugs" and the consequent prison boom on residents of poor
non-white neighborhoods (Ossorio and Duster 2005; Mauer 2006; Western 2006). These processes have yielded massive racial disparities in incarceration rates and have led to the "hyper-incarceration" (Wacquant 2010)
of young, black, poorly educated men. The same processes have generated
massive racial disparities in representation in DNA data banks. If black
male high school dropouts have a 60 percent chance of going to prison by
their mid-thirties, an even higher fraction of this group is no doubt represented in CODIS, which is becoming a "nearly universal database for
[poorly educated] urban black men" (Roberts 2011: 579).[31] Because of their
overrepresentation in CODIS, African Americans—and poorly educated
African Americans in particular—thus face a much higher probability of
being identified as suspects through "cold hits" generated by matching crime
scene samples with DNA profiles in CODIS. They are also at higher risk of
being falsely convicted because of laboratory error or the planting of evidence (Thompson 2008). This differential risk of implication by DNA ampli-
fies existing racial inequalities in the criminal justice system by adding a
new self-reinforcing loop.[32]

The expansion of DNA data banks reinforces existing racial inequalities, but it does not—unlike biomedical research—contribute to refashion-
ing race as a biologically grounded category. A second forensic application
of DNA, however, *does*—or at least *can*—work in this direction. This is
what is known as forensic DNA phenotyping (FDP), which seeks to predict the phenotype of an unknown suspect from crime scene DNA. Two
variants of FDP can be distinguished (Koops and Schellekens 2008). The
first uses "ancestry-informative markers"—genetic variants that are highly
variable across populations—to predict the ethnoracial self-identification
and biogeographic ancestry of a suspect and thus, indirectly, to predict
phenotypic features associated with that self-identification or ancestry.
The second seeks to predict phenotypic features such as skin, eye, and hair
color directly through an analysis of the genetic variants that code for these
traits.

Although there are virtually no "population-specific" alleles—genetic
variants found only in a single group—researchers have discovered hundreds of single-nucleotide polymorphisms (SNPs) with substantially differing allelic frequencies across geographically defined populations. Taken
individually, such genetic variants do not yield reliable information about
ancestry. Taken together, however, the variants found at hundreds of such

variable genetic loci can yield powerful estimates of ancestry and of individual ethnoracial self-identification. The notions of "population" and "ancestry," to be sure, are elusive and contested, and estimates of ancestry and self-identification work better in some contexts than in others. It is obviously much harder to predict the self-identification of someone whose grandparents have substantially differing biogeographic ancestries than of someone whose grandparents have similar biogeographic ancestries. Estimates of individual biogeographic ancestry, moreover—typically presented as percentages of ancestry attributable to three continental regions of "origin"—raise a host of conceptual and methodological problems and can generate anomalous or even nonsensical results in some contexts (Royal et al. 2010).

Still, it is clear that certain polymorphisms, taken in combination with one another, are indeed powerfully ancestry-informative and can be pragmatically useful in some forensic contexts. It is this that led the now-defunct company DNAPrint Genomics to market its panel of ancestry-informative markers not only to individuals seeking information about their ancestries but also to law enforcement agencies.[33] Its product DNA Witness, according to promotional material, would identify "the heritable component of race" and enable police to "determine race proportions from crime scene DNA": "This test provides not only the majority population affiliation (i.e. Indo European, Sub-Saharan African, East Asian or Native American), but the admixture, as well (i.e. 82% East Asian and 18% Indo-European mix)" (Shields and Thompson 2003).

DNAPrint's technology has been used in a few high-profile cases, the most notable of which involved a serial killer in Louisiana in 2001–2003. Crime scene DNA had yielded no hits in the database, and a police investigation—focused as a result of eyewitness testimony and an FBI profile on a young white man—had reached a dead end. DNAPrint's panel of ancestry-informative markers suggested that the investigation was on the wrong track: the ancestry of the suspect was estimated to be 85 percent sub-Saharan African and 15 percent Native American. The company's chief scientific officer, Tony Frudakis, could not categorically identify the suspect's ethnoracial self-identification—the suspect "could be African American or Afro-Caribbean." But he was categorical about one thing: "There is no chance that this is a Caucasian" (Newsome 2007). Having commissioned from DNAPrint the analysis of a few dozen test samples from known individuals, the task force charged with the investigation believed this analysis was credible. The investigation was reoriented, and an African American man who had come to the attention of police in other contexts was arrested and eventually convicted on the basis of a DNA match to crime scene evidence (Frudakis 2008: 599–603).

Despite this much-publicized success, DNAPrint went out of business in 2009. Law enforcement agencies in the United States have been hesitant to adopt forensic DNA phenotyping. While cost was one factor, political sensitivities—and specifically, concerns about a new form of racial profiling—appear to have played a role as well (Newsome 2007). Yet while DNAPrint did not survive, forensic DNA phenotyping is likely to become more rather than less widely used in the future as new techniques—emerging from the confluence of developments in population genetics, biomedical research, direct-to-consumer ancestry testing, and forensics—promise more accurate results. This may contribute to the naturalization of race and ethnicity by suggesting that race is ultimately "in our genes." Even as sophisticated an observer as Nicholas Kristof (2003) cited the Louisiana serial killer case in challenging the idea that race is "biologically meaningless": "DNA does tend to differ, very slightly, with race. . . . Genetics increasingly shows that racial and ethnic distinctions are real—but often fuzzy and greatly exaggerated."

Emergent techniques for predicting phenotypic traits directly from the genetic variants that code for them, according to some observers, offer a potential way to avoid the naturalization and reification of race. It may be possible in the foreseeable future to predict eye color, hair color, skin color, height, handedness, and other externally visible and therefore potentially forensically relevant features of an unknown suspect directly, without the intervening use of identifiers that index self-identified race or biogeographic ancestry.[34] In theory, such techniques could be deracializing: just as personalized medicine promises to bypass race by directly analyzing genetic variants linked to disease susceptibility or drug response, so forensic DNA phenotyping promises to bypass race by directly analyzing genetic variants that code for observable traits.[35]

In practice, however, direct forensic DNA phenotyping is more likely to reinforce than to transcend race (Sankar 2010). Features like skin color and facial structure are closely associated with socially defined racial categories and are likely to be interpreted through a racial lens. And since socially defined racial categories are deeply and pervasively embedded in the routine practices of policing, predicted phenotypic traits that are strongly associated with such categories (such as skin color) are more likely to be forensically relevant than those (such as height or handedness) that are not. Most fundamentally, racially associated phenotypic traits are themselves likely to be *differentially* relevant in forensic contexts (Ossorio

2006; M'Charek 2008: 402). Here the distinction between marked and unmarked traits and categories is useful. The most pragmatically relevant phenotypic traits in forensic contexts are likely to be those that are themselves marked *and* that are associated with marked racial categories around which policing activities are already organized. Unmarked traits like light skin and average stature are unlikely to generate a forensically relevant class of suspects.[36] Red hair is a marked phenotypic trait, but it is not associated in the United States with a marked ethnoracial category. Dark skin is a marked phenotypic trait, and it is locally associated with a marked racial category that is already pervasively embedded in police work. Because it meshes more closely with routine police practices, a forensic DNA phenotyping finding that predicts dark skin (or other traits associated with African Americans or with other marked local minorities) is likely to have more pragmatic force in forensic contexts than other findings.

One further way in which socially defined racial categories can be invested with biological authority involves the burgeoning field of behavioral genetics.[37] This is a point of intersection between biomedicine and criminology. The field's rapid expansion has been driven largely by NIH and other biomedically oriented funding in the hope of explaining variability in dispositions and behaviors that contribute to health outcomes. But the increasing sophistication and rapidly decreasing cost of sequencing technology have made it easy and inexpensive to include genetic data in studies that seek to explain dispositions and traits relevant to a wide range of outcomes and processes, including delinquency and criminality.

Behavioral genetics has no intrinsic connection with race: its fundamental concern is to explain individual differences, not group differences. Neither twin studies—designed to estimate the heritability of various dispositions or behaviors—nor more recent molecular-level efforts to link particular genetic variants to psychological or behavioral outcomes have any necessary connection to race. Yet in a context in which race is already deeply and pervasively implicated in the workings of the criminal justice system and in popular representations and understandings of crime, research focused on identifying possible genetic bases of aggression, impulsivity, sensation-seeking, and other dispositions or behaviors associated with crime is easily appropriated and translated into public discourse in ways that contribute to naturalizing the association between race and crime. This is particularly true for molecular genetic studies that posit a link between specific genetic variants and dispositions and behaviors associated with crime, especially when the variants in question (like some genetic variants that affect disease susceptibility and drug response) are found in differing frequencies across socially defined racial categories.

A case in point is the MAOA gene, which regulates the activity level of an enzyme that breaks down neurotransmitters such as serotonin and dopamine in the brain. A number of studies over the course of the past decade have suggested a connection between forms of this gene that generate low levels of the enzyme and various forms of "antisocial behavior." One widely cited study found that among those exposed to early childhood maltreatment and physical abuse, those with the low-activity form of the MAOA gene were more likely to develop forms of antisocial behavior as adults (Caspi et al. 2002). This study found no direct effect of the gene on behavioral outcomes (though it *did,* like other studies, find a direct effect of childhood maltreatment); instead it found evidence of a gene-environment interaction, in which the gene affected how individuals responded to adverse environmental experiences. Some other studies (for example, Huizinga et al. 2006) failed to replicate this result, though a meta-analysis (Kim-Cohen et al. 2006) provided support for it.

The qualified, complex, and contradictory findings about the MAOA gene—dubbed the "warrior gene" by a journalist in 2004—were appropriated in public discussion in a simplified, often sensationalized, and in some contexts overtly racialized manner. The Caspi et al. (2002) study had made no mention of race. But when a New Zealand scientist reported that more than half of the Maori men he had tested carried the low-activity form of the gene (roughly twice as many as in European populations), speculated that this may be linked to their historical seafaring and military prowess, and allegedly (though the scientist claimed he was misquoted) also linked this to contemporary problems of alcoholism and violence, the media ran stories attributing "Maori violence" to the "warrior gene" (Yong 2010). Similarly reductive and expressly racialized accounts linking a similar prevalence of the low-activity form of the MAOA gene to aggression and crime among African Americans are staples of the far-right blogosphere in the United States. (These accounts conveniently ignore the similar or higher prevalence of the low-activity form of the MAOA gene among East Asian populations [Lea and Chambers 2007]). Even apart from such sensationalized and overtly racialized accounts, behavioral genetic findings are likely to be assimilated in public understandings in ways that downplay complex gene-environment interactions and strengthen understandings of crime and aggression as rooted in genetic predispositions. In a context in which crime is already understood in pervasively racialized terms, this cannot help but contribute to the naturalization of the association between race and crime.

Behavioral genetic research using the DNA samples stored in forensic data banks would also contribute to the naturalization of the association between race and crime. This has not yet happened, but some experts are worried that it might. While the DNA *profiles* stored in the data banks and used for the purpose of matching crime scene DNA against that of an unknown suspect are simply strings of numbers, twenty-nine states store the actual *tissue samples* used to generate the profiles, and state-level restrictions on the uses of these samples are rather loose (Kimmelman 2000: 211–212). This raises the possibility that researchers might use such racially skewed data banks in an effort to identify the distinctiveness of what is publicly represented as "criminal DNA" (despite the fact that many of the samples are taken from persons arrested but never convicted).

The return of objectivist understandings of race and ethnicity has followed differing trajectories in the biomedical and forensic domains. Socially defined racial categories have accrued biological meaning in biomedical contexts through the ironic workings of a self-consciously progressive politics of inclusion, which mandates the pervasive use of an ethnoracial scheme of counting and accounting in biomedical research, and through the bureaucratic logic of categorical alignment, which requires the use of the same categories in epidemiological and etiological research. Racial categories have accrued biological meaning in forensic contexts through efforts to predict ethnoracial self-identification, ancestry, and phenotype from crime scene DNA, and—in the context of a pervasively racialized criminal justice system—through research on the genetic bases of dispositions linked to criminal behavior.

Yet on a deeper level, there are striking parallels between developments in biomedicine and forensics, specifically in the popular appropriation or misappropriation of research findings. Some public discourses, appealing to sociologically oriented epidemiological and criminological research, emphasize the social causes of racialized disparities in both health and criminal justice outcomes. Other public discourses, appealing to genetically oriented biomedical and behavioral research, posit a genetic basis of both health and, more or less explicitly, criminal justice disparities. In so doing they risk transforming disparity into difference (Kahn 2005: 125–126, 129; Rothenberg and Wang 2006: 359): a social problem that calls out for amelioration is reformulated as a biological fact that is refractory to public policy intervention.

In both biomedical and forensic domains, the immense public authority and prestige of genetics, the steady accumulation of genetic findings, and the circuits through which those findings are appropriated by journalists, filtered through prevailing essentialist schemes of interpretation, and disseminated to broader popular audiences have on balance bestowed new-found scientific—or putatively scientific—legitimacy on essentialist, natu-ralist, and objectivist understandings of race and ethnicity. Even efforts to bypass the use of socially defined racial categories in biomedical and be-havioral genetic research by identifying the causally significant genetic variants may in practice reinvest socially defined racial categories with bi-ological meaning. When putatively significant genetic variants exhibit non-trivial frequency differences between socially defined racial categories, this can reinforce the notion that race is "in our genes." And when the medical or behavioral outcome associated with the genetic variant is a stigmatized one, as in the case of the "warrior gene," biomedical and behavioral gene-tic research can contribute not only to naturalizing race but also to natu-ralizing the association between race and disease or between race and crime.

Genealogy

Developments in biomedicine and forensics affect popular understand-ings largely via the media: lay audiences are passive consumers of stories crafted by journalists (with the help of other intermediaries like university communications and media relations offices). In the domain of genetic ge-nealogy, by contrast, lay consumers of ancestry tests are actively involved in constructing stories about who they are and where they come from. What matters here are not prevailing media representations but the sense-making practices of large numbers of lay users, drawn by the relatively inexpensive tests that have been marketed since 2000 by a rapidly shift-ing landscape of companies (Greely 2008; Royal et al. 2010; Wagner et al. 2012).[38]

An emerging body of work suggests that people make sense of ancestry tests in complex and sometimes surprising ways. On the one hand, ancestry tests can of course reinforce and naturalize commonsense racial categories (Bolnick 2003). On the other hand, test results can destabilize previously taken-for-granted racial and ethnic identities; they can provide resources for constructing complex narratives of kinship and affiliation that are at variance with prevailing idioms of racial and ethnic identity. Moreover, ancestry tests are not self-interpreting. The companies that market them do provide various interpretive guides to the results, but the test results—along with other, nongenetic resources—are then enlisted in a process of "affiliative self-fashioning" (Nelson 2008a) that leaves considerable room for interpretation and choice (Hirschman and Panther-Yates 2008; Nash

2004; Hacking 2006). On balance, the literature suggests that genetic genealogy cannot be described as simply reinforcing essentialist or naturalist
understandings of race.

In biomedicine and forensics, ancestry is a marker or proxy for genes; in
genetic genealogy, genes are a marker for ancestry. Particular genetic variants are significant not as causal agents that predispose to disease, behavior, or appearance but as nonfunctional markers—differentially distributed as a result of ancient and recent migrations, genetic drift, and social
and geographic barriers to random mating—that can be used to make inferences about ancestry and to construct usable stories about who we are
and where we come from.

Two types of tests are commercially available (Royal et al. 2010). The
first (and until very recently by far the most common) uses mitochondrial
DNA markers transmitted from mothers to their children or Y-chromosome markers transmitted from fathers to sons to make inferences about
maternal or paternal lineages. Because mitochondrial DNA and Y-chromosome DNA (unlike the rest of our DNA) are transmitted without recombination from generation to generation, these tests can yield powerful
inferences about maternal and paternal lineages.[39] The inferences may
concern "deep ancestry" (Wells 2007) in a paleoanthropological time frame,
or they may concern the more recent ancestry that is relevant to those interested in tracing particular genealogical relationships or in learning
about the more proximate "origins" of a maternal or paternal lineage.

Deep ancestry tests place people in mitochondrial DNA or Y-chromosome haplogroups. These are groups that share a common maternal or
paternal ancestor and a distinctive genetic mutation—a "unique event
polymorphism"—originating with that ancestor.[40] Haplogroups represent
biological lineages (not to be confused with socially real or meaningful
lineages) whose origin in space and time can be estimated, whose subsequent main paths of migratory dispersion can be conjecturally traced, and
whose contemporary geographic distribution can be mapped. Deep ancestry tests allow consumers to focus on a single intuitively and concretely
meaningful maternal or paternal lineage, to follow the migration paths of
their ancient ancestors, and to participate vicariously in the "story of the
greatest journey ever told: how our ancestors migrated from their African
homeland to populate the Earth tens of thousands of years ago."[41]

For some test takers, haplogroups have become meaningful biosocial
identities. But for others, paleoanthropological time is too remote to be of
interest, and haplogroups are too abstract. Their very names are forbid-
dingly abstract: they bear labels like R1b (also known in an alternative
nomenclature as R-M343). Haplogroup frequencies do differ substantially

among contemporary populations defined by ethnicity, nationality, and region, and maps make the contemporary clinal geographic distributions of haplogroups intuitively graspable.[42] But a mitochondrial DNA or Y-chromosome haplogroup cannot be interpreted as an indicator of "deep" ethnic or racial identity, both because of the gross anachronism of projecting ethnic categories back into paleoanthropological time and because mitochondrial DNA and Y-chromosome tests necessarily ignore most biological ancestors—almost all of them, in fact—in order to reconstruct a single line of descent.[43]

For those interested in more recent ancestry, other mitochondrial DNA and Y-chromosome markers can be compared to reference databases in order to make probabilistic inferences about one's relatively proximate maternal- or paternal-line ancestry. This has appealed with particular poignancy to African Americans and other Afro-descendant populations who, inspired by the example of Alex Haley, have sought to reconstruct African ancestral roots so as to repair the massive breach in collective memory and continuity imposed by the Middle Passage (Nelson 2008a; Schramm 2012).[44] African Ancestry, the best-known company that targets such persons, promises to "determine which present-day African country and ethnic group you share ancestry with" on the maternal or paternal line and to provide a "premium personalized certificate" along with a map of Africa and a "Guide to African History and Cultures."[45] Test results have led some users not simply to revise their self-understanding but to visit their newly identified homeland and to take other steps to convert an abstract test result into a lived, experienced, and embodied identification (Nelson 2008a: 770–771; 2008b: 259–262; Schramm 2012).[46] But the severe truncation of ancestry imposed by mitochondrial DNA and Y-chromosome tests is brought home in the boldface disclaimer accompanying the description of African Ancestry's PatriClan test: "We cannot guarantee that your results will be African! Only 65% of the paternal lineages we trace result in African ancestry. There is a 35% chance that your results will not be African."[47] This risk results directly from considering just one of many ancestral strands. For those seeking to reconstruct their brutally severed genealogical ties to African ancestors, it may be a bitter irony to have this one strand traced back to Europe.[48]

To overcome the limitations of focusing on a single lineage, companies are increasingly promoting a second kind of test that uses autosomal DNA, inherited from both parents, instead of (or in addition to) mitochondrial DNA and Y-chromosome DNA. Because autosomal DNA is inherited from both parents through recombination, autosomal tests cannot trace specific lineages the way uniparentally inherited mitochondrial DNA and

Y-chromosome tests can. Instead they rely on rapidly accumulating data about the uneven distribution of genetic markers known as single nucleotide polymorphisms, or SNPs, to make inferences about ancestry—not about "deep" ancestry but about relatively recent ancestry, about "where your ancestors lived 500 years ago, before the advent of intercontinental travel."[49] Autosomal tests have become widely available only recently, as it has become technically and economically feasible to test large numbers of SNPs—700,000 to 1 million, at this writing—and to match the results statistically against growing databases of reference populations. And prices have dropped sharply in the past few years, with the major companies now offering autosomal tests for about $100.

Until recently, the reference populations were specified only in continental terms, as African, European, Asian, and Native American. In the past few years, however, companies offering autosomal tests have begun to use larger numbers of more finely distinguished reference populations. This shift, made possible by larger reference databases and by the testing of larger numbers of markers, responds to users' desire for more concrete and socially meaningful ancestries that can be enlisted in the construction of a "usable past" (Nelson 2008a). Continental categories do not provide useful social identities; they do not furnish a useful answer to the question "Where are you from?" (Schramm 2012: 180). The forms of multiculturalism that are institutionalized in U.S. schools, for example, create a demand for "ethnicity," for which continental racial identifications are not helpful. Schramm (2012: 179–180) makes this point with respect to the category "African," but the same holds for "European." Afro-descendant populations may have a particularly keen interest in reconstructing severed ancestral ties to Africa, but their desire to identify ties to particular regions or ethnic groups is shared by others.

Some commentators worry that autosomal ancestry tests work in the direction of reifying and naturalizing commonsense racial and ethnic categories. The concern is understandable. One leading company, Ancestry.com, explicitly promises to reveal the test taker's "genetic ethnicity" and to provide a breakdown of "the various ethnic groups contained in your DNA."[50] Here ethnicity is directly advertised to be "in your DNA." The other major companies are more circumspect. 23andMe and Family Tree DNA refer to "populations" rather than "ethnic groups," and the former cautions that "the population labels refer to genetically similar groups, rather than nationalities."[51] Even so, these and other autosomal tests—unlike deep ancestry mitochondrial DNA and Y-chromosome tests—use familiar racial, ethnic, national, and ethnoregional labels for their populations; and this facilitates the alignment of the genetically relatively homogeneous populations constructed by the ancestry testing companies with commonsense racial, ethnic, and national categories. As in the biomedical domain, such categorical alignment provides a conduit through which biological meaning is grafted onto social categories.

Yet there are grounds for a more sanguine view of autosomal ancestry tests. Mitochondrial DNA and Y-chromosome tests can underwrite understandings of singular identities and pure origins. "Are you a Viking?" and "Are you Jewish?" asks iGENEA in promoting such tests.[52] These tests focus on a single ancestral line whose mitochondrial or Y-chromosome DNA has remained identical for millennia (save for the rare mutations that make inferences about ancestry possible). That literal form of genetic identity—an identity unadulterated by recombination—can support understandings of an equally pure and unmixed ancient social identity. Customers can be "seduced by the promise of a pure, but fictive genealogy" (Brodwin 2002: 328; Nash 2008: 260–263).

Autosomal tests, by contrast, provide no support for understandings of "pure" identities. Indeed they directly challenge such understandings. Unlike mitochondrial and Y-chromosome DNA, autosomal DNA gets mixed up every generation through recombination. Ancestry tests cannot untangle that mixing; they cannot distinguish maternal from paternal contributions to one's DNA. Moreover, autosomal tests not only analyze biparentally inherited—and therefore "mixed"—DNA; they also reveal that virtually everyone derives genetic ancestry from a variety of ancestral populations. This emphasis on universal mixedness undermines typological forms of racial thinking.

To be sure, this notion of "mixedness" is not entirely innocent. As has often been observed (for example by Gilroy 2000: 250), the notion of "mixing"—like the notions of hybridity, creolization, or syncretism—implicitly posits some prior unmixed elements that the mixture comprises. And the parental populations to which autosomal tests assign ancestral proportions may, as noted earlier, be conflated with identically labeled commonsense racial, ethnic, and national categories in such a way that the relative genetic similarity used to construct the former is taken as proof of the biological existence of the latter. Short of such conflation, it may also be the case that autosomal tests encourage a view of the world as having consisted of largely isolated, stationary, and discrete populations five hundred years ago that only subsequently became mixed—a view that erases earlier histories of migration and mixing. This view may suit well enough the relative stability of European populations during the half-millennium preceding 1500, but it neglects the very different demographic histories of other parts of the world. This view may also foster the habit of dividing the world's population into relatively "pure" and "recently admixed" populations.

All these caveats are important. Yet they provide no warrant for concluding, as Bolnick (2003: 6) did in her pioneering analysis a decade ago, that genetic ancestry tests "suggest that race is biologically determined, and that humans can be divided into a small number of discrete groups." Ancestry testing is a dynamic and rapidly evolving field. As reference databases have grown, they have supported finer-grained discriminations among "populations." Attention has already shifted away from the continental-level categories aligned with folk notions of race to smaller-scale, more specific categories aligned with ethnicity, nationality, and region; this downward scalar shift is likely to continue. This may contribute to naturalizing ethnic, national, or even subethnic regional categories even as it weakens the hold of continental racial categories on the genealogical imagination. But a growing awareness of universal mixedness may also contribute to undermining notions of pure, bounded, and discrete racial, ethnic, *or* national categories. No doubt both processes will occur; genetic genealogy takes many forms, and its effects are likely to be contradictory and ambiguous.[53]

The Politics of Belonging

In the biomedical, forensic, and genealogical domains, genetic data are incorporated into specific, institutionalized organizational practices and routines. Genetic variants figure in these routines as causal agents that affect disease susceptibility and drug response, as individuating and identifying markers, and as indicators of proximate or remote ancestry. The domain of the politics of belonging is more diffuse. It is not centered on specific sets of institutionalized routines. It is defined rather by the ways genetic data—and the inferences they are held to support about individual and collective ancestry—are enlisted in the service of claims and struggles over identity, membership, and belonging (Skinner 2006). Accordingly, while the preceding sections focused primarily on distinctively U.S. institutional, organizational, and cultural contexts, this section is less U.S.-focused, reflecting the global diffusion of genetically inflected idioms of membership and belonging.

The politics of belonging is a politics of identity, but it is often at the same time a politics of interest: who *is* what has implications for who *gets* what. Identity and interest are intertwined on both individual and collective levels. Tests of ancestry or relatedness (on the individual level) and population genetics findings (on the collective level) can be enlisted to support claims to an identity or status to which rights or benefits are attached—or to challenge such claims.

Individual-level genetic data have become relevant to identity claims—or have been represented as relevant to such claims—in a number of contexts. The most salient context in the United States involves tribal membership claims, especially where tribal wealth confers substantial economic value on membership.[54] A handful of genetic testing companies have targeted the Native American market since around 2000, marketing their services both to individuals interested in validating Native American ancestry and to tribes interested in screening new applicants and existing members. Two very different kinds of tests have been promoted. The first—like the ancestry tests discussed in the preceding section—use uniparentally inherited mitochondrial or Y-chromosome DNA to make inferences about single-stranded maternal or paternal lineages, or they use biparentally inherited autosomal DNA to make inferences about the percentage of one's ancestry that is Native American. The second kind of test compares an individual's DNA to that of another known individual so as to establish the genealogical relationship, if any, between the two.

Individuals might occasionally be interested in tests of specific relationships, but the nature of their close genealogical relationships with living individuals is ordinarily not in doubt. In marketing their services to individuals, companies have therefore focused on tests of ancestry. But even if such tests could reliably ascertain the percentage of one's genetic ancestry that is Native American, or could identify a distinctively Native American Y-chromosome or mitochondrial DNA haplotype—and autosomal admixture tests are known to produce anomalous results in some cases—they cannot help establish a specific tribal affiliation. The ancestry that matters in validating a claim to tribal membership, in most cases, is *tribal* ancestry, not Native American ancestry. One's genetic and genealogical ancestry can be 100 percent Native American, yet one might still fail to satisfy the blood quantum requirements for membership in any particular tribe.[55]

Why, then, are individuals interested in ancestry tests that target Native Americans? Some may believe that such tests *can* support their claims to tribal membership. As Kimberly TallBear notes (2013b: 82–88), a number of companies have promoted their services with false or misleading claims. Other users, however, may seek testing to bolster or validate a claim to a Native American, not a specific tribal identity (Golbeck and Roth 2012). For some, this may be a strategic choice, as in the case of those who are considering identifying themselves as Native American—or, analogously, as African American—in college admission or employment contexts (as anecdotally suggested by Harmon 2006). The reluctance of liberal states to get involved in administering or policing ethnic or racial identity, coupled with the existence of policies that advantage members of certain ethnic or racial categories, creates opportunities—and incentives—for such strategic self-identification. Yet while self-identification is not formally controlled or policed, opportunistic self-identification is potentially vulnerable to challenge. Genetic evidence of a "useful" identity may embolden some individuals to make such strategic—and potentially controversial and challengeable—identity claims. Others, however, may be moved by ideal or symbolic interests—or by simple genealogical curiosity—to claim a Native American identity or explore possible Native American ancestry.[56]

Genetic tests of specific relationships have been marketed with greater success to tribes. For while such tests are seldom useful to individual consumers, they can be very useful to wealthy tribes that seek to tighten and rationalize their membership policies and procedures. Such tribes have turned increasingly to professional consultants, including genetic testing companies, to help them manage their enrollment systems by scrutinizing not only new applicants but also, in some cases, their entire existing membership in order to remove from the rolls those deemed not to qualify (TallBear 2013b: 88–99). The resultant large-scale disenrollments from some wealthy tribes have generated a storm of controversy (Dao 2011). But those disenrolled have no recourse beyond the tribe: as "domestic dependent nations," federally recognized tribes in the United States establish and enforce their own rules of membership.

Genetic testing has also emerged as an issue in connection with immigration proceedings. In family reunification contexts—in which certain family relationships confer immigration and citizenship benefits—genetic testing is increasingly used to confirm the claimed relationship (Taitz et al. 2002). Most of this testing is routine and publicly invisible, but in 2008 the State Department suspended a program to unite East African refugees with relatives living in the United States after genetic tests uncovered high rates of fraud (Jordan 2008). Since the tests used in immigration contexts turn not on ancestry but on immediate relatedness, they do not contribute to the geneticization of race or ethnicity. There is, however, one notorious exception. In 2009 the UK Border Agency launched a pilot Human Provenance program that would use DNA tests (in conjunction with language assessment and interviewing) to identify the country of origin of asylum seekers, in response to concerns that applicants claiming to be fleeing persecution in Somalia might actually be from another country (Travis 2009; Tutton et al. 2014). Even scientists who think ethnicity can be reliably inferred from DNA—and this is already controversial—objected to this blatant conflation of ethnicity with legal nationality. In response to wide-spread criticism of the program from scientists as well as refugee advocacy groups, the agency suspended and later ended the program (*Science* 2011).

Identity and interest are intertwined on the collective as well as the individual level. Population-level genetic data can be mobilized to support—or to challenge—claims to identities that carry with them certain rights or advantages. The nexus between genes, collective identity claims, and interests is revealed most starkly in contexts involving claims to indigeneity. Like nationhood, indigeneity is not an ethnodemographic fact; it is a political claim, which must be recognized, accepted, and institutionalized in order to become a socially effective and politically and legally consequential identity. And because claims to indigeneity are intrinsically relational and comparative, they have implications not only for the collectivity advancing the claim but also for others; they are therefore often contested.[57]

Claims to indigeneity link place, time, and population. It is therefore unsurprising that the findings of population genetics—which trace the histories of populations in space and time, albeit in a different register—can be enlisted to support or challenge such claims. It is also unsurprising that population genetic research projects that seek to reconstruct prehistoric migration and settlement patterns have become embroiled in political controversy (Pálsson 2008; Tallbear 2013a).

Consider, for example, the mobilization of genetic data in support of political claims by the Uros, a small group living primarily on floating islands in the reed beds of Lake Titicaca in Peru.[58] Anthropologists and state officials had long considered the Aymara-speaking Uros to be part of the much larger Aymara population in the region. But the Uros claim a distinct identity as descendants of the ancient Urus, the first major ethnic group to have settled in the Andes. And in the past fifteen years, they have enlisted genetic data in support of this claim, relying initially on work done by Peruvian geneticists, and subsequently on their collaboration with the international Genographic Project. Indigeneity per se is not at stake in the Uros' claim to a differentiated identity: the Aymaras (and the more numerous Quechuas) are socially and politically recognized as indigenous peoples. At stake, rather, is the establishment of a distinctive ultra-indigenous identity that would match—and underwrite monopolistic control over—a particular ecological and economic niche. As the floating islands have become a major tourist attraction in recent decades—the second most important in Peru—the stakes of struggles to control and profit from the tourist trade have risen. This has embroiled the Uros in conflicts with both the state and neighboring lakeshore Aymara groups. In this context, the assertion of a distinctive genetic profile—marking both their difference from the Aymaras and their similarity to groups in Bolivia that likewise claim descent from the ancient Urus—served to bolster claims to a distinct cultural identity, to a primordial link with the reed beds of Lake Titicaca, to an authentic mastery of an ancient and distinctive way of life, and, in a characteristically flexible twist, to an environmentalist ethos well suited to the preservation of the unique habitat of the floating islands.[59]

Genetic research creates political risks as well as opportunities; and among populations whose claims to indigenous status are securely recognized, the risks may be seen as substantially outweighing the opportunities (Kent 2013: 550). Studies documenting mixing or migrations, some fear, might be used to challenge the distinctive status of indigenous populations or to reduce indigenous rights (Tallbear 2013b: 153–154; Pálsson 2008: 553; Berthier-Foglar 2012: 4, 24–26; Collingwood-Whittick 2012: 305–307). In the context of a long history of mistrust of Western science, these concerns may help explain the unwillingness of many indigenous populations to participate in genetic research projects (Berthier-Foglar 2012).

Identity and interest are intertwined, but the politics of identity cannot be reduced to a politics of interest, narrowly understood. Genetically informed accounts of who is what and who comes from where have implications for who gets what, but they have a range of broader implications as well. The interests at stake are ideal or symbolic as well as material. For indigenous peoples, these may include interests in the integrity of constitutive myths and origins stories—stories that may be unsettled or undermined by genetic accounts (Davis 2004).[60] But genetically informed accounts of origins have broad implications for identity and belonging in a wide range of contexts, not only those involving claims to indigeneity. Population genetic studies have become entangled, for example, in arguments about the origins and antiquity of the caste system in India (Egorova 2010); in debates about national identity and *mestizaje* in Mexico (Schwartz-Marín and Silva-Zolezzi 2010; Benjamin 2013); and in disputes about miscegenation, racial classification, affirmative action, and "racial democracy" in Brazil (Santos and Maio 2004; Santos et al. 2009). More generally, population genetic studies have contributed to naturalizing understandings of nationhood, legitimizing the view that not only race and ethnicity but nationhood too is built on a distinct biological substrate (Benjamin 2009).

By supporting objectivist understandings of nationhood, genetically informed accounts of who is what and who comes from where can also raise questions about who (really) belongs where. The British National Party's magazine *Identity,* for example, has given sustained attention to population genetic research suggesting that the genetic landscape of Britain was largely fixed in the Neolithic era and that subsequent ancient migrations had surprisingly little effect on this basic landscape. These findings have been used by the BNP to bolster its discourse about the threats posed by immigration to the "indigenous population of Britain" (Bonifas 2008).[61]

Questions about who belongs where can also be suggested in a much more subtle way. Genetic understandings of relatedness play into the explicit, discursively articulated politics of belonging; but they also have implications for the tacit politics of what might be called "deep belonging." At stake are not only the formal, tangible, legally specified rights and benefits of belonging, and not only expressly articulated forms of recognition, but also the informal, symbolic, and invisible privileges of unmarked, unquestioned, and unproblematic belonging. Belonging is of course claimed, contested, and negotiated. But there are forms of belonging that are *not* claimed or asserted, that are not negotiated, that are not discursively articulated. Deep belonging is the product of a frictionless, tacit, taken-for-granted congruence of self-understandings and recognition by others. Beyond the manifold ways in which genetic accounts of origin and relatedness are articulated in public and private debate, such accounts may reinforce tacit understandings of who "really" belongs where.

This is shown in Catherine Nash's study of a project that sought to map the genetic heritage of the British population.[62] The People of the British Isles project was informed by a self-consciously inclusive and progressive discourse of diversity and multiculturalism. It expressly rejected the trope of purity, representing the British population as "mixed up," underscoring the diversity of the nation's genetic heritage, and highlighting the genetic legacy of successive waves of migration. But the project was built on an "implicit, yet crucial, distinction between different sorts of genetic diversity" (Nash 2013: 201). The diversity introduced by twentieth-century migrations was screened out in order to focus on the diversity introduced by the ancient migrations of Romans, Anglo-Saxons, Vikings, and Normans.[63] To ascertain the uneven regional distribution of this diverse genetic legacy, the project sampled only rural Britons whose parents and grandparents had lived in the same locality. This did not signal an "exclusionary model of belonging"; it was standard population genetic practice. But it meant that donors "had to be rural, rooted, and effectively white" (201)—an awkward circumstance for a study expressly framed as a survey of the national population.

Acknowledging that the project did not take account of recent immigrants, the project's leader, distinguished geneticist Walter Bodmer, observed that "their history relates to their country of origin, not to the British Isles." This was not an attempt to "delimit belonging through ancestry"; it was a gesture "imbued with the multicultural principles of sensitivity toward the diverse ethnic origins of people in Britain and the validity of expressing these heritages." Yet as Nash observes, such gestures "can imply that the history and heritage of Britain belongs to a certain portion of the British people of native descent and that other people—'ethnic minorities'— have their own equally valid but different heritages." In this way, "the culture of groups is imagined as a biological inheritance that is the natural possession of that group" (2013: 203). The People of the British Isles project thus reveals the "ambiguities and contradictions" that result from the encounter between multiculturalist and antiracist commitments and a "genetic model of belonging and relatedness"—even, implicitly, a "genetic model of the nation"—that suggests the congruence of "genes, geography, culture and identity" (193, 204). The subtle "genetic indigenization" (Fortier 2012) accomplished by this and similar projects of national genetic mapping, as well as by practices of genetic genealogy, can suggest that "the historic roots and true home of non-indigenous and implicitly non-white Europeans must be elsewhere" (Nash 2004: 23).

Nash has remarked on the "inescapably political dimensions of all accounts of origins and ancestors" (2008: 22), including genetic accounts. This applies not only to the varied forms of the politics of belonging discussed in this section but also to the practices discussed in previous sections: to the sampling strategies used by population geneticists in their construction of ancestral populations; to the use of self-identified race as a crude proxy for biogeographic ancestry in biomedical research, pharmaceutical development, and clinical practice; to the forensic use of "ancestry-informative markers" to predict the ethnoracial self-identification or phenotype of an unknown suspect; and to the growing popularity of genetic ancestry tests. All of these practices are controversial, and all have potentially far-reaching political implications.

This section has focused not on these broad political implications of the continued geneticization of biomedicine, forensics, and genealogy but on the more specific ways genetic ancestry testing and population genetic research bear on claims and struggles over—and tacit understandings of— identity, membership, and belonging. Having considered various ways in which genetic data are mobilized in the service of racial and ethnic identity claims, I should note that genetic data can also be mobilized *against* such identity claims—not simply against *particular* identity claims but against institutionalized practices of racial identification themselves. In Brazil, notably, genetic evidence has been used to challenge the legitimacy of official racial classification schemes, specifically the black-white scheme underlying racial quotas in university admissions (Schramm et al. 2012: 4–6). A 2008 open letter by left-wing opponents of racial classification, for example, cited population genetic studies showing that 30 percent of Brazilians who self-identified as white had African ancestry, while 20 percent of those who self-identified as "pardo" (brown) or "black" had none.[64] The analytical point worth underscoring here is the political indeterminacy of genetics (Benjamin 2013): just as genetic findings can be enlisted both for and against particular identity claims, so they can be enlisted both for and against practices of racial and ethnic identification in general.

Conclusion: A Constructivist Response

I return in conclusion to the challenge posed by the newly respectable objectivism and naturalism to subjectivist and constructivist theories of race and ethnicity. How might social scientists respond to this challenge without simply reasserting that socially defined racial categories have no biological reality and denying—in a self-marginalizing way—the relevance of biology to the social sciences?[65] Here I sketch nine elements of a constructivist response.

1. The foundational insight of the subjectivist and constructivist position should be reaffirmed. Race and ethnicity do not exist prior to or independently of people's beliefs and practices, in particular their practices of identification, classification, and categorization. Race is not—unlike species or, for that matter, sex—an objective division of the natural world, just as ethnicity is not an objective division of the cultural world. Race and ethnicity are *constituted* by practices of social classification and categorization and by practices of attributing meaning to social categories and organizing social life in accordance with them. These practices vary widely over time, place, and context. In this sense race and ethnicity are perspectives on the world, principles of vision and division of the world, not classification-independent things in the world.

2. There is much more genetic variation within than between socially defined racial categories. But this does not mean that there are *no* significant genetic differences between such categories.[66] Subjectivists and constructivists have often denied that significant differences exist. But the validity of subjectivist and constructivist accounts of race does not depend on the complete absence of such differences. It is possible, for example, that biomedical research may demonstrate some nontrivial genetically based differences in disease susceptibility or drug response between socially defined racial categories, beyond what is already known today. But identifying the biological *correlates* of a socially defined racial category—correlates resulting (in this example) from differences in allele frequencies between socially

defined racial categories—does not turn that social category into a biological one.[67] Race is not *constituted* by the facts of genetic difference, just as ethnicity is not constituted by the facts of cultural difference. People differ objectively—that is, in ways that do not depend on their beliefs or classification practices—in innumerable ways, including their genetic makeup. But there is an infinite multiplicity of such differences, and they are not constitutive of the phenomenon of race and ethnicity, even when some such differences are correlated with or captured by racial and ethnic categories.

3. There is structure in human genetic variation, and there are ongoing debates about the extent to which this variation is not only clinal but also involves some clustering (Serre and Pääbo 2004; Rosenberg et al. 2005; Handley et al. 2007; Feldman and Lewontin 2008). Researchers have shown that clustering algorithms can use data on polymorphic genetic markers to sort people into sets that closely match self-identified race. But clustering algorithms are highly sensitive to assumptions, parameter specifications, sampling procedures, and levels of aggregation (Bolnick 2008; Royal et al. 2010: 667–668; Kalinowski 2011). More fundamentally, the ability to predict self-identified race from genotype does not turn socially defined racial categories into biologically meaningful ones. One can infer ancestry or self-identified race from genotype, but one cannot infer a person's genotype from her ancestry or self-identified race (Feldman and Lewontin 2008: 93). At best, ancestry or self-identified race is a very crude proxy for the probability of possessing certain genetic variants.

4. For the great majority of genetic polymorphisms used to detect clustering, allele frequency differences between socially defined racial categories are quite small. Clustering "derives mainly from small differences in allele frequencies at large numbers of markers, not from diagnostic genotypes" (Feldman and Lewontin 2008: 92). Some genetic markers, however, show much greater frequency differences between socially defined racial categories. And certain rare genetic variants may be found primarily or even exclusively within a single population (though the relevant population may be smaller and more specific than "continental" racial categories). If the "common disease, rare variant" hypothesis turns out to be correct, or partially correct, these rare variants, singly or in combination, may play a significant role in predisposing to certain diseases. The discovery of such population-specific disease-predisposing rare variants, however, would not challenge the fundamental tenets of the subjectivist understanding of race. Such variants, rare by hypothesis, might in certain cases be *unique* to a particular socially defined racial category, but they would not be *definitive* of any socially defined racial category. They would be definitive of a very different kind of category: a specifically genetic "at-risk"

category, comprising all and only those who possess the variant (or combination of variants) in question (Novas and Rose 2000). There would be as many such categories as there would be disease-predisposing genetic variants. And none of these categories (being defined by rare variants) would coincide even roughly with any socially defined racial category, even if the variant in question were found primarily or exclusively within a single socially defined racial category. No genetic variants are shared by *all* and *only* members of a particular socially defined racial category.

5. The social reality of race and the biogeographic and biogenetic reality of ancestry are fundamentally different phenomena. The former is founded on acts of classification and categorization that establish sharp boundaries and make those boundaries matter. The latter is the accumulated precipitate, at once shared *and* differentiated, of the entire history of our species.[68] The subjectivist position is *not* that these two orders of phenomena are entirely unconnected. It is not that socially defined racial categories are entirely arbitrary, bearing no relation to biogeographic and biogenetic ancestry. Since social understandings of race and ethnicity emphasize origins and descent, it would be surprising if socially defined racial and ethnic categories did not capture, in a crude way, *some* information about biogeographic and biogenetic ancestry.[69] But it is also evident that socially defined racial categories may obscure rather than reveal ancestry. Perhaps the most striking example is the one-drop rule, which historically classified as black a person with any known African ancestry. And as is well known, African Americans in general have substantial amounts of European ancestry, estimated at around 15 to 20 percent on average, a fact of biogenetic ancestry that is obscured by the social category "black." Socially defined racial and ethnic categories have their own history and politics (Brubaker et al. 2004: 32–35); and as underscored earlier, they vary substantially over time, place, and context.

6. Socially defined racial categories—like categories in general—are *categorical*, not *gradational*. They have insides and outsides; they create sharp distinctions and boundaries. (This holds a fortiori when the categories are employed in organizational or administrative settings that require either-or categorization and do not allow for ambiguity.)[70] The phenomenon of race (and ethnicity) is constituted by the ways in which social life is organized around such distinctions and boundaries. These sharp boundaries do not exist in nature. Genetic variation does not take the form of discrete and sharply bounded groups.

7. While avoiding the *conflation* of the social and the biological, we should analyze their *interface*. The conflation of the social and the biological arises from the routine use of "groupist" language that blurs the distinction

between socially defined racial categories and "races" as substantial entities in the world; from the bureaucratic logic of "categorical alignment" that promotes the use of socially defined racial categories in biomedical contexts (etiological as well as epidemiological); and from the tendency to interpret residual racial differences in medically significant outcomes as suggesting genetic rather than social causes.

8. Yet the interface between the social and the biological is a crucial research frontier, and subjectivists and constructivists should not turn their backs on it (Benton 1991; Freese et al. 2003; Bone 2009; Rose 2013). At a moment in which nonreductionist and "post-genomic" modes of biological thinking are flourishing (Meloni 2014), the antipathy to the biological characteristic of subjectivist and constructivist stances has outlived whatever usefulness it might once have had. The circuits of social construction and social causation, after all, pass through the body, and attention to these pathways has enabled researchers to show, for example, "how [social] race becomes biology" (Gravlee 2009) and "how adversity gets under the skin" (Hyman 2009). We need a "biosocial constructivism," not a purely social constructivism that ignores the biological dimensions of our embodied being.[71] A biosocial constructivism would attend to the social shaping of biological processes as well as to the biological shaping of social processes.

9. Even if the new ethnic and racial objectivism and naturalism do not *invalidate* subjectivist and constructivist accounts, they do provide abundant *new data* for such accounts. Flawed as a *scientific* perspective on the world, ethnoracial objectivism is no less important as a *vernacular* perspective, a perspective that is implicated in a wide range of practices. The naturalization of race and ethnicity is of course nothing new. "Participants' primordialism" has long been a dominant vernacular perspective on race and ethnicity, and constructivists have had to come to terms with it. But geneticization is a new and distinctive form of naturalization. It has not simply reauthorized or reified existing understandings of race. Instead geneticization has transformed understandings and practices of race and ethnicity in a variety of domains, not just at the individual level but at the organizational and collective levels as well. The effort to understand these transformations has only just begun.

CHAPTER THREE

Language, Religion, and the Politics of Difference

L ANGUAGE AND RELIGION are arguably the two most socially and politically consequential domains of cultural difference in the modern world. The study of the political accommodation of cultural difference—or what might be called the political sociology of multiculturalism—would therefore seem to require sustained attention to both.

Yet there have been few efforts to compare language and religion, the outstanding exception—and an important inspiration for this chapter—being a paper by Aristide Zolberg and Litt Woon Long (1999). Language and religion are of course often discussed together in the literatures on ethnicity, nationalism, minority rights, and multiculturalism, but most such discussions involve passing juxtaposition rather than sustained comparison. And the more sustained discussions (see notably Bauböck 2002) tend to be normative rather than empirical.

It might be suggested that the lack of sustained comparison is not surprising since language and religion are simply not comparable. I do not want to get sidetracked here by a discussion of the meaning of comparison or the conditions of comparability. My interests are substantive, not methodological. One can certainly construe religion and language in such a way that they are not comparable. If one were to define religion in terms of beliefs and rituals, for example, there would be little leverage for

---

This chapter is dedicated to the memory of Aristide Zolberg.

comparison. And obviously religion (at least "organized religion") has an organizational dimension and a structure of authority that language lacks. But I want to argue that one can nonetheless construe language and religion in a way that makes comparison both possible and fruitful.

My strategy for doing so is to begin by aligning language and religion, provisionally, with ethnicity and nationhood and by sketching five ways in which language and religion are both similar to and similarly intertwined with ethnicity and nationhood. I will then identify some differences between language and religion and between modes of institutionalization of linguistic and religious pluralism in contemporary liberal societies; and I will draw out their implications for the politics of difference.

These implications—to anticipate—are ambivalent. Language is in certain respects more chronically and inescapably politicized today than religion is. The rules and practices governing the language of public life cannot help massively advantaging people with certain language repertoires, while disadvantaging others. Political and economic developments during the past several centuries have made language a crucial form of cultural capital and a key terrain of political struggle. During the same period, religion has become for many a more individual, private, and subjective affair.

Yet religion resists full relegation to the private sphere, and recent decades have seen a dramatic resurgence of public religious claims-making. Religious pluralism tends to be more intergenerationally robust and more deeply institutionalized than linguistic pluralism in contemporary liberal societies, and it entails deeper and more divisive forms of diversity. The upshot, I suggest, is that the most vexed and contentious conundrums of multiculturalism are increasingly grounded in the deep diversity of religious worldviews and ways of life. This recent tendency for religion to displace language as the cutting edge of contention over the political accommodation of cultural difference represents a striking reversal of the longer term historical process through which language had earlier displaced religion as the key terrain of contention.

Language and Religion in Relation to Ethnicity and Nationhood

Language and religion can be aligned with ethnicity and nationalism in several respects.[1] First, both language and religion are *domains of categorically differentiated cultural practice that simultaneously unite and divide.*

By "categorically differentiated," I mean that language and religion are understood by participants and observers alike as partitioned into discrete categories rather than as a continuous spectrum of variation. (That they are so understood is of course a product of history and politics, not least a history and politics of objectification, individuation, and boundary drawing that have carved out distinct "languages" from dialect continua and constructed and institutionalized distinct "religions" from fluid and varying sets of practices.)[2] In popular understandings, both language and religion sort people into distinct, bounded, and largely self-reproducing "communities"; in this respect they are both analogous to ethnic groups and nations and variously intertwined with them.

Second, language and religion are *basic sources and forms of social, cultural, and political identification.* They are ways of identifying oneself and others, construing sameness and difference, and naming fundamental social groups. Language and religion are again both analogous to ethnicity and nationalism in this respect and pervasively intertwined with them. Language, religion, or both are generally understood as central to or even constitutive of most ethnic and national identifications, and they frequently serve as the key diacritical markers, emblems, or symbols of such identifications.

Third, the family is a primary site of linguistic and religious socialization, as it is of ethnic and national socialization. Indeed language and religion are ordinarily more central to primary socialization in the family than are ethnicity and nationality. Language and religion are therefore often *deeply taken-for-granted and embodied identifications,* and both are routinely represented as primordial.

Fourth, however, neither religion nor language is in fact primordial or fixed. Like ethnicity and nationhood, religion and language are powerfully shaped by political, economic, and cultural processes, and they change as circumstances change. From an individual point of view, as Benedict Anderson said of nations, both religions and languages are "joinable in time" (1991: 145); and in the contemporary world, both are *increasingly chosen rather than given.* This shift is particularly marked for religion. Although initial religious identifications continue to be inherited, modalities and degrees of religious engagement can no longer be taken for granted, but—in the West at least—are increasingly reflexively negotiated and embraced (or rejected) (see, for example, Taylor 2007).

Fifth, many of the *claims* made in the name of religious or linguistic groups are similar to—and again, also intertwined with—claims made in the name of ethnic groups or nations. These include claims for economic resources, symbolic recognition, equal representation, cultural reproduction, and political autonomy.

In all these respects, language and religion are both *similar* to ethnicity and nationalism and *similarly intertwined* with them. This has led many scholars of ethnicity to treat language and religion—implicitly or explicitly—as functionally equivalent. Indeed ethnicity was constituted as an object of study precisely by abstracting from the specificities of language, religion, and other ascriptive markers such as phenotype, region of origin, and customary mode of livelihood. In the words of Joseph Rothschild, whose 1981 study *Ethnopolitics* was one of the first, and remains one of the best, to survey the field, it would be pointless to "separate out the notion of ethnic consciousness, solidarity, and assertiveness from religious, linguistic, racial, and other so-called primordial foci of consciousness, solidarity, and assertiveness." If this were to be done, "it is difficult to see what precisely would be left to, or meant by, the residual notion of ethnicity and ethnic groups" (9; cf. Geertz 1963: 109ff; Horowitz 1985: 41).

The call to abstract from cultural content was given its strongest formulation by Fredrik Barth (1969), who argued that the study of ethnicity should focus on the nature and dynamics of ethnic boundaries, not on what he somewhat dismissively called the "cultural stuff" these boundaries enclose. This perspective on ethnicity has been immensely fruitful, and it has been important for my own work. But it is also inevitably flattening since it neglects, by design, the specific cultural practices, understandings, and institutions that are implicated in the construction and working of ethnic identities and boundaries.

It is not fruitful, I believe, to talk about multiculturalism or the politics of difference in terms of highly generalized notions of ethnicity, culture, identity, or difference. It is necessary instead to attend to the specific logic and properties—the specific "affordances"—of differing modes of cultural difference. So in this chapter, following the lead of scholars such as Stephen Cornell (1996) and Richard Jenkins (1997: chapter 8), I want to return the "cultural stuff"—specifically language and religion—to the center of analytical attention.[3]

I want to register two caveats, however, about doing so. First, "cultural stuff" is potentially misleading if it is taken to imply an opposition between culture and social organization. I treat language and religion not only as cultural forms but also as modes of social organization and media of interaction. Second, the specific configuration of the contemporary politics of difference has been shaped not only by the intrinsic properties of language and religion—not only by the cultural and social-organizational "stuff," considered as an ahistorical constant—but also, and indeed more profoundly, by the specific historical trajectories through which states understood as "liberal" and "national" emerged, and were transformed, in and through their confrontation first with religious and later with linguistic heterogeneity.[4]

Before proceeding further, it is worth underscoring that religion is a much more elusive analytical object than language. For all their complexity, linguistic phenomena have a definiteness and regularity that religious phenomena lack. We know what we are talking about when we talk about language, but the same cannot be said for religion. It is not accidental that linguistics is a relatively well-defined discipline, while religious studies is a loose congeries of undertakings. Some have argued that religion is meaningless or useless as an analytical category (see, for example, Bloch 1996); I'm not aware that anyone has made this claim about language.

While fully acknowledging that "religion" is a problematic and deeply contested category—contested both as a category of analysis and as a category of practice—I do not want to enter here into the debate about the category. Since the scope of my argument is limited to contemporary liberal polities, I am content to work here with a relatively unreflexive, commonsense category of "religion" (cf. Casanova 2009: 5), limiting my attention primarily to what we call "organized religion," and within that field primarily to the Abrahamic religions.

Trajectories of Politicization and Depoliticization

There are good reasons for expecting language to be more deeply and chronically politicized than religion under modern conditions. Language, after all, is a *universal and pervasive medium of social life,* while religion is not. If one defines religion broadly enough, to be sure, then religion too can be seen as a universal social phenomenon. But it is not universal in the same way.[5] Language is a pervasive, inescapable medium of social interaction; religion is not.[6] Moreover, language is a necessary medium of public as well as private life. It is an inescapable medium of public discourse, government, administration, law, courts, education, media, and public signage. However one defines religion, it cannot be said to be an inescapable medium or necessary ground of action in any of these domains.

Public life can in principle be areligious, but it cannot be alinguistic. The modern state is characterized by direct rule, intensive interaction with citizens, universal public education, and a public sector that provides large numbers of jobs. As a result, the rules and practices that govern the language of public life directly affect the material and ideal interests of people with differing language repertoires (Zolberg and Long 1999: 21). This holds a fortiori in an economic context in which work is increasingly "semantic and communicative rather than physical" (Gellner 1997: 85), involving the manipulation of meanings, not of things. Language is therefore chronically and pervasively politicized in linguistically heterogeneous modern societies (Patten and Kymlicka 2003; May 2001).

Religion is also politicized, but it is politicized in different ways and for different reasons. The state must privilege a particular language or set of languages, but it need not privilege a particular religion, at least not in the same way and not to the same degree. Complete neutrality, to be sure, is now widely recognized as a myth (Bader 2007: 82ff), not least because the state cannot help but take a position on the question of what counts as "religion."[7] Moreover, one can easily identify pervasive traces of Christianity in the public life of Western liberal democracies, even in those with the strongest traditions of separation of church and state or of *laicité* (Alba 2005). One need think only of such taken-for-granted frameworks as the reckoning of dates according to the Christian calendar, the organization of holidays, or the privileging of Sunday as a day of rest—the domain of what Torpey (2010) calls "latent religiosity." Yet contemporary liberal polities— even those that still have some kind of established church, notably the UK and Scandinavia (apart from Sweden)—have made substantial, though contested, moves in the direction of a more neutral stance toward differing religions. Such moves have no counterpart in the domain of language. The state can approach neutrality with respect to religion, even if such moves are vulnerable to political pressures;[8] but it cannot even approach neutrality with respect to language (Zolberg and Long 1999: 21; Bauböck 2002: 175–176).

There is a second reason for thinking that language should be more deeply and chronically politicized than religion. According to secularization theory, modernity has entailed the progressive privatization and hence the depoliticization of religion. Events of the past three decades have made simplistic versions of secularization theory ripe for criticism. But as several leading analysts of religion have argued, secularization theory is more complex and interesting than many critics suggest, and it cannot be dismissed out of hand.[9] For many in the modern world, religion has indeed become a more individual, subjective, and private experience. To the extent that this is the case, religion indeed becomes depoliticized, and religious pluralism can flourish in the private realm without generating conflicts in the public sphere. Over the course of the past several centuries, religion has indeed become much *less* central to public life and less politically contentious in the West, while language has become much *more* central and more contentious (Rothschild 1981: 88).

Yet while secularization theory captures an important long-term trend, a powerful medium-term trend works in the other direction, toward the *deprivatization* and therefore the *repoliticization* of religion (Casanova 1994). On a time scale of decades rather than centuries, conflicts over religion have intensified, while conflicts over language, as I argue below, have eased.[10] As a result, while religion is not necessarily, chronically, and pervasively politicized the way language is, the challenges posed by religious pluralism today—or at least by some forms of religious pluralism—tend to be more complex and difficult than those posed by linguistic pluralism.

I want to develop this argument in two stages. I will begin by arguing that religious pluralism tends to be more robust than linguistic pluralism in contemporary liberal societies and polities. I will then argue that religious pluralism entails deeper and more divisive forms of diversity.

The Robustness of Religious Pluralism

The greater robustness of religious than linguistic pluralism results from the differing ways religious and linguistic pluralism are *generated, reproduced,* and *institutionalized* in contemporary liberal societies. I will consider each in turn, starting with the generation of pluralism, then moving on to address its reproduction and institutionalization.

Conquest, colonization, and especially (in the contemporary world) migration generate religious and linguistic pluralism in similar ways, by importing it *from without.* But religious pluralism is also generated *from within.* I'm not concerned here with relatively rare cases of religious splits and foundings, though historically these have been important internal sources of religious pluralism. I'm concerned rather with routine individual-level changes in religious affiliation and identity.

Individuals routinely change their linguistic repertoires as well. But they do so in differing ways and with differing consequences. For adults, at least, language change is mainly *additive,* though there may of course be some attrition of proficiency in languages that are seldom used. Religious change, on the other hand, is often *substitutive* and *transformative.* When adults add a new language to an existing repertory of languages, this may inflect their identity, but it is unlikely to transform it. Yet when they convert from one religion to another, or from one form of religious engagement to another, this can involve a basic transformation of identity (Snow and Machalek 1984). People do not ordinarily simply add a new religion to a repertory of religions, notwithstanding the flourishing of various forms of hybridity and syncretism, nor do they ordinarily "convert" from one language to another.

For children of immigrants, to be sure, language change is often substitutive rather than additive; but this *reduces* heterogeneity in the receiving country, while religious conversion often *increases* it. Conversion can also reduce heterogeneity, and some immigrant groups to the United States—Taiwanese, for example—exhibit high rates of conversion to Christianity. But pressures and incentives for conversion to the prevailing religion are on the whole relatively weak in contemporary liberal societies, while incentives to learn the prevailing language are strong. A whole series of factors, in addition to immigration, promote religious pluralization in contemporary liberal societies: new religious movements, organized proselytism, transnational religious networks, an open religious marketplace, and a general climate of spiritual experimentation. There are no analogous forces generating linguistic pluralization from within.

So religious conversion, broadly understood, is an important source of politically significant cultural heterogeneity, while individual-level language change is not. In contemporary liberal societies, new forms and degrees of linguistic pluralism are almost exclusively imported (through immigration), while new forms and degrees of religious pluralism are both imported and endogenously generated through conversion.

The second reason for the greater robustness of religious than linguistic pluralism is that religious pluralism is more easily reproduced. Here I shift my perspective from *intragenerational* to *intergenerational* change and reproduction. And I adopt a stylized—and of course grossly oversimplified—contrast between premodern and modern liberal societies.

In premodern societies, linguistic pluralism was more or less self-reproducing. Linguistic socialization occurred in families and local communities, and it did not require any specialized apparatus. Political authorities made no effort to impose linguistic homogeneity (though they often did impose religious homogeneity).

In contemporary liberal societies, the situation is reversed: it is now religious pluralism that is more or less self-reproducing. Religious socialization occurs in families and local religious communities, and political authorities make no effort to impose religious homogeneity. But linguistic reproduction now requires what Gellner (1983: chapter 3) called exo-socialization. It requires prolonged and expensive schooling on a scale that only the state is ordinarily in a position to provide. So the state is much more central to linguistic than to religious reproduction.

Children often acquire basic competence in a minority language from their parents and extended families, and this can be reinforced by minority-language media. But without comprehensive schooling in that language—and I mean schooling with that language as the medium of instruction, not simply as the object of instruction—it is difficult for the minority language to be fully reproduced. Some countries with long-established, territorially concentrated linguistic minorities do provide comprehensive minority-language schooling, but even this is not sufficient to ensure full reproduction. Minority-language populations are shrinking even where such schooling is available—as it is for the Swedish minority in Finland and the Hungarian minority in Romania. This happens as some children opt out of minority-language school systems and as intermarriage often leads to intergenerational assimilation (Brubaker et al. 2006: 297–298, 370–371).

Beyond comprehensive minority-language schooling, a linguistic regime that constrains people's choices may be necessary to ensure the reproduction of minority languages. This is what Philippe Van Parijs (2009: 163ff) has called a "linguistic territoriality regime." An example is the Quebec policy that restricts who can attend English-language schools (and notably requires almost all new immigrants to attend Francophone schools). This underscores the crucial role of the state in linguistic reproduction.

This argument might seem to be blatantly contradicted by the sharp increase in linguistic heterogeneity in the United States and other countries of immigration that do not provide comprehensive minority-language schooling or other strong state support for immigrant languages. Immigration does of course generally increase linguistic heterogeneity, and the effect is intensified when immigrants cluster in metropolitan areas that sustain dense networks of mother-tongue institutions. But this speaks to the *generation* of pluralism, not to its *reproduction*.

Continuing large-scale immigration masks substantial intergenerational linguistic assimilation. The Fishman model of language shift among second- and third-generation immigrants, set forth a half century ago (Fishman 1966; Veltman 1983), remains valid in its broad outlines. Thickening transnational ties, weakening assimilationist pressures, and the growth of substantial foreign-language media markets may have slowed down the process, at least for some groups. As Richard Alba and others have shown, this is notably the case for the descendants of Spanish-speaking immigrants in the United States. But even in this group, a majority of the third generation speak only English at home (Alba et al. 2002).[11] Samuel Huntington's (2004) alarmist scenario of ethnonational conflict in the American Southwest, based on a deepening language divide, has no basis in fact.

The reproduction of minority languages in contemporary liberal states, then, requires a massive and ordinarily state-provided educational apparatus, and it may also require a territorial regime that limits language choice. Such arrangements are in place in some historically multilingual states, as a legacy of earlier nationalist struggles over the language of public life. Examples include Canada, Belgium, Spain, Switzerland, and India. But no such arrangements protect minority languages generated by recent immigration. The various limited forms of de facto bilingualism or multilingualism that have emerged in the United States and other countries of immigration are significant as pragmatic ways of accommodating linguistic pluralism, but they neither aim at nor are capable of reproducing that pluralism intergenerationally.[12]

The religious pluralism generated by immigration is more easily reproduced. Of course it is not automatically reproduced. The religious landscape of contemporary liberal societies is fluid, especially in the United States, and I noted earlier the importance of conversion. But the intergenerational transmission of minority religions requires no state apparatus like a minority-language school system. And it requires no particular legal regime beyond the commitment to religious freedom that is a constitutive element of liberal polities. The transmission of religion, moreover, is not particularly costly. The transmission of a language—beyond what is simply picked up in the home, extended family, or neighborhood—requires a major effort and carries a substantial opportunity cost. But the transmission of a religious affiliation or identification does not.

What is transmitted, to be sure, may be little more than a nominal religious affiliation or identification (Gans 1994). But this nominal identity can later be revived or reconstructed. Some second- and third-generation Muslim immigrants in Western countries, for example, are more pious than their parents or grandparents or have constructed new forms of Muslim religiosity (Roy 2004; Duderija 2007); the same has been true of many American immigrant groups (Hirschman 2004).[13] The intergenerational staying power of religion results in significant part from the flexible adaptation of religious practices to changing circumstances. This has no real analogue in the domain of language.

So the religious pluralism generated by immigration is more likely to be intergenerationally persistent than the linguistic pluralism so generated. Admittedly, one should distinguish between nominal and substantive religious pluralism. In the United States, immigration has sharply increased the nominal pluralism of an already pluralistic religious landscape; at the same time, however, immigrant religions have become Americanized, notably by adopting prevailing congregational forms of religious organization and worship (Yang and Ebaugh 2001).

Still, among descendants of immigrants, religion offers a more enduring locus for cultural pluralism than language does.[14] This is especially true in the American context, characterized by high levels of religiosity. But elsewhere too there is nothing in the domain of religion analogous to the characteristic pattern of language shift for second- and third-generation immigrants. While linguistic competencies and identifications erode substantially across generations, religious practices and identifications are more likely to persist and in some cases may even grow stronger.

The final reason for the greater robustness of religious than linguistic pluralism is that religious pluralism is institutionalized and legitimated as an enduring presence in liberal societies in ways linguistic pluralism is not. Both ideologically and institutionally, as Zolberg and Long (1999: 31) observed, contemporary liberal states tend to be pluralist with respect to religion and monist or assimilationist with respect to language. Their stance toward religion is an attenuated pluralism, to be sure. A more far-reaching pluralism is found in some empires and postcolonial polities, where differing systems of personal law govern members of different religious communities. But this kind of legal pluralism is "incompatible with the structural character of modern nation-states" (14; see also Hirschl and Shachar 2009). Still, even this attenuated pluralism toward religion represents a sharp reversal of the historical pattern in the Christian world, where states were strongly *monist* with respect to religion and *pluralist* with respect to language (or, more precisely, simply *indifferent* to linguistic diversity).

Ideologically and normatively, the clearest expression of these different stances toward religion and language is that immigrants are *not* expected to adopt the prevailing religion but *are* expected to learn the prevailing language (or one of the prevailing languages). The liberal state is expected to be neutral with respect to religion, even if it can never be fully neutral in practice; but there is no such expectation of neutrality with respect to language. Language tests for citizenship are routine, but a religious test would be unthinkable in a liberal polity.

Enduring religious pluralism is not simply normatively accepted in liberal states but institutionally supported. To be sure, as I noted earlier, some historically multilingual states provide strong institutional support for linguistic pluralism.[15] But this strongly pluralist stance nowhere applies to immigrants.

I do not mean to suggest that liberal states generally adopt harshly or even actively assimilationist stances toward immigrant languages, although

there has been a shift in the past two decades back to a moderately assimilationist stance (Brubaker 2001). The point I want to underscore here is the
sharp distinction, both normative and institutional, between *endogenous*
and *imported* linguistic pluralism. International minority rights regimes
mandate expansive protection for long-established minority languages but
only minimal protection for immigrant languages. And states that provide
elaborate institutional support for historically established minority languages
provide nothing comparable for immigrant languages.[16]

Liberal countries of immigration do of course accommodate the linguistic diversity generated by immigration in various ways. They may provide
signage, information, voting materials, or bureaucratic forms in minority
languages; translators in medical, legal, or administrative settings; or various forms of bilingual education. But these pragmatic accommodations
are categorically distinct from the comprehensive parallel school systems or regimes of territorial autonomy that seek to facilitate the multi-
generational reproduction and preservation of multiple languages within a
single state.

There is thus a sharp distinction between endogenous and imported linguistic pluralism. But there is *no* sharp distinction between endogenous
and imported *religious* pluralism. This key point bears restating. Rights
and protections for long-established minority languages are nowhere extended to immigrant languages. Linguistic settlements, in other words, are
not expandable to include immigrant-borne languages. But religious settlements *are* expandable: not easily or automatically expandable, but expandable nonetheless. Many of the rights and recognitions enjoyed by
long-established religions *have* been extended to immigrant religions. Liberal states have differing historically conditioned modes of accommodating religious pluralism; but whatever their established mode of accommodation, they face nontrivial pressures to accommodate immigrant religions
on similar terms. These pressures have no counterpart in the domain of
language.

The most salient contemporary instance of course concerns the accommodation of Islam in northern and western Europe. It is impossible to do
justice to this vexed and complex issue here. Consider just one example,
from the domain of education. Accommodation on similar terms would
mean providing or permitting Islamic education in public schools in countries that provide or permit other forms of religious instruction; it would
also mean subsidizing private Islamic schools in countries that subsidize
other private religious schools. Moves to accommodate Islam in this and
other domains have been halting, uneven, and controversial; many Muslims claim with considerable justice that the measures taken have not even

come close to realizing equal treatment. And of course one can point to spectacular counterexamples in other domains, such as the ban on the face-covering niqab that has been enacted in France and Belgium and is under discussion elsewhere, and the Swiss referendum banning the construction of minarets. Yet if one looks beyond cases of highly mediatized contestation, one can see a steady if slow, contested, and often grudging move toward accommodation in the educational sphere and other domains. This has been driven by the courts on the one hand, which have been receptive to parity claims (Koenig 2010; Joppke and Torpey 2013), and by a statist and securitarian concern to manage and supervise Muslim populations on the other (Laurence 2012).

This part of the argument can be summed up as follows: Normative expectations, institutional frameworks, and individual incentives converge in fostering a deeper and more robust religious than linguistic pluralism in liberal societies. Not simply immigration but other factors too make for increasing, persistent, and institutionalized religious pluralism. Immigration generates at least as much linguistic as religious heterogeneity, but migration-generated linguistic heterogeneity is neither intergenerationally persistent nor institutionally supported. Continuing immigration and clustered settlement patterns sustain the appearance of increasing and persistent linguistic pluralism, but an ongoing intergenerational language shift tends to prevent the consolidation of self-reproducing linguistic minorities.

Religious Pluralism and Deep Diversity

Having argued that religious pluralism tends to be more robustly generated, reproduced, and institutionalized than linguistic pluralism in liberal polities, I now want to suggest that religious pluralism is also more likely to give rise to difficult and sometimes intractable problems of "deep diversity."[17]

This is obviously not true for *all* forms of religious pluralism. Insofar as religious pluralism involves individualized, "subjectivized," or otherwise privatized forms of religious experience, it is easily accommodated in liberal polities. Much of the recent pluralization of the religious landscape in liberal societies has involved the proliferation of new forms of individualized religiosity and spirituality that *do* conform to the expectations of secularization theory about the long-term privatization and depoliticization of religion. But as I mentioned earlier, recent decades have also witnessed a significant countertrend toward the deprivatization and repoliticization of religion. I'm concerned here with public, organized, and collective forms of religious life, not with private, individualized forms.[18]

Much of the discussion of public or political religion has focused on Islam, and for good reason. Privatized and individualized forms of religiosity are more common among Muslims, especially those living in the West, than essentialist accounts of Islam as an intrinsically public and political religion would suggest (Cesari 2002). But these have been overshadowed by the centrality of various forms of public or political Islam to political contestation in both Muslim-majority and Muslim-minority settings. Public religion is of course not unique to Islam; strong forms of public religion can be found in Christian, Jewish, Hindu, and Buddhist traditions, among others. Yet the claims of public Islam pose a particularly difficult challenge to liberal states.

I am concerned here, however, with religion and language more generally. In the era of modern nationalism, language has been widely understood as the chief criterion and main cultural substrate of nationhood. Territorially concentrated linguistic minorities have therefore been understood—by ethnopolitical entrepreneurs on the one hand and central state elites on the other—as potential nations, and linguistic pluralism has been construed as a threat to national identity and to the territorial integrity of the state. Even where secession or territorial autonomy has been implausible, language conflicts have been endemic. The expansion of state employment, the introduction of universal schooling and universal male military service, and the growing importance of what Gellner (1983: chapter 3) calls "context-free communication" in an urban, mobile, and literate society have made language a crucial form of cultural capital, a central focus of personal and collective identity, and a key terrain of political struggle.

Yet I want to argue that language conflict has lost some of its intensity and transformative potential in recent decades, as the high noon of language-based nationalist conflicts appears to have passed. The vast reorganization of political space along national (and for the most part broadly linguistic) lines throughout Europe and Eurasia has reduced, though of course not eliminated, the scope for new language-based nationalist claims. This has not only involved the disintegration of multinational empires into linguistically more homogeneous successor states; it has also involved the internal reorganization of multilevel states to create linguistically more homogeneous constituent states, as in India. Forms of federalism and devolution that have allowed autonomous but nonsovereign polities like Quebec, Catalonia, the Basque Country, and Wales to pursue their own language agendas are part of the same trend. Older language-based nationalist and ethnopolitical conflicts of course remain alive, but—with some exceptions—they have become less urgent and less destabilizing.

In the geopolitically relaxed zones of northern and western Europe, the Americas, and Australia–New Zealand, states no longer seek to impose the tight coupling of culture, territory, and population that was central to the nationalizing projects of a century ago; linguistic diversity is not only tolerated but in some cases even celebrated. Even in central and eastern Europe, historically the locus classicus of nationalist language conflicts, the eastward expansion of the European Union and the institutionalization of minority language rights have taken some of the edge off formerly intractable ethnolinguistic conflicts. In the United States, conflicts over the status of Spanish flare up periodically, focused for example on bilingual education or the symbolic question of an official language. More striking, however, is the continuing piecemeal, pragmatic, and largely uncontested accommodation of Spanish and other languages in a variety of less visible settings.

Language continues to be a terrain of chronic struggle in multilingual polities worldwide, especially where linguistic minorities are territorially concentrated. But in liberal polities, those struggles—again with some exceptions, most obviously in Belgium—have become less intense and intractable. Yet while language conflicts have eased somewhat in recent decades, conflicts over religion have intensified, driven by the resurgence of public religion.

As a universal and inescapable medium of public life, language can never be fully privatized or depoliticized. Religion could *in principle* be fully privatized and depoliticized, but the mid-twentieth-century Western vision of a fully privatized religion has proved entirely chimerical. And to the extent that religion is *not* privatized or depoliticized, the conflicts arising from religious pluralism tend to be deeper and more intractable than those arising from linguistic pluralism.

The reasons for this are found in the most elementary differences between language and religion. Language is a medium of communication; it is not a structure of authority, and it has no intrinsic normative content. In Herderian, Humboldtian, or Whorfian perspective, to be sure, languages may be seen as constitutive of culture and as carriers of distinctive world views. But strong versions of this constitutivist view are untenable, at least in contemporary settings. Whatever normative content languages might have is relatively thin.[19] Religion, however, and especially public religion, often involves an authoritative, binding, and comprehensive set of norms.

These norms do not simply regulate private behavior; they reach into the public realm, addressing such matters as gender, sexuality, family life, education, social policy, the economy, and even international affairs and war.[20]

Gender, sexuality, and family life are particularly important (and of course contested) domains of religious regulation (Friedland 2002; Casanova 2009: 17–18). Some religious norms constitute systems of law that directly and comprehensively regulate family matters, as Jewish and Islamic norms do for marriage, divorce, and inheritance. But nearly all forms of organized religion seek to regulate gender, sexuality, and family life.

The claims of public religion to provide binding and authoritative norms for the regulation of public and private life challenge the state's claim to monopolize the regulation of public life (and to authoritatively regulate certain areas of private life as well). They also create conflicts with competing forms of public religion and with those segments of the public (including those who profess the same religion) who reject the claims of public religion.

These are often deep conflicts of principle, involving fundamental differences of worldview. It is these that warrant speaking of "deep diversity." Language conflicts do not involve such conflicts of principle or worldview. As Gellner puts it in another context (1983: 117–118), they are conflicts between people who "speak the same language," as it were, even when they do not speak the same language.

Liberal states are committed to a far-reaching accommodation of religious pluralism, but this commitment can generate quandaries. Liberal states may be obliged to accommodate forms of religion that promote illiberal ideas or practices, or they may be obliged to act illiberally in restricting religious or other freedoms in the name of other values (see, for example, Joppke 2009: 4–5, Triadafilopoulos 2011).

Consider a few examples from the domain of education. Should the state exempt Christian children from exposure to "secular humanist" views in school, as some fundamentalist Christian parents in Tennessee requested (Stolzenberg 1993)? Should it exempt Muslim children from co-educational physical education classes, as some Muslim parents in European countries have requested (see, for example, German Islam Conference 2009: 20–22)? Should it allow teachers or students to wear religious clothing, including the face-covering niqab (Joppke 2009; Joppke and Torpey 2013: chapter 2)? How much leeway should it grant, and what kind of financial or other support should it provide, to conservative religious schools (or to forms of home schooling) that cultivate ways of life at odds with the state's interest in fostering the development of autonomous individuals and responsible citizens (Reich 2002: chapter 6)? Or consider the question that was brought into focus by the Rushdie affair in the late 1990s and revived by the Danish cartoon affair some years later: Should the state restrict potentially hurtful or offensive speech or expression so as to protect the sensibilities of members of religious communities (Parekh

2000: chapter 10)? No comparable quandaries arise in the domain of language.

Conclusion

Language and religion have seldom been studied together in a sustained way. To specialists in either subject, language and religion have seemed too *different,* while to students of ethnicity, they have seemed too *similar.* I have argued that language and religion are similar enough, if construed in a certain way, to make comparison possible, yet different enough to make it interesting.

As fundamental domains of cultural difference, language and religion have much in common. Both are ways of identifying oneself and others, of construing sameness and difference. In Bourdieusian language, both are basic principles of vision and division of the social world. Both divide the world, in popular understandings, into distinct, bounded, and self-reproducing communities. And claims are made in the name of both kinds of communities for recognition, resources, and reproduction.

These and other similarities have led students of ethnicity to treat language and religion as functionally equivalent and as theoretically uninteresting forms of "cultural stuff," significant primarily as grist for the mill of ethnic classification and boundary formation. But this perspective is flattening. It neglects important differences in the social organization and political expression of language and religion in liberal societies and polities.

Language is an inescapable medium of public as well as private life; religion is not. The state must privilege a particular language or set of languages, but it need not privilege a particular religion. Language is chronically and pervasively politicized in the modern world, while much of religion has become privatized and depoliticized. Yet deprivatization is an important countertrend, and the claims of public religion to authoritatively regulate public and private life have no counterpart in the domain of language. Immigration generates new forms and degrees of both linguistic and religious pluralism, but the religious pluralism generated by immigration is more intergenerationally robust and more deeply institutionalized than the linguistic pluralism. The result is that religion has tended to displace language as the cutting edge of contestation over the political accommodation of cultural difference in Western liberal democracies—a striking reversal of the longer term process through which language had previously displaced religion as the primary focus of contention.

CHAPTER FOUR

Religion and Nationalism

RELIGION AND *NATIONALISM* have long been contested terms. On almost any understanding, both designate large and multidimensional fields of phenomena. Given the lack of agreement on what we are talking about when we talk about religion or nationalism, it is no surprise that one encounters seemingly antithetical assertions about the relation between the two—for example, that nationalism is intrinsically secular, and that it is intrinsically religious; that nationalism emerged from the decline of religion, and that it emerged in a period of intensified religious feeling.

Since both terms can designate a whole world of different things, few statements about nationalism per se or religion per se, or about the relation between the two, are likely to be tenable, interesting, or even meaningful. A differentiated analytical strategy is required. Rather than ask *what* the relation between religion and nationalism is—a question too blunt to yield interesting answers—I seek in this chapter to specify *how* that relation can fruitfully be studied. Building on the literature produced by a recent surge of interest in the topic, I delineate, develop, and critically engage four distinct ways of studying the connection between religion and nationalism.[1] The first is to treat religion and nationalism, along with ethnicity and race, as *analogous* phenomena. The second is to specify how religion helps *explain* things about nationalism—its origin, its power, or its distinctive character in particular cases. The third is to treat religion as *part* of nationalism and to specify modes of interpenetration and intertwining.

The fourth is to posit a distinctively religious *form* of nationalism. I conclude by defending a qualified version of the much-criticized understanding of nationalism as a distinctively secular phenomenon.

Religion and Nationalism as Analogous Phenomena

Consider first the strategy of treating religion and nationalism as analogous phenomena. One way of doing so is exemplified by efforts to define or characterize nationalism by specifying its similarity to religion or by simply characterizing nationalism *as* a religion. An early statement of this approach, which can be traced back to Durkheim's *Elementary Forms of Religious Life* (1995: 215–216, 221ff, 429; A. Smith 2003: 26), is found in the work of Carlton Hayes, who devoted one chapter of his 1926 book *Essays on Nationalism* to "nationalism as a religion." According to Hayes, nationalism mobilizes a "deep and compelling emotion" that is "essentially religious." Like other religions, nationalism involves faith in some external power, feelings of awe and reverence, and ceremonial rites, focused on the flag. Straining a bit to sustain the metaphor, Hayes argues that nationalism has its gods—"the patron or personification of [the] fatherland"; its "speculative theology or mythology," describing the "eternal past . . . and everlasting future" of the nation; its notions of salvation and immortality; its canon of holy scripture; its feasts, fasts, processions, pilgrimages, and holy days; and its supreme sacrifice. But while most world religions serve to unify, nationalism "re-enshrines the earlier tribal mission of a chosen people," with its "tribal selfishness and vainglory."[2]

More recently, Anthony Smith has provided a more sophisticated, and more sympathetic, account of nationalism as a "new religion of the people"—a religion as "binding, ritually repetitive, and collectively enthusing" as any other. According to Smith, nationalism is a religion both in a substantive sense, insofar as it entails a quest for a kind of this-worldly collective "salvation," and in a functional sense, insofar as it involves a "system of beliefs and practices that distinguishes the sacred from the profane and unites its adherents in a single moral community of the faithful." In this new religion, which both "parallels and competes with traditional religions," authenticity is the functional equivalent of sanctity; patriotic heroes and national geniuses, who embody and exemplify this authenticity and sacrifice themselves for the community, are the equivalent of prophets and messiah-saviors; and posterity, in which their legendary deeds live on, is the equivalent of the afterlife. It is this religious quality of nationalism, on Smith's account, that explains the durability and emotional potency of national identities and the "scope, depth, and intensity of the feelings and loyalties that nations and nationalism so often evoke" (2003: 4–5, 15, 26, 40–42).

While such characterizations of nationalism as a religion are suggestive and fruitful, I want to propose an alternative strategy for considering nationalism and religion as analogous phenomena. Rather than characterize nationalism with terms drawn from the field of religion, as Hayes and, to a certain extent, Smith do—faith, reverence, liturgy, cult, god, salvation, scripture, sacred objects, and holy days—it may be useful to connect both phenomena to more general social structures and processes. Without any claim to exhaustiveness, I briefly discuss three ways of considering religion and nationalism (and ethnicity as well) under more encompassing conceptual rubrics: as a mode of identification, a mode of social organization, and a way of framing political claims.

Ethnicity and nationalism have been characterized as basic sources and forms of social and cultural identification. As such, they are ways of identifying oneself and others, of construing sameness and difference, and of situating and placing oneself in relation to others. Understood as perspectives on the world rather than things in the world, they are ways of understanding and identifying oneself, making sense of one's problems and predicaments, identifying one's interests, and orienting one's actions (Brubaker 2004). Religion too can be understood in this manner. As a principle of vision and division of the social world, to use Bourdieu's phrase, religion provides a way of identifying and naming fundamental social groups, a powerful framework for imagining community, and a set of schemas, templates, and metaphors for making sense of the social world (and of course the supramundane world as well).[3]

Second, like ethnicity and nationalism, religion can be understood as a mode of social organization, a way of framing, channeling, and organizing social relations. I'm not referring here to churches, ethnic associations, or nationalist organizations per se. I'm referring rather to the ways religion, ethnicity, and nationality can serve as more or less pervasive axes of social segmentation in heterogeneous societies, even without territorial concentration along religious, ethnic, or national lines. This is in part a matter of what Van den Berghe, in an effort to distinguish structural from cultural pluralism, called "institutional duplication" (1967: 34). Even when they are territorially intermixed, members of different religious, ethnic, or national communities may participate in separate, parallel institutional worlds, which can include school systems, universities, media, political parties, hospitals, nursing homes, and institutionalized sporting, cultural, and recreational activities as well as churches and ethnic associations (Brubaker et al. 2006: chapter 9).[4]

Even outside such parallel institutional worlds, though more often in conjunction with them, religion, ethnicity, and nationality can channel informal social relations in ways that generate and sustain social segmentation. The key mechanism here is religious or ethnic endogamy, whether more or less deliberately pursued from the inside or imposed from the outside.[5] Religious injunctions against intermarriage, together with clerical control or influence over marriage, have often helped reproduce socioreligious segmentation. This, in turn, has helped reproduce religious, ethnic, and national communities over the long run and has worked to prevent their dissolution through assimilation (Smith 1986: 123).

Third, from a political point of view, claims made in the name of religion—or in the name of particular religious groups—can be considered alongside claims made in the name of ethnicity, race, or nationhood. The similarities are particularly striking insofar as claims are made for economic resources, political representation, symbolic recognition, or cultural reproduction (the last by means of institutional or territorial autonomy, where institutional autonomy involves control of one's own agencies of socialization, crucially schools). These claims are part of the general phenomenon of politicized ethnicity, broadly understood as encompassing claims made on the basis of ethnoreligious, ethnonational, ethnoracial, ethnoregional, or otherwise ethnocultural identifications, which have proliferated in both the developed and the developing world in the past half-century.[6] Widening the analytical lens still further, claims made in the name of religious communities can fruitfully be seen as part of a very general pattern of the politicization of culture and the culturalization of politics.[7]

In this perspective, religion figures as a way of identifying "groups" or political claimants, not as a distinctive way of specifying the *content* of political claims. Of course, politicized religion involves not only claims for resources, representation, recognition, or reproduction; it also involves claims to restructure public life in accordance with religious principles. I will return to this issue later, when I discuss the question of whether there is a distinctively religious form of nationalism, defined by the distinctive content of its claims.

The three perspectives I have sketched suggest potentially fruitful ways of treating religion, ethnicity, and nationalism as analogous phenomena and as parts of a more encompassing domain. But all three abstract from the specific content of religious belief or practice, the specific ways in which belief may shape life conduct, and the specific role played by religious organizations and their relation to the state. As a result, their treatment of religion remains inevitably flattening, and they miss much of what is distinctive and interesting about religion and its relation to nationalism.

Religion as a Cause or Explanation
of Nationalism

A second way of analyzing the relation between religion and nationalism seeks to specify how religion helps explain nationalism. Such arguments can be cast in several ways, depending on what it is about nationalism that is said to be explained (for example, its origins, persistence, emotional power, content, or form) and what it is about religion that is said to explain it (religious ideas, institutions, practices, or events).

Most of the literature in this tradition focuses on particular cases, showing how particular religious traditions have shaped particular forms of nationalism. Scholars have traced the influence of Calvinism on Dutch and English nationalism (Gorski 2000b; Kohn 1940; Greenfeld 1992), of Pietism on German nationalism (Lehmann 1982), of Catholicism on Polish nationalism (for a critical review, see Zubrzycki 2006), of Orthodoxy on nationalism in the Balkans (Leustean 2008), of Shinto on Japanese nationalism (Fukase-Indergaard and Indergaard 2008), of Buddhism on Sinhalese nationalism (Kapferer 1988), and of the Hebraic idea of covenant on Northern Irish, Afrikaner, and Israeli nationalism (Akenson 1992).

A number of scholars, however, have advanced broader arguments about the centrality of religion in the origins and development of nationalism. One important cluster of work has shown how religious motifs, narratives, and symbols were transposed into the political domain and used to construct the first recognizably nationalist (or at least proto-nationalist) claims. Much of this work has focused on the motif of chosenness, or what Smith (2003) calls the "myth of ethnic election."[8] This and associated motifs, narratives, and symbols from the Hebrew Bible were central to political rhetoric and iconography in the Netherlands (Schama 1988: 93–125; Gorski 2000b) and England (Hill 1993) during the tumultuous and tightly interlinked religious and political struggles of the sixteenth and seventeenth centuries. Gorski has argued forcefully that this early modern "Mosaic moment" was distinctively nationalist in scope and content. Smith now agrees that this period saw the birth of movements and programs that he calls "covenantal nationalisms" (2008: chapter 5).[9] Chosenness and other religious motifs and symbols, he argues, are "deep cultural resources" that continue to provide the "basic cultural and ideological building blocks for nationalists" (2003: 254–255; see also Hutchison and Lehmann 1994).

Religion contributed to the origin and development of nationalism not only through the political appropriation of religious symbols and narratives but also in more indirect ways. Scholars have suggested, for example, that the Protestant Reformation and the broader process of "confessionalization" contributed to the development of nationalism in three ways: by generating new modes of imagining and constructing social and political relationships, promoting literacy in and standardization of vernacular languages, and bringing polity and culture into tighter alignment.

The new ways of imagining and institutionalizing religious community fostered by the Reformation provided new models for political community. This line of argument emphasizes the egalitarian potential inherent in the notion of the priesthood of all believers, the individualism involved in the emphasis on the direct study of scripture, and the direct and unmediated relationship between individuals and God. These new ways of imagining religious community have a striking affinity with understandings of "the nation" as an internally undifferentiated, egalitarian community to which individuals belong directly and immediately.[10] Practices of congregational self-rule in sectarian Protestantism, moreover, furnished models for democratic and national self-rule (Calhoun 1997: 72). A complementary argument about new modes of imagining community focuses on the long-term trajectory of Christianity, furthered by though not originating in Protestantism. Drawing on Gauchet (1997) and Baker (1994), for example, Bell (2001: 24–26) has argued that the intensification of the perceived gap between human and divine allowed the social world to be conceived in terms of its own autonomous laws. New understandings of nation—along with related foundational notions, including society, *patrie,* civilization, and public—emerged in this context.

Second, by fostering literacy in and prompting the standardization of vernacular languages, the Reformation laid the groundwork for imagining nationhood through the medium of language.[11] The Protestant emphasis on direct, unmediated access to scripture promoted the development of mass literacy, while the concern to make the Bible accessible to the widest possible audience—and the explosion of popular religious tracts occasioned by multiplying religious disputes—generated a surge in printing and publishing in vernacular languages. The proliferation of printed material, in turn, gave a powerful impetus to the standardization of vernacular languages. In Anderson's argument about "print-capitalism," the publishers of religious tracts and other materials sought wider markets and assembled varied idiolects into smaller numbers of increasingly standardized "print languages"; these "laid the bases for national consciousness" by creating "unified fields of exchange and communication below Latin and above the spoken vernacular" (1991: 44).[12]

The third line of argument focuses not on the Reformation per se but on the broader Reformation-era process of "confessionalization" that embraced Catholic as well as Protestant regions and involved "the emergence of three doctrinally, liturgically, and organizationally distinct 'confessions' [Catholicism, Lutheranism, and Calvinism], and their gradual imposition on an often passive population" (Gorski 2000a: 152). Confessionalization substantially tightened the relation between political organization and religious belief and practice. In so doing it provided a model for and a matrix of the congruence between culture and polity that is at the core of nationalism.

Confessionalization involved the fusion of politics and religion through the emergence of territorial churches that were subordinated (more or less fully and explicitly) to secular political control. Intensified religious discipline and new forms of social control heightened pressures for conformity. The persecution of dissent and consequent waves of refugees generated an "unmixing of confessions" that anticipated the later ethnic and nationalist "unmixing of peoples" (Gorski 2000a: 157–158). Rulers' explicit concern with the religious homogeneity of their subjects marked a sharp departure from the generic prenationalist condition portrayed in stylized fashion by Gellner (1994: 62) in which rulers "were interested in the tribute and labour potential of their subjects, not in their culture." Rulers were now very much interested in the culture of their subjects, though not in their language. The state-led cultural homogenization that was licensed by the formula *cuius regio, eius religio* provided a model for later, expressly nationalist modes of statist national homogenization.

Nationalism centrally involves a distinctive organization of sameness and difference: nationalist ideology demands—and nationalist social, political, and cultural processes tend to generate—cultural homogeneity *within* political units and cultural heterogeneity *between* them. The territorialization and pluralization of religion entailed by the process of confessionalization and codified in settlements such as the 1555 Peace of Augsburg and the 1648 Peace of Westphalia institutionalized and legitimated this distinctive pattern.[13] Religious homogeneity—a model for (and often a component of) national cultural homogeneity—was produced and legitimized on the level of the individual polity, while religious pluralism was institutionalized within the wider state system. More broadly, the territorialization and pluralization of religion entailed by the process of confessionalization placed religion "in a competitive, comparative field," in

Anderson's phrase (1991: 17). The emergence of such a field—replacing the single vast field of medieval Christendom—made it easier to imagine a world of distinct, bounded nations.[14]

As this brief and highly selective sampling suggests, religion can be understood as contributing to the origins and development of nationalism in a great variety of ways. What these arguments have in common is their rejection of an older understanding that nationalism arose from the decline of—and as an antithesis to—religion. Of course some nationalist claims *are* formulated in direct opposition to religious claims, but even in these cases—most strikingly in the French Revolution—nationalism may assume a religious quality, taking over some of the forms and functions of religion. Moreover, earlier forms of nationalist (or proto-nationalist) politics and national (or proto-national) consciousness emerged in a period of intensified rather than declining religiosity. And recent scholarship has suggestively traced the paths by which nationalism, like capitalism on Weber's account, emerged in part as an unintended consequence of religious developments (Gorski 2003).

Religion as Imbricated or Intertwined
with Nationalism

A third way of analyzing the connection between religion and nationalism sees religion not as something outside of nationalism that helps to explain it, but as so deeply imbricated or intertwined with nationalism as to be part of the phenomenon rather than an external explanation of it.

One kind of intertwining involves the coincidence of religious and national boundaries.[15] This has stronger and weaker variants. In the stronger variant, the nation is imagined as composed of *all* and *only* those who belong to a particular religion. This is illustrated by at least certain forms of Sikh nationalism and Jewish nationalism. In a weaker variant, local religious boundaries coincide with national boundaries, and religion may serve as the primary diacritical marker that enables one to identify ethnicity or nationality, but the religious community extends beyond the nation. This is illustrated by the doubling of religious and ethnonational identities in Northern Ireland and by the role of religious affiliation as a diacritical marker distinguishing Catholic Croats from Orthodox Serbs in the former Yugoslavia, where both groups spoke what used to be considered one and the same language.

In a second kind of intertwining, religion does not necessarily define the boundaries of the nation, but it supplies myths, metaphors, and symbols that are central to the discursive or iconic representation of the nation. This theme has been developed most fully in the work of Smith (1986, 2003, 2008). The question that religious resources help answer in this case is not necessarily "Who belongs?" but rather "Who are we?" and "What is distinctive about us as a people, in terms of our history, character, identity, mission, or destiny?"

This second kind of intertwining involves the religious inflection of nationalist discourse. If one interprets nationalist discourse broadly as embracing not only the discourse that accompanies and informs nationalist movements or specific forms of nationalist politics but any form of public or private talk about particular "nations" or countries, then this offers a broad and fertile terrain for studying the connection between religion and nationalism.

There is, for example, a large literature on the religious or religiously tinged language and imagery that infuse American political rhetoric. Although this rhetoric is not for the most part linked to distinctively nationalist forms of politics, it can be seen as part of the phenomenon of nationalism or nationhood in a broader sense. Historically, religious language and imagery have deeply informed and infused ways of thinking and talking about America and "Americanism," about the origins of the nation, its mission, its destiny, its role in the world, the "righteousness" of its causes, and the "evil" of its enemies. America has been represented as a nation uniquely blessed by God, indeed chosen by God for a "redemptive" role in the world and ordained to serve as a "New Israel," whose providential mission is to serve in exemplary fashion as a "beacon unto the nations" or, in its interventionist Wilsonian form, to take the lead in recasting and regenerating the world order, to "lead the world in the assertion of the rights of peoples and the rights of free nations" (Woodrow Wilson, quoted in Stephanson 1995: 117).

The legacy of this discourse is evident today, even if the notion of a distinctive mission is seldom cast, in mainstream political rhetoric, in expressly religious terms. It may be difficult to imagine an American president declaring, as Theodore Roosevelt famously did in the 1912 campaign, "We stand at Armageddon, and we battle for the Lord." But just days after 9/11, President George W. Bush did declare it "our responsibility to history" to "rid the world of evil." It may be hard to imagine a speech on the floor of the Senate today using exactly the language of Albert Beveridge, who in 1900 justified the war against the Filipino independence movement by claiming that God had made "the English-speaking and Teutonic peoples . . . master organizers of the world to establish system where chaos reigned," to "overwhelm the forces of reaction throughout the earth," to "administer government among savage and senile peoples," and to prevent the world from "relaps[ing] into barbarism and night," marking "the American people as His chosen nation to finally lead in the redemption of the world" (quoted in Tuveson 1968: vii; Bellah 1975: 38). Yet a century later, the rhetoric of mission used in connection with the war in Iraq and, more broadly, in connection with the "global war on terror" and the mission of "spreading freedom," has certain evident similarities.

Yet while it is easy enough to show how religious or religiously tinged language and imagery are used to frame talk about the special character, mission, or destiny of a nation, it is more difficult to specify the precise nature of the connection between religion and nationalism or nationhood in such cases. Consider briefly three conceptual and methodological difficulties.

First, what is religious about the religious or religiously tinged language, narratives, tropes, or images that are used to frame or color nation- or country-talk? Consider the political uses of the language of "sacredness." When state representatives or nationalists speak of "sacred" ideals, "sacred" territory, or "sacred" causes, does this signal an intertwining of religion and nation (or state)? Or can it be considered simply one of many metaphorical traces of originally religious language? Allusions to the Bible permeate all of English literature, even literature that is in no way religious. Should we think of this in terms of the intertwining of religion and literature? Or should we note that, while the modern English language has indeed been profoundly shaped by religion, metaphors and other figures of speech that derive ultimately from religious texts and traditions can be used, in English as in any other language, to communicate in ways that are not distinctively religious? After all, sometimes a metaphor is just a metaphor.

When reference is made today to America's distinctive mission in the world, is this evidence of the religious nature of American nationalism? Or, if one were to trace the rhetoric of mission from the New England colonies of the seventeenth century through the present, would one be more struck by the progressive secularization of that rhetoric? The specifically religious resonance or force of the rhetoric of national mission would seem to be much weaker today than in the New England colonies or seventeenth-century Netherlands. In the peroration to the *Protestant Ethic*, Weber (1958) spoke of victorious capitalism no longer needing the support of religion. Whatever the role of religion in the origins of nationalism, we might well say the same thing about victorious nationalism today (cf. Greenfeld 1992: 77).

One question, then, is what counts as religious language and imagery, as opposed to religiously tinged or originally religious but subsequently secularized language and imagery. A second issue concerns how to judge in comparative perspective—whether over time or across cases—the salience or pervasiveness of religious language or imagery. In almost any setting, the field of nation-talk is vast, heterogeneous, and chronically contested; one cannot judge the degree to which nation-talk is framed in religious terms simply by giving examples of such religious framing, no matter how numerous or vivid. To judge the relative importance of distinctively religious ways of framing nation-talk, as opposed to other ways of framing such talk, in different times and places, one would need a systematic discourse-analytic study of the field of nation-talk as a whole.

A further issue concerns the resonance or effectiveness of religiously framed, coded, or tinged nation-talk. The force, meaning, and resonance of national or nationalist rhetoric, like that of any other form of rhetoric, depend not on the rhetoric itself or the intentions of the speaker but on the schemas through which the rhetoric is interpreted. This suggests that the intertwining of religious and nationalist discourse should be studied not only on the "production" side but also on the "reception" side. In the American case, for example, even if the rhetoric of national mission used to justify post-9/11 foreign policy is not in and of itself distinctively religious, and indeed is cast in much more secular form today than in the past, that rhetoric may have religious resonance, and may be interpreted in religious terms, by some of those to whom it is addressed. It might therefore be claimed that the distinctive degrees and forms of American religiosity help explain the initially broad-based public acceptance of post-9/11 American foreign policy, and of the invasion of Iraq in particular. But how exactly to study the intertwining of religious schemas of interpretation and nation-talk on the "reception" side is far from evident.

Scholars have studied not only the religious inflection of nationalist discourse but also the inverse phenomenon: the national or nationalist inflection of religious discourse. More broadly, they have studied the "nationalization" of religion in its organizational and practical as well as discursive aspects, showing how religions—particularly supraethnic, "universal" religions such as Christianity and Islam—have been transformed by their encounter with nationalism and the nation-state (Haupt and Langewiesche 2004: 12f; Schulze Wessel 2006: 7–14).

In the Christian context, nationalization is in part a matter of what might more precisely be called the "étatization" of religion, through which states have sought to establish control over church affairs, appointments, and property. In the realm of Orthodox Christianity, especially in southeastern Europe, the nationalization of Christianity involved the fragmentation of Eastern Christendom into a series of autocephalous national churches, which provided a key institutional framework for nationalist movements and promoted a strong symbiosis of religious and national traditions. The nationalization of religion is also a matter of the varying cultural inflections of religious thought and practice in different state and national contexts. This cultural inflection of religious practice has been fostered by the fact that Christianity, unlike Islam, has never been tied to a unifying sacred language but has been from the start a "religion of translation" (Hastings 1997: 194). Although universalistic tendencies in Islam have been stronger than those in Christianity, scholars have studied the nationalization of Islam as well, showing how Islam has accommodated itself to—and been inflected by—differing national and state contexts (Lapidus 2001).

Religious Nationalism as a Distinctive Kind of Nationalism

The fourth and final way of analyzing the connection between religion and nationalism involves the claim that religious nationalism is a distinctive kind of nationalism. The claim is not simply that nationalist rhetoric may be suffused with religious imagery or that nationalist claims may be framed and formulated in religious or religiously tinged language. This is indisputably true. It is not simply a claim about a religio-national symbiosis or interpenetration, which no doubt often exists. The argument I want to examine here concerns not the *rhetorical form* of nationalist claims, or the *language or imagery* used to frame them, but the *content* of those claims. It is an argument that there is a distinctively religious type of nationalist program that represents a distinct alternative to secular nationalism.

The claim for a distinctively religious form of nationalism has been most fully articulated by Roger Friedland (2002; see also Juergensmeyer 1993). Friedland defines nationalism in statist terms. He characterizes nationalism as "a state-centered form of collective subject formation"; as "a program for the co-constitution of the state and the territorially bounded population in whose name it speaks"; and as "a set of discursive practices by which the territorial identity of a state and the cultural identity of the people whose collective representation it claims are constituted as a singular fact" (2002: 386).

This statist definition allows Friedland to conceptualize religious nationalism as a particular type of nationalism. Nationalism is understood as a *form* with variable *content*. The form prescribes the "joining of state, territoriality, and culture" (2002: 387) but does not specify *how* they are to be joined. It leaves open the *content* of state-centered collective subject formation, the content of the discursive practices through which the territorial identity of a state and the cultural identity of a people are "constituted as a singular fact." Religion provides one way of specifying this content. It provides a distinctive way—or a distinctive family of ways—of joining state, territoriality, and culture.

Religion is able to do so, on Friedland's account, because it provides "models of authority" and "imaginations of an ordering power" (2002: 390). Religion is a "totalizing order capable of regulating every aspect of life" (390)—though Friedland acknowledges that this is less true of Christianity, given its origins as a stateless faith. Religious nationalism joins state, territory, and culture primarily by focusing on family, gender, and sexuality: by defending the family's powers of social reproduction and moral socialization against economic and cultural forces that weaken them; by upholding traditional gendered divisions of labor within and outside the family; and by seeking to contain sexuality within the family.

This is a sophisticated and interesting argument. It usefully focuses attention on the distinctively religious content of programs for the ordering and regulating of public and private life rather than on the religious inflection of political rhetoric or the religious identities of political contestants. Neither of the latter is necessarily associated with a distinctively religious nationalist program. In Northern Ireland, for example, political rhetoric is often inflected by religious motifs, images, and symbols, and religion is the key diacritical marker that defines the parties to the conflict. Yet the conflict is not "about" religion; no major claims are made about ordering and regulating public life according to religious principles. This is a classical nationalist conflict, not a case of a distinctively religious kind of nationalism (Jenkins 1997: chapter 8).

What, then, *is* a case of religious nationalism in this strong sense? Friedland casts his definitional net widely; he sees religious nationalism at work in a wide range of settings, including the United States, India, Iran, Israel, Palestine, Turkey, Algeria, Egypt, and Pakistan. But while he discusses Christian fundamentalism and Hindu nationalism in some detail and touches on Jewish nationalism, he devotes his most sustained attention to Islamist movements. Since these pose in sharp form certain questions about the category of religious nationalism, I will focus on these.

There are certain striking similarities between Islamist movements and familiar forms of nationalism. Islamist movements invoke a putatively homogeneous prepolitical identity (the umma, or community of Muslims) that ought, on some accounts, to have its own state, a restored caliphate. They hold that public life should safeguard and promote the distinctive values of this community. They seek to awaken people to their "true" identities and to bring culture and polity into close alignment. They protest against the "alien" rule of non-Muslims over Muslims or of governments that are only nominally Muslim, and they seek to purify the polity of corrupting forms of alien influence (moral, cultural, or economic). In Friedland's terms, they seek to join state, territory, and culture. In these and other ways, Islamist movements partake of the underlying "grammar" of modern nationalism even when they are ostensibly antinationalist or supranational. Islamists, moreover, have often allied with nationalist movements, and they have sometimes fused with them. Hamas, for example, combines a classical state-seeking nationalist agenda with a distinctively religious program of Islamization, though not without considerable tension (Aburaiya 2009; Pelham and Rodenbeck 2009). Yet most Islamist movements, although they work through the *state*, are not oriented to the *nation*.

The territorial nation-state remains the dominant political reality of our time; reports of its death or debility have been greatly exaggerated. Islamist movements—like other forms of politicized religion—accommodate themselves to this reality, even when they have transnational commitments or aspirations. The claim of the nation-state to regulate all aspects of life makes it an inescapable arena of engagement. In pervasively state-organized societies, "no movement that aspires to more than mere belief or inconsequential talk in public can remain indifferent to state power" (Asad 2003: 200). But the fact that Islamist movements seek to gain or influence the exercise of power within particular nation-states does not make them nationalist (Arjomand 1994; Asad 2003: chapter 6).

Nationalism is a useful concept only if it is not overstretched. If the concept is not to lose its discriminating power, it must be limited to forms of politics, ideology, or discourse that involve a central orientation to "the nation"; it cannot be extended to encompass all forms of politics that work in and through nation-states (cf. Smith 1991: 74). There is no compelling reason to speak of "nationalism" unless the imagined community of the nation is widely understood as a primary focus of value, source of legitimacy, object of loyalty, and basis of identity. But the nation is not understood in this way by most Islamist movements. This points to the limits of Friedland's state-centered understanding of nationalism. If Islamism is a form of nationalism, it is nationalism without a central role for "the nation."

Some scholars have argued that the umma—the worldwide community of Muslim believers—is a kind of nation. On this account, the forms of transborder politicized Islam that have taken root especially among marginalized second- and third-generation immigrant youth in Europe—oriented to the global umma, nurtured primarily in cyberspace, articulated increasingly in English, and promoted by a new class of Internet-based interpreters of Islam (Anderson 2003)—are therefore a kind of deterritorialized nationalism (Saunders 2008). Abstracting from the ethnic and national identities and the traditional religious beliefs and practices of their parents and grandparents, "Muslim" has indeed become a powerful categorical identity in Europe (Brubaker 2013). This holds even among the nonobservant, so it is correct to say that "Muslim" is not simply a religious identity. But there is no compelling reason for regarding "Muslim" as a specifically *national* identity. A key distinguishing feature of nation as an imagined community—and of nationalism as an ideology—is that any given nation is imagined as limited, as just one among many other such nations (Anderson 1991: 7). The social ontology of nationalism is in this sense "polycentric" or "pluralist" (Smith 1983:158–159, 170–171). The umma is not imagined as limited in this way, as one nation alongside others. Nor is the umma imagined as actually or potentially sovereign—as the ultimate source of political legitimacy (Asad 2003: 197–198). The forms of politics built around this categorical identity are therefore not usefully characterized as nationalist.

Nationalism and Secularization Revisited

The four ways of studying the relation between religion and nationalism that I have distinguished and delineated are neither exhaustive nor mutually exclusive. They do not represent alternative theories; they do not provide different answers to the same questions but ask different kinds of questions. My aim has not been to argue for the merits of one of the four approaches over the others; all represent interesting and valuable lines of research. I have sought rather to give a sense of the range and variety of questions that can be asked about the relation between the large and multidimensional fields of phenomena we call *religion* and *nationalism*.

I would like to conclude this chapter by reconsidering the much-criticized understanding of nationalism as a distinctively secular phenomenon. A secularist bias in the study of nationalism, like the secularist bias in many other domains of social science, long obscured interesting connections and affinities between religion and nationalism. Long-dominant modernizationist arguments, emphasizing socioeconomic modernity (Gellner 1983; Deutsch 1953), political modernity (Breuilly 1994; Tilly 1996; Hechter

2000), or cultural modernity (Anderson 1991), neglected religion or saw it as superseded by nationalism. The paradigmatic instances addressed in the literature were European nationalisms between the late eighteenth and early twentieth century; this truncated range of cases marginalized others—from early modern Europe, South Asia, or the Middle East, for example—in which religion was more obviously central. A widely shared understanding of the modern nation-state—an understanding at once normative and predictive—relegated religion to the realm of the private.

This secularist bias has been powerfully challenged in recent years (Van der Veer 1994; Asad 2003; Spohn 2003), and a substantial body of work, several strands of which I have discussed in this chapter, has explored the multiple connections and affinities between religion and nationalism. This work has highlighted the religious matrix of the category of the secular itself, and it has challenged the notion that modernity requires the privatization of religion (Casanova 1994). These developments are entirely salutary. But is there perhaps something in the secularist understanding of nationalism that, reformulated and shorn of various palpably untenable claims and expectations, might be worth preserving?

As a distinctive form of politics, nationalism involves demands for congruence between "the nation"—however defined—and the state or polity; in a slightly different idiom, it involves claims that "the nation" should be fully expressed in and protected by an existing or projected state or polity. The fundamental point of reference of nationalist politics is "the nation"; its social ontology posits nations as fundamental social units (Smith 1983: 178). Nations are seen as legitimately entitled to "their own" polities and as "owning" those polities once they are established; authority is seen as legitimate only if it arises from "the nation." This complex structure of political argument and cultural understanding involves a distinctive social ontology, a particular social imaginary (Anderson 1991; Taylor 2007: chapter 4), and an "ascending" doctrine of political authority and legitimacy (Calhoun 1997).

The development and diffusion of this structure of political argument and cultural understanding, it can be argued, were made possible in part by a process of secularization. By secularization, I do not mean the decline of religion or the relegation of religion to the private realm. As noted above, early forms of national consciousness and nationalist or proto-nationalist politics emerged in a period of intensified rather than declining religiosity and of prevailingly public rather than private religion. As a general account of religion in the modern world, the secularization thesis is untenable if it is taken to refer to either the decline or the privatization of religion. But the core of the secularization thesis—the claim that the differentiation of various autonomous realms of human activity from religious institutions and norms has been central to, even constitutive of, Western modernity—remains compelling (Casanova 1994). And this process of differentiation—in particular the emergence of understandings of economy, society, and polity as autonomous realms—was arguably a precondition for the emergence and widespread naturalization of the social ontology, social imaginary, and ascending understanding of political legitimacy characteristic of modern nationalism.

Moreover, nationalist politics—based on claims made in the name of "the nation"—remain distinct from, even as they are intertwined with, forms of religious politics that seek to transform public life not in the name of the nation, but in the name of God. To be sure, as I discussed earlier, nationalism and religion are often deeply intertwined; political actors may make claims *both* in the name of the nation *and* in the name of God. Nationalist politics can accommodate the claims of religion, and nationalist rhetoric often deploys religious language, imagery, and symbolism; similarly, religion can accommodate the claims of the nation-state, and religious movements can deploy nationalist language.

Yet intertwining is not identity; the very metaphor of intertwining implies a distinction between the intertwined strands. As I have argued, religious movements that pursue a comprehensive transformation of public life do not become nationalist simply by working through the nation-state; nor do they become nationalist by allying with secular nationalists in anticolonial struggles or by deploying the rhetoric of anticolonial nationalism. Similarly, nationalist movements do not turn into specifically religious movements by virtue of deploying religious symbols, emphasizing religious traditions, or even making religious affiliation a criterion of full membership of the nation. Languages of religion and nation, like all forms of language, can be pervasively intertwined. But even when the languages are intertwined, the fundamental ontologies and structures of justification differ. We can be sensitive both to discursive intertwining and to this fundamental difference.

CHAPTER FIVE

The "Diaspora" Diaspora

A QUARTER OF A CENTURY AGO, writing in the inaugural issue of the journal *Diaspora*, William Safran observed that most scholarly discussions of ethnicity and immigration paid "little if any attention ... to diasporas" (1991: 83). This claim was beginning to be out of date—as Safran recognized—even by the time it appeared in print. And obviously no one would think of making such a claim today. There has been a veritable explosion of interest in diasporas since the late 1980s. The words *diaspora* and *diasporic* appear in titles or abstracts of only twelve dissertations during the entire 1970s, in about ten per year in the late 1980s, in about sixty per year in the late 1990s, and in more than two hundred per year since 2008.[1] Diaspora yields half a million Google Scholar results and 15 million general Google hits, a large majority of them nonacademic.

As the term has proliferated, its meaning has been stretched to accommodate a broadening variety of intellectual, cultural, and political agendas. This has resulted in what one might call a "'diaspora' diaspora"—a dispersion of the meanings of the term in semantic, conceptual, and disciplinary space.[2]

Most early discussions of diaspora were firmly rooted in a conceptual "homeland"; they were concerned with a paradigmatic case or a small number of core cases. The paradigmatic case was of course the Jewish diaspora; until recently, some dictionary definitions of diaspora did not simply *illustrate* but *defined* the word with reference to that case (Sheffer 2003: 9).

The modern use of the word *diaspora*, as Stéphane Dufoix has shown, derives from the Septuagint, the first Greek translation of the Hebrew Bible.[3] The word is used there to describe not the *fact* of dispersion but the *threat* of dispersion that will befall the Jews, as divine punishment, if they do not respect God's commandments. Later, in the first century of the Christian era, the word came to be applied to the actual dispersion of the Jews following the destruction of the Second Temple, and it was then applied by extension to the early Christian dispersion. For nearly two millennia the term functioned as a proper noun, or at least as a category with a strictly limited membership; diaspora simply *was* the Jewish dispersion, or the early Christian dispersion. Later still, in the context of the Reformation, the term was used with reference to the links between Protestant evangelical missions in different countries. But until perhaps fifty years ago, the term was limited to specifically Jewish and Christian religious contexts.

As discussions of diasporas began to branch out to include other cases, they remained oriented, at least initially, to the paradigmatic Jewish case. When historian George Shepperson introduced the notion of the African diaspora, he did so by expressly engaging the Jewish experience of forcible dispersion (Shepperson 1966; Edwards 2001; Alpers 2001). The Palestinian diaspora too has been construed as a "catastrophic" diaspora or a "victim diaspora" (Cohen 1997) on the model of the Jewish case. The concept of the trading diaspora—or the "mobilized diaspora" (Armstrong 1976)—was constructed on the model of another aspect of the Jewish, as well as the Greek and Armenian, experience.[4] An orientation to this paradigmatic case also informs a number of influential overviews, including those of Safran (1991), Clifford (1994), and Cohen (1997).

In several more recent extensions of the term, however, the reference to the paradigmatic case has become more attenuated. Some emigrant groups—characterized as "long-distance nationalists" by Anderson (1998)—have been construed as diasporas because of their continued involvement in homeland politics.[5] In a further extension, the term has come to embrace labor migrants and their descendants who maintain (to some degree) emotional and social ties with a homeland.[6] Even older populations of migrant origin that have been largely assimilated, like Italians in the United States, have been characterized as diasporas.[7] The study of diaspora has become coextensive with the study of social formations emerging from any kind of migration: "to say 'migration,'" as Roger Waldinger (2008: xi) has put it, "is now to say 'diaspora.'"

Some further extensions go even beyond migration. Diasporas are said to result from the movement of borders over people, not simply from that of people over borders. Hungarians, Russians, and other ethnonational communities separated by a political frontier from their putative national home-land have been conceptualized as diasporas in this sense.[8] Transborder lin-guistic categories too—such as Francophone, Anglophone, and Lusophone "communities" (a word that should be used only in quotation marks [Bau-mann 1996])—have been conceptualized as diasporas, as have global reli-gious "communities," yielding Hindu, Sikh, Buddhist, Confucian, Hugue-not, Muslim, and Catholic diasporas.[9] It appears to be little more than sheer dispersion that underwrites the formulation of such populations as "diasporas."

And then there is a grab bag of putative diasporas of other sorts: the Dixie diaspora, the Yankee diaspora, the white diaspora, the liberal dias-pora, the conservative diaspora, the gay diaspora, the deaf diaspora, the queer diaspora, the redneck diaspora, the digital diaspora, the fundamen-talist diaspora, the terrorist diaspora, the shamanic diaspora, the foodie diaspora, and, underlying them all, the human diaspora.[10]

One dimension of dispersion, then, involves the application of the term to an ever-broadening set of cases—to any and every nameable population category that is in some way dispersed in space. The problem with this latitudinarian, "let a thousand diasporas bloom" approach is that the cat-egory risks being stretched to the point of uselessness (Sartori 1970). If everyone is diasporic, then no one is distinctively so. To the extent that the term "now shares meanings with a larger semantic domain that includes words like immigrant, expatriate, refugee, guest-worker, exile community, overseas community, ethnic community"—a problem already evident to a discerning observer in 1991 (Tölölyan 1991: 4)—it loses its discriminating power. The universalization of diaspora, paradoxically, means the disap-pearance of diaspora.

James Clifford (1994: 305, 325–327) and others have argued persuasively that there is no reason to privilege the Jewish experience, not least because that experience is internally complex, ambivalent, and by no means straight-forwardly "diasporic" in the strict sense of the term. But there is no reason to speak of the diasporization of every more or less dispersed population. Even the editor of the journal *Diaspora*—a key vehicle for the prolifera-tion of academic diaspora-talk—noted in the journal's sixth year that dias-pora "is in danger of becoming a promiscuously capacious category" and urged at least some "stringency of definition" (Tölölyan 1996: 8, 30).

Besides the nomination of new candidates for diaspora status, the "dias-pora" diaspora also involves a dispersion in disciplinary and social space. Within the academy, the term is now used throughout the humanities and social sciences. A sampling of forty recent dissertations on diaspora showed that they were distributed among forty-five different fields and subfields, ranging from various subfields of history, literature, anthropology, and sociology through Black studies, women's studies, religion, philosophy, communications, folklore, and education, to art history, cinema, dance, music, and theater. As Tölölyan (1996: 27) has observed, the "theory-driven revolution in the humanities" has been central to this disciplinary (and transdisciplinary) dispersion.

Dispersion has been even more striking outside the academy: in the media, on the web, and in the self-representations of a wide range of groups and initiatives.[11] In this respect the trajectory of *diaspora* resembles that of *identity*, which moved from being a technical term of philosophy and psychoanalysis to a key term throughout the humanities and social sciences, and which came to be very widely used in the media and popular culture (Gleason 1983; Brubaker and Cooper 2000).[12]

Criteria

Notwithstanding the dispersion in semantic and conceptual space, one can identify three core elements that remain widely understood to be constitutive of diaspora. Some subset or combination of these, variously weighted, underlies most definitions and discussions of the phenomenon.[13] The first is dispersion in space; the second, orientation to a "homeland"; and the third, boundary maintenance. Consideration of the changing significance accorded these elements—and of the various ways they have been interpreted—provides leverage for a more analytical appraisal of the "diaspora" diaspora.

Dispersion

Dispersion in space is today the most widely accepted criterion of diaspora and also the most straightforward. It can be interpreted strictly as forced or otherwise traumatic dispersion;[14] more broadly as any kind of dispersion in space, provided that the dispersion crosses state borders; or (in the increasingly common metaphorical extensions of the term) more broadly still, so that dispersion *within* state borders may suffice.

Although dispersion is widely accepted as a criterion of diaspora, it is not universally accepted. Some substitute division for dispersion, defining diasporas as "ethnic communities divided by state frontiers" (King and Melvin 1999: 108; see also King and Melvin 1998) or as "that segment of a people living outside the homeland" (Connor 1986: 16). This allows even compactly settled populations to count as diasporas when part of the population lives as a minority outside its ethnonational "homeland."

Homeland Orientation

The second constitutive criterion is the orientation to a real or imagined "homeland" as an authoritative source of value, identity, and loyalty. Here a significant shift can be discerned in recent discussions. Earlier discussions strongly emphasized this criterion. Four of the six criteria specified by Safran (1991), for example, concern the orientation to a homeland.[15] These include maintaining a collective memory or myth about the homeland; regarding the "ancestral homeland as their true, ideal home and as the place to which they or their descendants would (or should) eventually return"; being collectively "committed to the maintenance or restoration of the homeland and to its safety and prosperity"; and "continu[ing] to relate, personally or vicariously," to the homeland, in a way that significantly shapes one's identity and solidarity (83–84).

Several more recent discussions de-emphasize homeland orientation (Clifford 1994; Anthias 1998; Falzon 2003). Clifford, for example, has criticized what he calls the "centered" model of Safran and others, in which diasporas are by definition "oriented by continuous cultural connections to a [single] source and by a teleology of 'return.'" On this strict definition, as Clifford notes, many aspects of the Jewish experience itself do not qualify. Nor would the experience of dispersed African, Caribbean, or South Asian populations; the South Asian diaspora, for example, is "not so much oriented to roots in a specific place and a desire for return as around an ability to recreate a culture in diverse locations." For Clifford, "decentered, lateral connections may be as important as those formed around a teleology of origin/return" (1994: 305–306). Cohen (2009) has sought to stake out a middle ground between classical homeland-focused and "postmodern" homeland-deconstructing accounts of diaspora; he distinguishes between "solid," "ductile" (flexible), and "liquid" (virtual) understandings of homeland and finds empirical support for all three.[16]

Boundary Maintenance

The third constitutive criterion is what, following Armstrong (1976: 394–397), I call boundary maintenance, involving the preservation of a distinctive identity vis-à-vis the host society (or societies). Armstrong invokes Barth's seminal 1969 contribution to emphasize the importance of boundaries for collectivities that do not have "their own" territorial polity: "Clearly, a diaspora is something more than, say, a collection of persons distinguished by some secondary characteristic such as, for example, all persons with Scottish names in Wisconsin. . . . The mobilized diaspora . . . has often constituted for centuries a *separate society or quasi-society* in a larger polity" (Armstrong 1976: 393–394, emphasis added). Boundaries can be maintained in two ways that are very different in principle, though often intertwined in practice (as in the paradigmatic Jewish case): they may be internally generated (through endogamy, self-segregation, or resistance to assimilation [Armstrong 1976: 394–395; Smith 1986]); or they may be externally generated (by various forms of external categorization, differential treatment, and social exclusion [Laitin 1995]).

On most accounts, boundary maintenance is an indispensable criterion of diaspora (for example, Armstrong 1976; Safran 1991: 83; Tölölyan 1996: 14; Cohen 1997: 24). It is this that enables one to speak of a diaspora as a distinctive "community," held together by a distinctive, active solidarity, as well as by relatively dense social relationships that cut across state boundaries and link members of the diaspora in different states into a single "transnational community."

Yet here there is an interesting ambivalence in the literature. Although boundary maintenance and the preservation of identity are ordinarily emphasized, a strong countercurrent emphasizes hybridity, fluidity, creolization, and syncretism. In an oft-quoted remark by Stuart Hall, the "diaspora experience . . . is defined, not by essence or purity, but by the recognition of a necessary heterogeneity and diversity; by a conception of 'identity' which lives with and through, not despite, difference; by *hybridity*" (1990: 235). This countercurrent is especially characteristic of the literature on transnationalism, which has tended to fuse in recent years with that on diaspora. There is thus a tension in the literature between *boundary maintenance* and *boundary erosion*. The tension is only occasionally acknowledged, and then sometimes only implicitly. In his discussion of Gilroy, for example, Clifford resorts to oxymoron, referring to the problem of the "changing same," to "something endlessly hybridized and in process but persistently there" (1994: 320).

A final point about boundary-maintenance is that it must occur over an extended time. This is seldom made explicit, but it is crucial. The erosion of boundaries through assimilation is always a temporally extended, intergenerational process (Alba and Nee 1997, 2003; Brubaker 2001). As a result, boundary maintenance becomes sociologically interesting, as it were, only when it persists over generations. That migrants themselves maintain boundaries is only to be expected; the interesting question, and the question relevant to the existence of a diaspora, is to what extent and in what forms boundaries are maintained by second, third, and subsequent generations. Classical diasporas—as Armstrong (1976, 1982: 206–213) and others have emphasized—were a phenomenon of the *longue durée*.

Whether the various diasporas that have been nominated into existence in recent decades will have this kind of multigenerational staying power is by no means clear.[17]

A Radical Break?

What are we to make of the proliferation of diasporas and of diaspora-talk, inside and outside the academy? And how should one interpret it? Are we seeing a proliferation of diasporas in the world—or perhaps even the dawning of an age of diaspora? Or (to put the question in deliberately exaggerated form) are we seeing simply a proliferation of diaspora-talk, a change in idiom rather than in the world?

I want to consider two sorts of claims about novelty and discontinuity. One concerns a putatively sharp break in ways of looking at the world, the other a putatively sharp transformation in the world itself. The two claims are of course closely related and are usually advanced together; the radical shift in perspective is presented as a way of coming to terms, analytically and politically, with fundamental changes in the world.

On the one hand, the literature on diaspora claims to mark a sharp shift in perspective. The old perspective, it is suggested, was immigrationist, assimilationist, (methodologically) nationalist,[18] and teleological. It took nation-states as units of analysis and assumed that immigrants made a sharp and definitive break with their homelands, that migration trajectories were unidirectional, and that migration inexorably led to assimilation. The new perspective does not make these assumptions. It is said to "transcend" the old assimilationist, immigrationist paradigm. In one representative statement, "it is no longer assumed that immigrants make a sharp break from their homelands. Rather, premigration networks, cultures, and capital remain salient. The sojourn itself is neither unidirectional nor final. . . . Movements . . . follow multifarious trajectories and sustain diverse networks. Rather than the singular immigrant, scholars now detail the diversity of immigration circumstances, class backgrounds, gendered transitions, and the sheer multitude of migration experiences" (Lie 1995: 304).[19] This greatly exaggerates the shift in perspective, at least in the American context. Long before *diaspora* became fashionable, historians and sociologists of immigration had abandoned—if indeed they ever held—simplistic assumptions about unidirectional trajectories, sharp and definitive breaks with home countries, and a singular path of assimilation. If Glazer and Moynihan's (1963: v) observation that "the point about the melting pot . . . is that it did not happen" was iconoclastic when first made, it had become widely accepted by the end of the 1960s. So much emphasis was placed on ethnic persistence in the historical and sociological literature between about 1965 and 1985—again, before the "diaspora" explosion—that there has even been, in reaction, a certain "return of assimilation" (Brubaker 2001) in the past two decades (albeit of a more subtle, multidimensional, and normatively ambivalent concept of assimilation).

More important than the alleged novelty and originality of the literature is the alleged novelty and import of the phenomenon itself. Does diaspora—along with kindred terms such as transnationalism, postnationalism, globalization, deterritorialization, postcolonialism, creolization, transculturalism, and postmodernity—name something fundamentally new in the world? Do these terms mark—or at least augur—an epochal shift, as some theorists have suggested (Kearney 1991; Appadurai 1996)? Have we passed from the age of the nation-state to the age of diaspora?

More specifically, does the "unprecedented porosity" of borders (Sheffer 2003: 22)—the unprecedented circulation of people, goods, messages, images, ideas, and cultural products—signify a basic realignment of the relationship between politics and culture, territorial state and deterritorialized identities? Does this entail the transcendence of the nation-state, based on territorial closure, exclusive claims on citizens' loyalty, and a homogenizing, nationalizing, assimilationist logic? Does the age of diaspora open up new possibilities for what Clifford has called "non-exclusive practices of community, politics, and cultural difference" (1994: 302)? Does it offer "an alternative to life in territorially and nationally marked groups"?[20]

Obviously the world has changed, and so have our ways of talking about it. But one should be skeptical of grand claims about radical breaks and epochal shifts (Favell 2001). Can one in fact speak of an unprecedented porosity of borders? Not with regard to the movement of people. Over the course of the past century and a half, states have gained rather than lost the capacity to monitor and control the movement of people through increasingly sophisticated technologies of identification and control, including citizenship, passports, visas, surveillance, integrated databases, and biometric devices.[21] The shock of 9/11 has only pushed states further and faster along a path on which they were already moving. No liberal state, to be sure, can absolutely seal its borders. On balance, however, the world's poor who seek work or refuge in prosperous and peaceful countries encounter a tighter mesh of state regulation and have fewer opportunities for migration to prosperous and peaceful countries than they did a century ago (Hirst and Thompson 1999: 30–31, 267).

Is migration today unprecedented in volume and velocity? How one answers this question depends, of course, on one's units of analysis. Migrant flows of recent decades to the United States are in fact much smaller, in relation both to the population of the United States and to the population of the rest of the world, than those of a century ago. And while contemporary migrations worldwide are "more geographically extensive than the great global migrations of the modern era," they have been characterized as "on balance slightly *less* intensive" (Held et al. 1999: 326, emphasis added). Even though there are more than 200 million migrants worldwide, this amounts to only 3 percent of the global population, and fewer than half of these are involved in south-north migration (International Organization for Migration 2013: 55); the mobility of the great majority, as I argued in Chapter 1, remains severely limited by the morally arbitrary facts of birthplace and inherited citizenship and by the exclusionary policies of states.

Is migration today neither unidirectional nor permanent? Of course not, in many cases; but it was neither unidirectional nor permanent, in many cases, a century ago. Historians have long highlighted the very high rates of return migration from North America to various European countries of origin in the late nineteenth and early twentieth centuries. Do migrants make a sharp and definitive break with their homelands? Of course not. But nor did they do so a century ago, as an abundant historical literature has made clear. Do migrants sustain ties with their country of origin? They do indeed, but they managed to do so by nonelectronic means a century ago (Morawska 2001; Hollinger 1995: 151ff; Waldinger and Fitzgerald 2004). This is not to say that nothing has changed or that distance-eclipsing technologies of communication and transportation do not matter; it, is, however, to caution against exaggerated claims of an epochal break.

Have the exclusive claims of the nation-state been eroded? They have indeed. But *the* nation-state—as opposed to the multifarious particular nation-states—is a figment of the sociological imagination. "The" nation-state is the primary conceptual "other" against which diaspora is defined—and often celebrated (Tölölyan 1991; Clifford 1994: 307). But there is a risk of essentializing "the" nation-state, a risk of attributing to it a timeless, self-actualizing, homogenizing "logic."[22] Sophisticated discussions are sensitive to the heterogeneity of diasporas, but they are not always as sensitive to the heterogeneity of nation-states. Discussions of diaspora are often informed by a strikingly idealist, teleological understanding of the nation-state, which is seen as the unfolding of an idea, the idea of nationalizing and homogenizing the population.[23] The conceptual antithesis between nation-state and diaspora obscures more than it reveals, occluding the persisting significance (and great empirical variety) of nation-states (Mann 1997).

Beyond Groupism: Diaspora as Idiom,
Stance, and Claim

Like nation, ethnic group, and minority—terms with which it shares an overlapping semantic field (Tölölyan 1991, 1996)—diaspora is often characterized in substantialist terms as an "entity." As one example among many, consider the beginning of a book by Gabriel Sheffer:

> The highly motivated Koreans and Vietnamese toiling hard to become prosperous in bustling Los Angeles, the haggard Palestinians living in dreary refugee camps near Beirut and Amman, the beleaguered Turks dwelling in cramped apartments in Berlin, and the frustrated Russians in Estonia, all have much in common. All of them, along with Indians, Chinese, Japanese, Africans, African-Americans, Jews, Palestinians, Greeks, Gypsies, Romanians, Poles, Kurds, Armenians, and numerous other groups permanently residing outside of their countries of origin, but maintaining contacts with people back in their old homelands, are members of ethno-national diasporas. (2003: 1)

Diasporas are treated here as "bona fide actual entities" (245) and cast as unitary actors. They are seen as possessing countable, quantifiable memberships. And indeed they are counted. Sheffer claims to have made the "first attempt to estimate the *real numbers* of the main historical, modern, and incipient diasporas" (104, emphasis added).[24]

Sheffer recognizes in principle the difference between "core," "marginal," and "dormant" members of diasporas (2003: 100), but his numerical estimates—which seem designed to be maximally inclusive—take no account of differing degrees and modes of diasporic engagement. The very notion of "dormant members" of a diaspora is problematic: if they are really dormant—if they have "assimilated or fully integrated" into a host society and merely "know or feel that their roots are in the diaspora group" (100)—then why should they count, and be counted, as "members" of the diaspora at all?

What is it that Sheffer and others are counting when they count "members" of diasporas? It appears that what is usually counted—or rather estimated—is ancestry. But if one takes seriously boundary maintenance, lateral ties to fellow diaspora members in other states, and vertical ties to the homeland, then ancestry is surely a poor proxy for membership in a diaspora. Enumerations such as this suggest that discussions of diaspora opportunistically combine elements of strong and weak definitions.[25] Strong definitions are used to emphasize the distinctiveness of diaspora as a social form; weak definitions, to emphasize numbers (and thereby the import of the phenomenon).

Not all discussions of diaspora, to be sure, emphasize boundary maintenance. Some discussions, as I indicated, emphasize hybridity, fluidity, creolization, and syncretism and offer an alternative to the groupist portrayal of diasporas as tangible, quantifiable, and bounded entities. But these discussions too tend to speak of diasporas as distinctive communities with distinctive identities, without explaining how such distinctive communities and identities can emerge if all is hybrid, fluid, creolized, and syncretic.

Where boundary maintenance and distinctive identity are emphasized, as they are in most discussions, familiar problems of "groupism" arise (Brubaker 2002). The metaphysics of the nation-state as a bounded territorial community may have been overcome, but the metaphysics of "community" and "identity" remain. Diaspora can be seen as an *alternative* to the essentialization of belonging, but it can also represent a nonterritorial *form* of essentialized belonging.[26] Talk of the deterritorialization of identity is all well and good, yet it still presupposes that there is "an identity" that is reconfigured, stretched in space to cross state boundaries, but on some level fundamentally the same. Yet if, as Homi Bhabha put it, "there is no such whole as the nation, the culture, or even the self," then why should there be any such whole as the Indian or Chinese or Jewish or Armenian or Kurdish diaspora?[27]

To overcome these problems of groupism, I want to argue that we should think of diaspora not in substantialist terms as a bounded entity but rather as an idiom, a stance, a claim. We should think of diaspora in the first instance as a *category of practice*—and only then ask whether and how it can fruitfully be used as a category of analysis.[28] As a category of practice, "diaspora" is used to make claims, articulate projects, formulate expectations, mobilize energies, and appeal to loyalties.[29] It often carries a strong normative change. It does not so much *describe* the world as seek to *remake* it.

As idiom, stance, and claim, diaspora is a way of formulating the identities and loyalties of a population. It is a way of imagining or projecting a community among a dispersed, cross-border population (Sökefeld 2006). Those who do the formulating may themselves belong to the population in question, or they may be speaking in the name of a putative homeland state.[30] In either case, not all those whom others claim as members of putative diasporas themselves claim a diasporic identity. Those who consistently adopt a diasporic stance are often only a small minority of the population that political or cultural entrepreneurs formulate as a diaspora (Tölölyan 1996: 19). What is casually called "the Armenian diaspora" in the United States, for example, is not very diasporic at all, according to a comprehensive sociological analysis (Bakalian 1993; cf. Tölölyan 1996: 15).

And it is becoming less rather than more so over time, as the large majority of those who identify as Armenians distance themselves from diasporic
stances, from links to the homeland, and from links to Armenians in other
countries. Their "Armenianness" is closer to what Herbert Gans (1979)
long ago called "symbolic ethnicity."

There is of course a committed diasporan or diasporic fraction, as Tölölyan
(1996: 18) calls it, among Armenians and many other dispersed populations.
And they have good reason to refer to all dispersed Armenians as a "diaspora." For them, diaspora is a category of practice and central to their project. But why should we, as analysts, use diaspora to refer to all persons of
Armenian descent living outside Armenia? The disadvantage of doing so is
that it occludes the difference between the actively diasporan fraction and
the majority who are not committed to the diasporic project.

In sum, rather than speak of "a diaspora" or "the diaspora" as an entity,
a bounded group, or an ethnodemographic or ethnocultural fact, it may be
more fruitful—and it would certainly be more precise—to speak of diasporic stances, projects, claims, idioms, and practices. We can then explore
to what extent, and in what circumstances, those claimed as members of
putative diasporas actively support, passively sympathize with, or are indifferent or even hostile to the diasporic projects pursued in their name.[31]

Scholars have suggested that diaspora provides an alternative to teleological, nation-statist understandings of immigration and assimilation. But
theories of diaspora have their own teleologies. Diaspora is often seen as
destiny—a destiny to which previously dormant members (or previously
dormant diasporas in their entirety) are now "awakening" (Sheffer 2003:
21). Embedded in the teleological language of "awakening"—the language, not coincidentally, of many nationalist movements—are essentialist
assumptions about "true" identities. Little is gained if we escape from one
teleology only to fall into another.

The point is not to deflate diaspora but rather to desubstantialize it. The
"groupness" of putative diasporas, like that of putative "nations," is contingent and variable. It is the stake of practical struggles—political, social,
and cultural—over the making and remaking of groups. We should not, as
analysts, prejudge the outcome of such struggles by imposing groupness
through definitional fiat. We should seek rather to bring the struggles themselves into focus. To this end, we should treat diaspora as a category of
practice, project, claim, and stance rather than as a bounded group.

CHAPTER SIX

Migration, Membership, and the Nation-State

W HAT ARE WE TALKING ABOUT when we talk about the nation-state? The term is often used to designate all polities that recognize one an-other's (nominal) independence. Yet this usage is analytically vacuous, since such polities vary enormously in all fundamental dimensions and aspects of stateness and nationness: they vary in size, structure, strength, capacity, wealth, cohesiveness, cultural homogeneity, and many other attributes.[1]

More analytically interesting is the use of "nation-state" to designate an analytical or normative ideal-type. As an *analytical* ideal-type, the nation-state is a model *of* political, social, and cultural organization; as a *normative* ideal-type, it is a model *for* political, social, and cultural organization.[2] In the former sense, "nation-state" is a category of *analysis,* used to make sense of the social world. In the latter, it is a category of *practice,* a consti-tutive part of the social world, a core term in the modern political lexicon, deployed in struggles to make and remake the social world.[3]

In both guises—as part of the analytical idiom of social science and as part of the practical idiom of modern politics—"the" nation-state is often understood and represented in a highly idealized manner. I mean "idealized" first and foremost in a logical sense, not necessarily in a normative sense; even sharp critics of the nation-state invoke an idealized conceptual model that is said to capture the basic "logic" or nature of "the" nation-state.

The idealized conceptual model of the nation-state, which began to take shape during the French Revolution and was elaborated through both theoretical reflection and political practice during most of the subsequent two centuries, posits a tight coupling or congruence of nation and state. More specifically, the model posits a set of mappings or congruencies linking state territory, national territory, national culture, and citizenry (Wimmer 2002: chapter 3; Brubaker 1990: 380–381). According to this model, the frontiers of the state as an actually existing territorial organization should match the frontiers of the nation as an "imagined community" (Anderson 1991). Polity and culture should be congruent: a distinctive national culture should be diffused throughout the territory of the state, but it should stop at the frontiers of the state; there should be cultural homogeneity *within* states but sharp cultural boundaries *between* them. State territory and citizenry should be congruent: all permanent residents of the state should be full citizens, and all citizens, ideally, should be residents. Finally, cultural nationality and legal citizenship should be coextensive: all ethnocultural nationals should be citizens, and all citizens should be nationals.

This model has important corollaries for mobility and membership. It construes the nation-state as an internally fluid but externally bounded space, a space of free geographic and social mobility, in both vertical and horizontal dimensions (Gellner 1983). But geographic mobility (like the circulation of goods, ideas, messages, and cultural patterns) is understood as sharply bounded. Mobility within nation-states is understood as normal and as something that should be facilitated (in that it contributes to the smooth functioning of labor markets and to cultural homogenization); but mobility between nation-states is understood as anomalous. Insofar as actual regimes of mobility approximate this idealized model, mobility is reciprocally linked to homogeneity within and heterogeneity between states: the internal mobility of persons is both cause and consequence of internal cultural homogeneity, while the external barriers to mobility are likewise both cause and consequence of cultural differences between states.

The Politics of Belonging

This idealized conceptual model of the nation-state might seem to have little relevance to the politics of belonging in a globalizing, transnational world. But I argue that the model not only helps *illuminate* the main lineaments of the contemporary politics of membership or belonging but also helps to *generate* the contemporary politics of belonging. While it is anachronistic as a model *of* political, social, and cultural organization, it remains relevant in practice as a model *for* political, social, and cultural organization. Demands to establish or restore congruence—between culture and polity, permanent residence and full membership, cultural nationality and legal citizenship—continue to inform the politics of belonging today. Some of the demands have been reinterpreted to fit contemporary circumstances, but the reinterpretation is evidence of the flexible adaptability of the conceptual model of the nation-state, not its transcendence.

I begin by drawing four distinctions. First, I am concerned with the politics of belonging only at the level of the nation-state, not at other levels or in other sites. In the broadest sense, the politics of membership plays itself out in a great variety of sites. The question "Who belongs?" can be contested—and hence, in the broadest sense, politicized—in sites as diverse as cities, neighborhoods, workplaces, clubs, associations, churches, unions, parties, tribes, and even families (Walzer 1983; Bauböck 2003).

Yet while the nation-state is only one locus of contestation over membership, it remains a uniquely consequential one. Indeed in longer term historical perspective, we can appreciate the *increasing* importance of the nation-state as a locus of belonging, as increasingly direct, intrusive, and centralized forms of rule entailed what might be called the "étatization of membership" (following Noiriel 1997: 28, who draws in turn on Foucault 1984: 318). Access to many important goods has come to be mediated through membership in a state, as the state has taken over the provision of goods that had been provided—if they were provided at all—by other organizations or associations (Loveman 2005).[4]

Second, the politics of citizenship *in* the nation-state can be distinguished analytically from the politics of belonging *to* the nation-state, though the two are often closely linked in practice. For some marginal or minority populations, there is no doubt or contestation about their *formal* state membership: they unambiguously belong to one and only one state, the state in which they reside. But in such cases, there often is doubt or contestation about their *substantive* membership or citizenship status—that is, about their access to and enjoyment of the substantive rights of citizenship or about their substantive acceptance as full members of a putatively national "society." In these cases, the politics of belonging is not generated by migration, at least not in any proximate sense, but by various forms of social closure, discrimination, or marginalization. The Anglo-American political sociology of citizenship of the early postwar era, for example, associated with T. H. Marshall (1950) and Reinhard Bendix (1977), was concerned with this kind of substantive civic belonging, specifically with the civic incorporation of the working class, whose formal membership in the nation-state was not in doubt. A related current of work addressed the civic incorporation of African Americans (Parsons 1965).

Even where the politics of belonging arises in response to migration, one can distinguish the politics of substantive membership or citizenship in the state from the politics of formal belonging to the state. Much work on the civil, political, and social rights of migrant workers in Europe, for example, has been concerned with substantive citizenship, not formal belonging; such work has focused on rights that are not contingent on a particular membership status in the state (Brubaker 1989; Soysal 1994; Chauvin and Garcés-Mascareñas 2012).

Third, I want to distinguish *formal* and *informal* aspects of the politics of belonging. Certain kinds of membership—legal nationality or state membership, for example—are administered by specialized personnel using formal, codified rules. Nation membership in a more informal sense, however, is administered not by specialized personnel but by ordinary people in the course of everyday life, using tacit understandings of who belongs and who does not, of us and them.[5] These everyday membership practices of identification and categorization, and of inclusion and exclusion, are often at variance with codified forms of official, formal membership. Persons may be formally included but informally excluded, as suggested by the expression *français de papier* (paper Frenchman), or they may be formally excluded but informally included, as suggested by the literature on the support undocumented migrants have found from NGOs, schools, churches, and other local institutions.[6]

Fourth, and most important for the discussion that follows, I want to distinguish *internal* and *external* dimensions or sites of the politics of belonging. The internal politics of belonging concerns populations that are durably situated within the territorial ambit of the state yet are not—or not fully—members of that state, or whose terms of membership in the state are contested. The external politics of belonging concerns populations that are durably situated outside the territorial ambit and jurisdiction of the state yet claim—or are claimed—to belong, in some sense, to the state or to "its" nation.

The internal and external politics of belonging can be connected in three ways. (1) They can be *reciprocally connected between states:* a population that is the focus of an internal politics of membership in one state may be the focus of an external politics of membership in another. This reciprocal link arises in many cases through migration. As immigrants, for example, Mexican migrants and their descendants are the subjects and objects of an internal politics of belonging in the United States; as emigrants, they are the subjects and objects of an external politics of belonging in Mexico (Fitzgerald 2009). But the reciprocal connection between internal and external membership politics can also arise without migration. To take a case from postcommunist eastern Europe, the ethnic Hungarian minority is the focus of an internal politics of belonging in states neighboring Hungary; at the same time, it is the focus of an external politics of belonging in Hungary itself (Brubaker et al. 2006).

(2) The internal and external politics of belonging may become *intertwined within a particular state* at a particular political conjuncture. Such was the case in Germany in the 1990s, when debates about the privileged immigration and citizenship status of ethnic German migrants from eastern Europe and the former Soviet Union (the so-called *Aussiedler*) became entangled with debates about the exclusion of guest workers and their children from German citizenship. The weak knowledge of German displayed by *Aussiedler*—especially by the increasing number of them arriving from the former Soviet Union—invited comparison with the fluent German spoken by the German-born children of guest workers. This raised the question: Why were the children of Turkish guest workers still overwhelmingly foreigners, despite being born and raised in Germany and speaking fluent German, while *Aussiedler* enjoyed all the rights of citizenship, and special privileges to boot, despite speaking little or no German?

(3) The internal and external politics of belonging may be linked *sequentially*. This can happen when a state's external membership politics facilitate or induce the immigration of external members. The internalization of external members through large-scale resettlement can generate a new internal politics of membership if—as regularly happens—resettlers are not fully integrated or accepted, or if the privileges or benefits they receive come to be resented or challenged. Germany's policies toward ethnic Germans of eastern Europe again furnish an example. The external politics of membership established immigration and citizenship privileges for these transborder ethnic "kin" during the 1950s, but the flow of resettlers was limited by exit restrictions throughout the cold war era. The lifting of these restrictions in the late 1980s generated a huge influx of resettlers. The various special rights and benefits they enjoyed, as well as their conspicuous lack of integration, generated a new internal politics of membership, contesting their privileged terms of incorporation (Brubaker and Kim 2011).

The Idealized Model of Membership
and the Politics of Belonging

I noted earlier that a series of congruencies—of territory and citizenry, state and nation, polity and culture, legal citizenship and ethnocultural nationality—are central to the idealized conceptual model of the nation-state. In practice, of course, these congruencies are seldom if ever fully realized. But this does not mean that the idealized model is irrelevant. It is precisely the *lack of congruence*—represented as problematic with explicit or implicit reference to the idealized model—that generates both internal and external forms of the politics of belonging.

In a hypothetical world of "perfect" nation-states ("perfect" in a logical or conceptual sense, not in a normative sense), characterized by the congruencies sketched earlier, there would be no politics of membership. It would be clear who belongs where; there would be no "matter out of place" (Douglas 1994), no internal or external politics of belonging *to* the nation-state.

Nor would there be a politics of membership *in* the nation-state. This hypothetical world of "perfect" nation-states would, by definition, contain no marginal, unincorporated minority populations. The nation-state would be just what the idealized conceptual model represents it to be: an undifferentiated, fluid totality, without fundamental class, regional, ethnic, or caste divisions; a space of internal equality and mobility; and an internally homogeneous and externally bounded sociocultural and sociopolitical realm.

Actual states, of course, do not conform to this idealized model. Specifying *how* they do not conform can help identify the sources of the internal and external politics of belonging. Migration is the most obvious source. It is easy to see how migration—insofar as it leads to substantial and more or less permanent settlement in another state—disturbs the congruencies central to the idealized model of the nation-state. Before discussing migration, however, I want to sketch three other sources of the internal and external politics of belonging.

In one configuration, characteristic of the aftermath of empire, the internal and external membership politics are generated not by the *movement of people over borders* but by the *movement of borders over people*. The locus classicus of this configuration was interwar central and eastern Europe after the breakup of the multinational Habsburg, Ottoman, and Romanov empires; a similar configuration was produced by the breakup of the Soviet Union, Yugoslavia, and Czechoslovakia in the 1990s. The massive reorganization of political space in the aftermath of empire, in which a series of new (or newly reconfigured) self-styled nation-states emerge on the territory of the sprawling multinational states that preceded them, regularly leaves large populations stranded on the "wrong" side of new nation-state frontiers. These populations belong to one state by residence and (usually) legal citizenship but to a neighboring state by ethnocultural nationality. This lack of congruence between ethnocultural nationality and legal citizenship, in turn, generates both an internal and an external politics of belonging. The most fateful instance of this during the interwar period involved large ethnic German minorities in Poland, Czechoslovakia, and other states who were the subjects and objects of an internal politics of belonging in their states of residence and of an external politics of belonging vis-à-vis Weimar and then Nazi Germany. In the post–cold war configuration, large Russian or Russophone minorities participate in an internal politics of belonging in Ukraine, Kazakhstan, Estonia, Latvia, and other Soviet successor states, and in an external politics of belonging vis-à-vis Russia (Brubaker 1996, 2011b).

A second configuration does not entail this sort of reciprocal connection between the internal politics of belonging in one state and the external politics of belonging in another. In this second configuration, the contested membership status is that of marginal or minority populations that do not have external "homeland" states. Here the politics of belonging are generated not by the movement of people across borders or by the movement of borders across people but by the *absence* of movement or mobility—in social space, not geographic space. Ernest Gellner characterized this immobility as an instance of "obstacles to entropy," by which he meant traits, structures, and processes that resist the prevailing modern tendency for the fixed structures, divisions, and subgroupings of agrarian society to erode in the "fluid totality" of the nation-state, with its "need for [a] random-seeming, entropic mobility and distribution of individuals" throughout social space (1983: 63–64).[7] Entropy-resisting groupings are not "evenly dispersed throughout the entire society" but instead remain "concentrated in one part or another of the total society," notably—in the cases of interest here—in the lower regions of social space (64–65). Key examples for Gellner were ethnoracially and some ethnoreligiously distinct populations (African Americans or Muslim immigrants and their descendants in Europe, for example), since markers of racial and (in some cases) religious distinctiveness—and the uneven distributions in economic and social space with which they are associated—often persist across generations. Measured against the ideal conceptual model of the nation-state as a fluid and egalitarian social space, this state of affairs constitutes a major anomaly; it generates an internal politics of belonging focused on the substantive membership or citizenship status of these groups.[8]

The third source of internal membership politics is the persisting legacy of empire. This legacy is often conveniently forgotten or seen as marginal (Kymlicka 1995: 20ff).[9] In the American context, the self-representation as a country of immigrants overlooks those "whose ancestors did not come to the U.S. either voluntarily or involuntarily. Instead, the United States came to them in the course of its relentless expansion across the continent and into the Caribbean and Pacific" (Thernstrom 1983: 248, quoted in Kymlicka 1995: 21; Mann 2005: chapter 4). Populations originally incorporated by conquest—to the extent they were not destroyed by murder, disease, or lethal deportations, and to the extent that they were never fully integrated or assimilated—can become the focus of an internal politics of membership. This politics can play out on two levels: on the level of the wider polity as a whole and on the level of the incorporated smaller polities (federally recognized tribes in the American context, or incorporated territories with a special status like Puerto Rico) whose autonomy and—within limits—sovereignty is recognized by the wider polity.[10]

Common to these sources of membership politics is that they cannot be understood as disturbing the congruencies that are central to the idealized conceptual model of the nation-state. More precisely, they can be understood from an atemporal, *logical* perspective as deviating from the conceptual model, but they cannot be understood in *historical* perspective as departing from or disturbing a previous condition of congruence. These are not new incongruencies: they have characterized self-styled nation-states from their inception.

Migration and the Politics of Belonging

A similar point can be made about migration as a source of the internal and external politics of membership. Large-scale transborder migrations leading to more or less permanent settlement do introduce new incongruencies or accentuate existing ones. But the incongruencies generated by migration have been part of the actual workings of the system of nation-states from the beginning. Only in an atemporal, logical sense, not in a historical sense, can migration be said to disturb the congruencies that constitute the idealized conceptual model of the nation-state.

With this caveat in mind, it can still be heuristically useful to consider how migration disturbs the idealized model. First, and most obviously, migration leading to settlement engenders a discrepancy between long-term residence and citizenship; and this, in turn, generates an internal—and reciprocally, an external—politics of membership. Internally, this involves contestation over the terms of access to full formal citizenship, as well as over substantive forms of membership and civic incorporation. In an inclusive vein, this internal politics of belonging is focused on efforts to bring the formal and substantive membership status of migrants (or their descendants) into alignment with their position as long-term residents whose lives— notwithstanding certain transborder engagements—are firmly anchored in the country of settlement.

The anomaly of settlement without citizenship is particularly salient for second- and third-generation immigrants. In countries without provisions for automatic civic incorporation through *jus soli* (which confers citizenship based on birth in a particular territory), immigrants and their descendants can remain indefinitely without citizenship in the country of settlement, even though they may be residing in the only country they have ever known. This sort of predicament was crucial to the debates that led to the introduction of certain elements of *jus soli* in Germany in 1999 (Triadafilopoulos and Faist 2006). But even where second- and third-generation immigrants are *formally* citizens, they may not be full members or citizens in a *substantive* sense. As the most glaring anomalies of multigenerational residence without formal citizenship are resolved, the politics of belonging for second- and third-generation immigrants in Europe turns increasingly on struggles over full substantive civil, political, and socioeconomic citizenship.

But migration engenders not only a discrepancy between residence and citizenship. Insofar as migrants (and in some cases their descendants) are understood to remain outside the imagined national community of their state of settlement, migration also engenders a discrepancy or incongruence between nation and state or, in slightly different terms, between culture and polity. This second incongruence can generate a more restrictive, or at least a more assimilationist, politics of belonging, premised on the claim that migrants must become members of the nation before they can become full members of the state. In many European countries, the center of gravity in struggles over the terms of membership has shifted back in this assimilationist direction in the past two decades, after a period of experimentation with more differentialist policies and practices (Brubaker 2001; Joppke 2004). This has led some analysts to speak of a "culturalization of citizenship" (Hurenkamp et al. 2012).

By virtue of the discrepancy between long-term residence and citizenship, migration can engender not only an internal politics of belonging in the state of settlement but also an external politics of belonging in the state of origin. The discrepancy between residence and citizenship may be seen as a *problem* in the homeland state, which may prevent emigrants from retaining citizenship or transmitting it to their children. But in recent decades it has been increasingly seen as an *opportunity*. From this standpoint, the politics of belonging is about maintaining ties with emigrants; mobilizing their resources and expertise; making it easier for them to retain citizenship, even when they acquire citizenship elsewhere; and facilitating home-country involvement in such matters as voting, property ownership, and remittances.[11]

Transborder Kin and the External Politics of Belonging

The emerging literature on the external politics of belonging focuses primarily on recent migrations. This is in keeping with the literature's emphasis on recent transformations of polity, economy, culture, technology, and social relations, transformations that are usually subsumed under the heading of globalization or transnationalism. According to this view, as discussed in Chapter 5, these transformations have engendered a world of newly pervasive and largely uncontrollable cross-border flows of people, goods, images, data, ideas, political projects, and social movements, in which loyalties, identities, solidarities, and membership structures increasingly cut across state borders.

The literature gives scant attention to the external politics of belonging generated by earlier migration flows. As a result, its understanding of the external politics of belonging is too presentist. It neglects sources of the external politics of belonging that antedate the current phase of capitalist globalization, recent advances in communication and transportation infrastructures, and the putative epochal shift toward a transnational, diasporic, postnational, or postmodern world.

Consider two cases that highlight a key issue neglected in the recent literature about migration and the external politics of belonging.[12] The German population in eastern Europe and the former Soviet Union and the Korean population in Japan and China share three characteristics from the perspective of their putative "homeland" states: (1) They have long resided outside the territory of the state—or indeed, in the case of many Germans, have never resided in that state. (2) They do not (for the most part) possess citizenship in that state. In fact they *could* not (for the most part) possess German or Korean citizenship since neither Germany nor Korea existed as a modern nation-state with its own citizenship when their ancestors emigrated. Yet (3) these transborder populations have been represented as belonging to the German or Korean nation and have been understood, though not uncontroversially, as having a legitimate claim on the "homeland" state.

Why have West Germany, postunification Germany, South Korea, and, in certain contexts, North Korea treated these transborder populations as "their own" and extended rights and privileges to them? More generally, how and why are certain populations, but not others, construed as "belonging" in some respect to states other than those in which they are settled?

This is a question that has seldom been raised in the literature. The literature on the external politics of belonging has tended to take the existence of such transborder populations for granted. It has not been centrally concerned with the social and political processes through which states identify and constitute some—but not other—transborder populations as "their own." It has focused on configurations in which the identification of transborder kin has been relatively unproblematic, by virtue of the recent movement of people over borders or borders over people, which generates relatively clear-cut relations between home states and their transborder emigrant populations or between territorially restructured, often "downsized" states and their newly transborder ethnonational kin. In both configurations, the transborder populations are relatively clearly bounded and identifiable because they are not simply emigrants or ethnonational kin but are also either citizens or former citizens of the "homeland" state in question or descendants of such persons.

In the German and Korean cases, the identification of transborder kin has been much more complicated. For most of their centuries-long existence, the German-speaking settlements of central and eastern Europe had no particular connection to Germany, which, after all, did not even exist as a unified state until 1871. Even after 1871, the ties between scattered German-speaking communities and Germany were tenuous and—until World War I—politically insignificant. It was only a complex chain of events that led the postwar West German state to embrace these populations as transborder coethnics and to extend certain rights and privileges to them. These included German defeat in World War I; the rise of *völkisch* nationalism; the Nazi eastward expansion and Nazi resettlement initiatives for transborder Germans; the Soviet deportations of Germans to Central Asia; the postwar expulsions of ethnic Germans from Czechoslovakia, Poland, and other countries; and the restrictive exit policies (and assimilationist cultural policies) of East European communist regimes. In the post–cold war era, the privileges extended to these transborder coethnics became increasingly difficult to justify and were gradually withdrawn. Transborder Germans of eastern Europe and the former Soviet Union were thus only contingently and temporarily defined as belonging to Germany.

Identification of transborder kin in the Korean case was problematic and contested for different reasons. Large-scale emigration from the Korean peninsula to northeastern China, Japan, and the maritime provinces of Russia began only in the late nineteenth century and intensified under Japanese colonial rule. These emigrants and their descendants were clearly considered Koreans in vernacular understandings, which the colonial regime reinforced by establishing a separate family registry for Koreans, regardless of where they resided in the empire. But the collapse of the empire and the division of Korea confounded the question of belonging. Colonial-era migrants had never possessed Korean nationality since the precolonial dynasty had not adopted modern nationality legislation. Their connection to the two postcolonial states was therefore legally ambiguous.

During the cold war era, North Korea sought (with some success) to induce the repatriation of Korean Japanese, while South Korea courted their political alignment, urging them to register as South Korean nationals. Both states neglected transborder Koreans in the Soviet Union and China. The easing of geopolitical tensions in the aftermath of the cold war prompted renewed South Korean interest in Korean Chinese, who (after sustained contestation) were recognized as transborder "kin." The Korean case thus highlights the contested and conjuncturally specific processes through which the state has embraced some—but not other—transborder coethnics. Like the German case, it reveals the social and political processes through which states constitute, recognize, or claim certain external populations as "their own."

The Nation-State and Nationalism: Resilience and Rearticulation

Migration is as old as human history, and so too are questions of membership and belonging. The development of the modern nation-state fundamentally recast both migration and membership, subjecting both to the classificatory and regulatory grid of the nation-state. Some argue that a movement beyond the nation-state is currently recasting migration and membership again in a postnational mode, but there is little evidence for such an epochal shift.

Far from escaping the control of the state, migration is subjected to ever more sophisticated technologies of regulation and control. Borders are not hermetically sealed, but states (and the Schengen zone) have not lost their capacity to regulate the movement of persons across them. Nor has membership been recast in a way that bypasses or transcends the nation-state. The nation-state remains the decisive locus of membership even in a globalizing world; struggles over belonging *in* and *to* the nation-state remain the most consequential forms of membership politics.

By disturbing the congruencies—between residence and citizenship, between nation membership and state membership, and between culture and polity—central to the idealized model of the nation-state, migration has long generated, and continues to generate, both an internal and an external politics of belonging. The former concerns those who are long-term residents but not full members of a state, the latter those who are long-term residents (and often citizens) of *other* states yet who can be represented as belonging, in some sense, to a "homeland" or "kin" state or to "its" eponymous nation.

Recent scholarly attention has focused primarily on the external politics of belonging. New forms of external membership have indeed been instituted in recent years, but they are hardly unprecedented; numerous examples of external membership politics are available from the late nineteenth and early twentieth centuries. Moreover, the recent forms of the external politics of belonging are neither postnational nor transnational; they are forms of transborder *nationalism*. They do not presage the transcendence of the nation-state; they indicate rather the resilience and continued relevance of the nation-state model.

Nationalism is a remarkably flexible and adaptable political idiom. Recent trends in external membership politics demonstrate this adaptability. Today the language of nationalism is used to identify and constitute certain transborder populations as members of a nation and to justify maintaining or reestablishing ties with them; in other contexts, that language has been used in effect to "excommunicate" such populations.

We are not witnessing a shift from a national to a postnational mode of membership politics, and still less a shift from a state-centered to a nonstate mode of organizing migration and membership. We see, rather, an expansion and strengthening of states' ties to transborder populations and of transborder populations' claims on "homeland" states, both legitimated in the language of nationalism.

Ways of construing the conceptual model of the nation-state, however, are changing. The various idealized congruencies I have highlighted—between the boundaries of the state and those of the nation, between polity and culture, between long-term residence and full membership, and between cultural nationality and legal citizenship—are not all of a piece.

They can be prioritized and interpreted in different ways. The recent wave of external membership policies reflects a shift to a less *territorialized* way of interpreting these congruencies. Congruence between state and nation, for example, can mean that the territorial frontiers of the state should match the (imagined) territorial boundaries of the nation. In interwar Europe, this territorial interpretation of congruence generated powerfully destabilizing irredentist claims. But congruence between state and nation can be given a different interpretation, one that extends the reach of the polity to embrace transborder members of the nation who do not reside within the territory of the state. This interpretation, rather than the territorial one, has informed most recent forms of external membership politics.

In this regard, the transnationalism and postnationalism literatures are correct to stress the diminished significance of territoriality. The point should not be overstated: the nation-state remains fundamentally a territorial organization. But it is also a membership association (Brubaker 1992: 22–23), and the frontiers of membership increasingly extend beyond the territorial borders of the state. These new forms of external membership, however, are neither trans-state nor transnational; as forms of transborder nationalism, they represent an extension and adaptation of the nation-state model, not its transcendence.

CHAPTER SEVEN

Nationalism, Ethnicity, and Modernity

T HE NOTION OF MULTIPLE MODERNITIES has been central to so-phisticated discussions of modernity in recent years. Proponents of the idea sharply distinguish their understanding of modernity from that of midcentury modernization theory. While midcentury theorists envisioned a convergence around a single, originally Western pattern of institutions and cultural understandings, contemporary theorists of multiple modernities reject the notion of convergence and emphasize the irreducible multiplicity of institutional patterns and cultural and political programs and models.

Ethnicity, nationalism, and the nation-state have figured centrally in discussions of multiple modernity. Midcentury modernization theorists are said to have had a radically mistaken understanding of these subjects. They are said to have dismissed ethnicity (along with religion) as a vestigial private matter, of no public significance; to have treated nationalism as axiomatically civic, secular, and inclusive; and to have vastly overemphasized the power of the nation-state to bind loyalties and generate attractive and inclusive national identities. The multiple modernities perspective, by contrast, is held to offer a superior understanding of the contemporary resurgence of politicized ethnicity; of the persistence of ethnic, religious, and otherwise exclusive forms of nationalism; and of the limited integrative power of the nation-state.

The multiple modernities literature has made a major contribution to the revitalization of the study of modernity (Spohn 2001). A case can be made, however, for the continued relevance of the notion of a "single modernity." I sketch the outline of such a case in this chapter, focusing on the domain of ethnicity, nationalism, and the nation-state. The argument is in three parts. I begin by identifying a paradoxical feature of the multiple modernities argument; I then seek to qualify the familiar critique of the failures of modernization theory with respect to ethnicity, nationalism, and the nation-state; and I conclude by outlining the advantages of a "single modernity" perspective on nationalism and politicized ethnicity.

Modernity: One or Many?

Two analytically distinct questions are central to the multiple modernities argument.[1] The first is the question of convergence. Do contemporary societies converge around a single institutional pattern or a single cultural-political program or model?[2] Or do we see the persistence or indeed the emergence of multiple institutional patterns and multiple cultural and political programs and models? The collapse of communism and the end of the cold war occasioned a renewed appreciation of modernization theory and a revival of the notion of convergence (Alexander 1995; Fukuyama 1992). But that revival was short-lived; and while qualified versions of convergence arguments continue to be advanced (Marsh 2008; Schmidt 2010, 2011), few theorists today endorse the sweeping midcentury arguments that projected a convergence around specifically Western institutional patterns and cultural and political programs. There is broad agreement on the enduring significance of multiple institutional patterns in political, economic, legal, religious, and other domains, as well as multiple—and in many contexts sharply differing—cultural and political programs and models.

The second question concerns the modernity of these multiple institutional patterns and cultural and political programs. Should some be characterized as modern, others as traditional or antimodern? Can they be ranked by their degree of modernity? Or are they all equally modern, representing not differing *degrees* but differing *kinds* of modernity? The contrast between tradition and modernity remains common in journalism and public argument, and some empirical research projects continue to operationalize modernity in a way that allows ranking of different societies on a scale of modernity. But many, perhaps most comparative historical scholars today would hesitate to rank varying institutional arrangements on such a scale. And there is a broad consensus among scholars that precisely the most vehemently antimodern and expressly "traditionalist" cultural and political programs are not "traditional" in any useful analytic sense but are best understood as distinctively modern, at least in certain respects.

But by what criteria are expressly antimodern cultural and political programs or social movements characterized as distinctively modern? The answer given by Shmuel Eisenstadt, the most persuasive proponent of the multiple modernities thesis, goes something like this: Putatively antimodern programs and movements are in fact characteristically modern in three ways. They are modern, first, in their reflexivity, that is, in their sense of a range of alternative social and political possibilities that can be realized "through autonomous human agency."[3] Second, such programs and movements are modern in their "highly political and ideological" character, in their modalities of protest and institution building. Third, they are modern in their "Jacobinism," by which Eisenstadt means their commitment to the "total reconstruction of personality, [and] of individual and collective identities, [through] conscious . . . political action" (2000: 3, 19, 21).

This is certainly an interesting argument. But it is also paradoxical: Eisenstadt appeals to an understanding of a *single* modernity in order to validate his argument about *multiple* modernities. On one level, there are multiple modernities; on another, more fundamental and abstract level, there is only one. The notion of a single modernity would seem to be more fundamental analytically, for this is what allows Eisenstadt to characterize a wide range of institutional patterns and cultural and political models, programs, and movements—even avowedly antimodern ones—as "modern."[4]

Eisenstadt himself does not always seem fully comfortable with the language of "multiple modernities," and there are suggestions in his work of an alternative analytical language. He writes, for example, of the "continual reinterpretation of the cultural program of modernity." In this alternative idiom, modernity is understood as a singular phenomenon, though it is of course subject to continual contestation and reinterpretation. And much of this contestation involves challenges to Western models, programs, and institutional patterns. As Eisenstadt says, such challenges seek to deprive the West "of its monopoly on modernity" (2000: 24).

I will adopt this alternative language. I want to consider nationalism and politicized ethnicity as characteristically modern phenomena. As is evident to any student of the subject, these phenomena display no single pattern but rather multiple configurations, patterns, and programs. Yet I want to treat nationalism and politicized ethnicity as manifestations of modernity understood as a singular historical phenomenon, though one that is dynamically changing and, of course, subject to chronic contestation.

Revisiting the Critique of Modernization Theory

The weaknesses of midcentury modernization theory's understanding of ethnicity, nationalism, and the nation-state have long come in for criticism. In the first place, modernization theory—according to the familiar critique—dismissed ethnicity as vestigial and therefore failed to theorize the persisting and indeed renewed significance of politicized ethnicity. Second, it was committed to an untenable form of the secularization thesis that confined religion to the private sphere; it therefore failed to theorize the continued and indeed renewed vitality of various forms of public religion. Third, modernization theory worked with a restricted understanding of modern forms of nationalism as axiomatically civic, secular, and inclusive and therefore failed to appreciate the persisting and indeed renewed significance of ethnic, religious, and exclusive forms of nationalism. Fourth, modernization theory overestimated the power of the modern state to elicit loyalty, instill solidarity, reshape subjectivities, and reframe social relations; it therefore failed to anticipate the continued and indeed renewed significance of substate or cross-state loyalties, solidarities, subjectivities, and social relations.

There is of course considerable truth to this critical characterization of certain forms of midcentury modernization theory. But the critique is exaggerated and overgeneralized.[5] This can be seen by considering three figures whose important work on ethnicity and nationalism in the 1950s and early 1960s was powerfully influenced by modernization theory: Karl Deutsch, Ernest Gellner, and Clifford Geertz.

Deutsch's 1953 book *Nationalism and Social Communication* was among the first self-consciously social-scientific studies of nationalism, and it remains one of the most interesting, though it will certainly strike any contemporary reader as dated in many ways. For Deutsch, modernity meant social mobilization, as indicated by the growing share of the population that was residing in towns, working in nonagricultural occupations, exposed to the mass media, subject to military conscription, educated in schools, and so on (100). In Deutsch's account, this mobilized population posed a challenge to projects and processes of national integration. Deutsch had a deep personal familiarity with the complex and refractory nature of the "national question" in his native Bohemia and in central and eastern Europe as a whole; there was nothing complacent or teleological about his understanding of such projects of nation and state building. He was agnostic about whether such projects would succeed or fail, about whether they would lead to assimilation and consolidated nation-statehood or to dissimilation, nationalist conflict, and possible state breakup.

Deutsch's book is certainly limited by its social-structural and quasi-demographic reductionism and by its treatment of political and cultural struggles as epiphenomenal. But it is not guilty of the standard charges leveled against modernization theory. It remains significant as a pioneering effort to think about ways of mapping social processes, relations, and networks in a complex and dynamic manner. It served recently as a model for Neil Fligstein's (2008) study of the dynamics of social integration on a European scale. And it can still be read with profit by anyone interested in mapping, modeling, or measuring flows, networks, and dynamic processes on subnational, national, or transnational scales.

Ernest Gellner's theory of nationalism is best known from his 1983 book, but his argument was first worked out twenty years earlier ([1964] 1974). Gellner was an unabashed if idiosyncratic exponent of modernization theory, and his theory of nationalism is at its core a theory of modernity. For Gellner, the primary generative fact of modernity was a complex, continuously changing division of labor, which generated a relatively fluid and mobile social order. This required—leaving aside here the well-known problems arising from the functionalist mode of argument—a new style of communication (what Gellner calls "context-free communication"), and it required a new kind of education, namely an extended, generic, state-provided "exo-education" that would teach literacy and impersonal communication skills in a standardized language and culture rather than a local dialect. The increased importance of routine communication with strangers in this new type of social order placed a subjective and objective premium on culture and especially language as a central marker of identity. This in turn helps explain the intense politicization of language that was personally familiar to Gellner from his central European background.[6]

As in Deutsch's work, there is little room for political struggles or cultural creativity in Gellner's account; he too can be charged with socioeconomic reductionism. But Gellner does provide a powerful and parsimonious account of why culture matters to politics under modern conditions in a way that it did not matter before—an account of the politicization of culture, or the culturalization of politics.[7]

Clifford Geertz may be the most interesting of the three for present purposes. He is not known today as a modernization theorist or, for that matter, as a major theorist of nationalism or ethnicity. But he was closely associated with Talcott Parsons and modernization theory as a graduate student in social relations at Harvard, and his early work was in that tradition. This early work includes his major contribution to the analysis of ethnicity and nationalism, namely the long essay "The Integrative Revolution" that appeared in the 1963 volume he edited, entitled *Old Societies and New States,* with the characteristic subtitle *The Quest for Modernity in Asia and Africa.*

When this essay is cited today, it is usually in connection with discussions of "primordialism." Criticizing primordialist accounts of ethnicity from a constructivist, circumstantialist, or instrumentalist point of view has been something of a minor industry in the past few decades. The problem with such critiques is not that they are wrong; it is that they are too obviously right to be interesting and that they have no serious target. Such critiques often cite Geertz's essay as an example of a primordialist account. This is no doubt because he described the modernizing postcolonial state—in his inimitable language—as roiling the parapolitical vortices of primordial sentiments (1963: 126–127). For many readers today, this language may suggest a crude dichotomy between the rational, civil modernizing state and the "vortices" of irrational, traditional primordial attachments. But Geertz's analysis is far more interesting and subtle than this.

Geertz's account of politicized ethnicity was anything but primordialist. By "primordial attachments," he meant ties that are assumed (in vernacular understandings) to be natural, prepolitical, and unalterable, or ties that are represented as such in vernacular discourse. He did not himself treat such ties as natural, prepolitical, or unalterable. In fact his own analysis showed that such attachments were being rearticulated and aggregated in postcolonial states into larger, more diffuse ethnic blocs, constructed along the lines of region, race, language, or religion, and stretched, as it were, to fit the scale of the state as a whole. The resulting structure of ethnic attachments, with its simplified and concentrated patterning of statewide group antagonisms, was in no sense the residue of "tradition." As Geertz emphasized, it was a product of modernity—a response to the structure and scale of political life in postcolonial polities (1963: 155). Far from seeing ethnicity as primordial or vestigial, or as destined to fade into merely private relevance, Geertz saw politicized ethnicity as intensifying precisely under modern political conditions.

Nor can Geertz be said to have drastically overestimated the power of the modern state to elicit loyalty, instill solidarity, and reshape identities. The "integrative revolution" to which his title alludes does not refer to "national integration" as envisioned by nationalist elites—or by less sophisticated modernization theorists; it does not project an end-state of successful or complete "national integration." Geertz was even more sensitive than Deutsch to the complexities and difficulties besetting nation-building projects in postcolonial states. The "integrative revolution" refers to the momentous political transformation through which extraordinarily heterogeneous populations were brought together in a single ostensibly democratic and national state—a state that styled itself as the state of and for the people over which it ruled. This new kind of state became much more significant than the preceding colonial state as a target, a prize, and an arena for action. Precisely this transformation is what elicited the reorganization of putatively primordial attachments that I have just mentioned and the intensification of politicized ethnicity. National integration as envisioned by postcolonial nationalist elites was largely a myth, but the "integrative revolution" described by Geertz was a fact.

A "Single Modernity" Perspective on Ethnicity and Nationalism

I return now to the question of multiple modernities. Willfried Spohn has recently made the case for analyzing contemporary forms of nationalism through the theoretical prism of multiple modernity. Spohn argues that a multiple modernities perspective is needed to make sense of the persisting though variable significance of religion and of "ethnic-primordial" elements as "constitutive dimensions of modern national identities and modern forms of nationalism" (2003: 269). He then goes on to survey in comparative-civilizational perspective the differing configurations and trajectories of nationalism, religion, and secularization processes in differing world regions.

Spohn's account is nuanced and insightful. But I am not persuaded that it requires the notion of multiple modernities. He is certainly right that understandings and representations of national identities are intertwined with religion in different ways in different world regions. And the substantial comparativist literature that has developed in the past three decades has identified many other ways in which configurations and trajectories of nationalism, ethnicity, and race have varied over time and place. But I want to argue that this is entirely consistent with an understanding of modernity as a single historical phenomenon, though of course one that is internally complex and chronically contested.

I see two advantages of a "single modernity" perspective in the study of nationalism and ethnicity. First, such a perspective brings into focus the global nature of the processes—socioeconomic, political, and cultural—that have generated and sustained nationalism and politicized ethnicity as basic principles of vision and division of the social world, as fundamental ways of identifying self and other, and as elementary templates for making claims.

Socioeconomic processes include the social mobilization and changing division of labor described by Deutsch and Gellner. Political processes include the diffusion of a new kind of polity and a cluster of associated ideas that I will describe in a moment. Cultural processes include those I mentioned earlier in my discussion of Eisenstadt: the development of a new reflexivity, an expanded understanding of autonomous human agency, and an enlarged sense of the possibilities of social change through political action. To emphasize the global nature of these processes is not to posit their uniformity; it is to underscore their scale, scope, and interconnectedness.

The second advantage of a "single modernity" perspective is that it highlights the diffusion of a set of organizational forms and political-cultural templates that provide the more immediate institutional and cultural materials for various forms of nationalism and politicized ethnicity. The notion of diffusion was central to midcentury modernization theory, and it has fallen into a certain disrepute. It is easy to criticize certain forms of modernization theory for their naïve and teleological understanding of the diffusion of a Western model of a civic, secular nation-state. But this does not mean we should dispense with the notion of diffusion altogether. Diffusion does indeed occur, though what is diffused and how diffusion works need to be better specified.

The language of nationalism was from the beginning an internationally circulating discourse. This does not mean it was mechanically copied from one setting to another. As it was taken up in new settings, it was adapted to local circumstances and struggles, translated into idioms with specific local resonances, and blended with various indigenous discursive traditions (Anderson 1991; Chatterjee 1986; Calhoun 1997: 107). Still, the linked ideas, ideals, and organizational models of nation, state, citizenship, and popular sovereignty form a kind of package. This package has a certain common core, underlying the varying adaptations, appropriations, and transformations. And one can speak of the global diffusion of this "package" in the two centuries following the French Revolution.

The package has an organizational and institutional component and a cultural and ideological component. The organizational component includes the basic form of the bureaucratic territorial state. Of course there is a great range of variation in the form of contemporary states. But in longer term historical perspective, what is striking is the global diffusion of one broad type of polity—the relatively centralized and intrusive territorial state, exercising direct rather than indirect rule and governing through what Weber called legal authority with a bureaucratic administrative staff—at the expense of many other types of polities. Also striking in longer term perspective is the convergence—across a wide range of variation in state size, efficacy, and regime type—in domains of state activity: almost all contemporary states assume at least nominal responsibility for such matters as education, health, social welfare, dispute resolution, the regulation of economic life, and so on (Meyer 1987).

The cultural or ideological component—analyzed from a different angle in Chapter 6—includes the linked ideas of peoplehood, nationhood, and citizenship. Those over whom a state rules are understood not as subjects but—at least potentially—as active citizens. These citizens are understood to constitute a coherent collectivity, a "people" or nation. This people or nation is understood as relatively homogeneous and as possessing a distinct unity, identity, or character. Finally, state authority is legitimated by some kind of reference to the sovereignty or "ownership" of "the people" or "the nation": the state is understood as the state of and for a particular "nation."

This language of peoplehood, nationhood, and citizenship is extremely flexible and adaptable. It can be used *by* states but also *against* them. It can be used to legitimize a polity but also to challenge its legitimacy, to demand a new polity, or to claim autonomy or resources. And the content of the idea of peoplehood or nationhood—that which gives a people or nation its unity, its character, its particular and distinctive identity—can be specified in various ways. It may be understood as shaped by the state and by shared political experience, or it may be understood as prepolitical, existing prior to and independently of the state. It may be understood as grounded in citizenship, history, language, way of life, descent, race, or religion.

On this account, we do not need the notion of "multiple modernities" to make sense of ethnic or religious nationalisms; a single modernity perspective can do just as well. The question becomes not "How many modernities?" but how to characterize modernity per se. If we work with an outmoded, narrow, complacently Eurocentric account of modernity, then the notion of multiple modernity may be compelling. But if "modernity" is characterized in a more supple and sophisticated manner—and there is a substantial literature that does just this—then the case for a multiple modernities perspective weakens considerably.

What does this mean in the domain of nationalism and ethnicity? If we work with an outmoded understanding of the modern nation-state and modern nationalism as purely secular and civic, with religion and ethnicity confined to the private realm, then a multiple modernities perspective may be compelling. But as I suggested in reviewing the work of Deutsch, Gellner, and Geertz, this narrow understanding was by no means the only one available even in the 1960s, let alone today. A more supple understanding of political modernity has long been available (see for example Wimmer 2002). This understanding allows for the flexible adaptability and chronic contestation of internationally circulating models of state, nation, people, and citizenship.

This chapter has advanced two arguments for a "single modernity" perspective, one logical, the other sociological. The logical argument is this: in order to characterize multiple institutional patterns and cultural and political programs, even ostensibly antimodern ones, as "modern," we need some criterion; this criterion depends—at least at an abstract conceptual level—on a single notion of modernity.

The sociological argument is twofold: it emphasizes the globally interconnected socioeconomic, political, and cultural processes that have generated and sustained nationalism and politicized ethnicity as basic forms of cultural and political understanding, identification, and claims-making; and it emphasizes both the common core and the flexible adaptability of the package of ideas and organizational models of state, nation, people, and citizenship that has diffused worldwide in the past two centuries.

Notes
References
Index

Notes

Introduction

1. White House, "Remarks by the President on Economic Mobility," December 4, 2013, http://www.whitehouse.gov/the-press-office/2013/12/04/remarks-president-economic-mobility.
2. Wide-ranging recent accounts include Noah 2012; Hacker and Pierson 2010; Stiglitz 2012; Grusky 2012; Saez 2013; Jenkins and Micklewright 2007; Neckerman and Torche 2007; Wilkinson and Pickett 2009; Weeden and Grusky 2012; DiMaggio and Garip 2012.
3. Fraser (1995) offered an influential early diagnosis of this shift.
4. See, for example, Wimmer 2013; Lamont et al. 2014; Emirbayer and Desmond forthcoming. Not coincidentally, Bourdieu is an important inspiration for all three works; on Bourdieu see Wacquant 2013.

1. Difference and Inequality

1. This represents a substantial shift from the first two-thirds of the twentieth century, when the very rich derived most of their income from capital. "The share of wage and salary income [in the top income percentile] has increased sharply from the 1920s to the present, and especially since the 1970s . . . a significant fraction of the surge in top incomes since 1970 is due to an explosion of top wages and salaries" (Saez 2013). As Saez notes, however, "such a pattern might not last for very long": drastic cuts in the federal estate tax "could certainly accelerate the path toward the reconstitution of the great wealth concentration that existed in the U.S. economy before the Great Depression." Saez's longtime

collaborator, Thomas Piketty (2014), has analyzed the "return of the rentier" (Milanovic 2014) in advanced capitalist economies.

2. The distinction between internal and external categories is relative (Tilly 1998: 77). Citizenship, for example, is an internal category with respect to the state as a whole insofar as it is an internal position or status defined by the state as an organization. But it is at the same time an external category with respect to particular organizations or programs that are nested within or financed by the state, in the sense that it is taken by those organizations and programs as given and predefined. Citizenship is of course also an external category outside the sphere of the state.

3. Exploitation and opportunity hoarding, Tilly writes, "establish" categorical inequality; two further mechanisms, emulation and adaptation, which I do not consider here, work to "cement" such arrangements (1998: 10).

4. Tilly is of course aware of the complexities of the system of racial classification under apartheid. But he argues that the workings of multicategorical systems of classification can be resolved analytically into the workings of categorical pairs (1998: 7).

5. It is therefore puzzling, as Mann (1999: 29) has observed about the book, that while "we clearly see ethnicity, race, and gender—and many occupational categories— . . . we only dimly glimpse capitalism." This is indeed, as Mann suggested, "quite an omission," particularly since Tilly (1998: 38) was moved to write the book by his belief that "the intensity of capitalist inequality causes unnecessary suffering."

6. This reflects differences in the resources involved. The resource controlled by insiders in the case of exploitation is a "labor-demanding resource, from which they can extract returns only by harnessing the effort of others" (Tilly 1998: 86–87); the resource controlled by insiders in the case of opportunity hoarding can be enjoyed without mobilizing the labor of others.

7. On the "anticategorical imperative" that informs network analysis, see Emirbayer and Goodwin 1994: 1414. Networks are almost always homophilous in one respect or another (McPherson et al. 2001), and networks that are homophilous with respect to individual-level characteristics associated with the adoption of welfare-enhancing practices can exacerbate original levels of inequality when (via externalities, social learning, or normative influence) the networks affect the likelihood of adopting the practice (DiMaggio and Garip 2012). The network-mediated, inequality-amplifying processes reviewed by DiMaggio and Garip do not require categorically bounded networks, exclusion, or opportunity hoarding; they do not depend on a boundary between insiders who control a valuable resource and outsiders who do not. However, *high degrees* of homophily—insofar as they go well beyond baseline levels of homophily attributable to opportunity structures such as differential group size (McPherson et al. 2001)—can be understood as shading over into categorical closure. This suggests a way of connecting Tilly's methodologically structuralist line of argument with the generally methodologically individualist research reviewed by DiMaggio and Garip (2012).

8. I borrow here a phrase used by Epstein (2007: 255) in a different context.

9. Even permanent residents, it should be noted, remain probationary residents, without the fully secure rights of residence and re-entry enjoyed by citizens; they can be deported or barred from re-entry into the territory for a range of reasons, including relatively minor criminal convictions.

10. In practice, to be sure, dual citizenship is increasingly common. But the basic structure of the interstate system, a system comprising formally coordinate and independent units, remains profoundly segmentary. On segmentation, stratification, and functional differentiation as three basic modes of differentiation, see Luhmann 1977.

11. For various ways of estimating the "excess demand" for migration to rich countries, see Pritchett 2006: 65ff. According to Gallup global survey data collected between 2009 and 2011, 13 percent of the world's adults—some 650 million people—would like to permanently leave their country (http://www.gallup.com/poll/153992/150-million-adults-worldwide-migrate.aspx).

12. Three recent books highlight the globally exclusive logic of citizenship: Pritchett (2006), writing from the perspective of development economics; Shachar (2009), writing from the perspective of law and normative political theory; and Korzeniewicz and Moran (2009), writing from the perspective of historical sociology. The normative case for open borders was first developed by Carens (1987).

13. This is why states have increasingly adopted strategies of territorial insulation or buffering to prevent unwanted migrants from gaining any kind of territorial foothold. This prevents such migrants from filing asylum claims or otherwise gaining access to procedural protections available to those present in the territory. Undocumented immigrants in liberal democracies are in a much more favorable position than those excluded from the territory. Though they are often treated as utterly lacking in rights and resources, Chauvin and Garcés-Mascareñas (2012) show that the reality is much more differentiated and complex and that one can speak of a limited but nontrivial form of civic incorporation, both formal and informal, of undocumented immigrants. The territorial excludability of noncitizens prevents many (though obviously not all) potential migrants even from gaining access to the status of undocumented immigrant, lowly though that status is. Borders do not have to be fully sealed for such citizenship-based regimes of territorial exclusion to be powerfully effective. The excluded are specifically those with a "bad" or stigmatized citizenship, who need visas just to get a foot in the door. Those with a "good" citizenship can enter the territory without a visa and thus can become undocumented simply by overstaying their visa. Although the paradigmatic undocumented immigrant is the clandestine border-crosser, nearly half of undocumented immigrants are visa overstayers, who need not attempt costly and dangerous clandestine entry (Pew Hispanic Center 2006). Given the association between citizenship and other resources, people with a "good" citizenship are also often able to blend in more effectively and thus are at a lower risk of detection and deportation.

14. Shachar's (2009) argument that citizenship is a form of inherited property casts in a new light the fact that contemporary states are understood as the states *of* and *for* their citizens. It suggests that membership in the state—and thus, more broadly, one's position in the interstate system—is "owned" by citizens and their

descendants. This marks a striking contrast to positions in the division of labor, which, in modern settings, are not owned by their incumbents—and still less by their descendants. This throws into sharp relief the contrast between the segmentary rigidity of the political organization of the world and the fluidity of the division of labor.

15. On the indeterminacy of the law and the broad scope of administrative discretion in the context of the Chinese Exclusion Acts, see Calavita 2000.

16. State prohibitions against discrimination govern not only state officials; they extend to private actors such as employers, universities, and clubs. Strong constitutional protections of the free exercise of religion, however, mean that religious organizations retain the right to discriminate on the basis of sex—for example, by excluding women from the Catholic priesthood—and on certain other grounds (Greenawalt 2006: chapter 20).

17. In some contexts, to be sure, everyday social relations are much more segregated by sex than they are in contemporary liberal democratic societies.

18. To explore this complexity is beyond the scope of this chapter. Suffice it to note that while taking households as units of analysis (as in much stratification research) can mask gender inequalities within households, taking individuals as units of analysis (as in the research I review here) can mask the centrality of the household as a social, economic, and affective unit.

19. Daniel H. Weinberg, "Evidence from Census 2000 about Earnings by Detailed Occupation for Men and Women," May 2004, http://www.census.gov/prod/2004pubs/censr-15.pdf.

20. This and the next paragraph follow closely the account given in Charles and Grusky (2004: chapter 1). The distinction between vertical and horizontal aspects of occupational sex segregation is an old one, but Charles and Grusky offer a new conceptualization and operationalization of this distinction.

21. See Budig and England (2001) on the motherhood penalty, part of which, they hypothesize, derives from women with children being less productive at work.

22. Citizenship can be central to self-understandings in certain contexts, but it is not routinely, chronically, and pervasively implicated in everyday life the way gender is.

23. On the distinction between automatic and deliberative cognition, see D'Andrade 1995; DiMaggio 1997.

24. Variation in the opportunity to discriminate, and in the likely costs of discrimination, suggests that large organizations are more likely to discriminate at the point of hiring than in the promotion, compensation, or dismissal of existing employees, since the latter have better information about discriminatory practices and more ability and incentive to file complaints. Consistent with these expectations, firm-level data on professional, managerial, and administrative employees in one large firm showed male-female differentials in job level and salary at point of hiring, consistent either with discrimination or with differential experience, but no indication of post-hiring discrimination (Petersen and Saporta 2004).

25. By ethnicity-like forms of religion, I mean forms of religious belonging that are understood to be inherited largely in families and to constitute parallel and largely self-reproducing communities. On the advantages of a broadly inclu-

sive understanding of ethnicity, see Rothschild 1981: 86–96; Brubaker 2009: 25–28; Wimmer 2013: 7–9.

26. These deeply institutionalized facts are not forever frozen. Although there is no evidence of change in the ubiquity of sex categorization and little evidence of significant change in essentialist understandings of difference, patterns of occupational sex segregation and the division of household labor have changed in nontrivial ways in recent decades. But they have changed very slowly, far more slowly than labor force participation rates, attitudes about gender equality, or levels of educational attainment.

27. The phrase is from Pettigrew (1979: 122). The most sustained analysis of residential segregation is Massey and Denton (1993). My account builds on that book and on Wacquant (2008).

28. For a broader review of studies of racial discrimination in employment, credit, and consumer as well as housing markets, see Pager and Shepherd 2008.

29. Black-white school segregation, on the other hand, has increased since the early 1990s, thanks to Supreme Court decisions effectively allowing a return to segregated neighborhood schools (Orfield and Lee 2006).

30. In 1999 the cumulative risk of incarceration by age thirty to thirty-four for African American men born in the late 1960s was about seven times the risk for white men of the same cohort. But the cumulative risk of incarceration for African American men without a high school degree was *twelve* times the risk for African American men with some college education; among white men, the risk was *sixteen* times higher for those without a high school degree than for those with some college. Strikingly, moreover, while the cumulative risk of incarceration more than doubled (from 12 to 30 percent) between 1979 and 1999 for young black men with a high school education or less, the cumulative risk of incarceration actually *declined* (from 6 to 5 percent) for young black men with some college (Pettit and Western 2004: 162; Wacquant 2010: 79–80). Racial disparities in prison experience have remained approximately stable, but class disparities within racial categories have increased dramatically. Virtually all of the huge increase in the risk of incarceration between 1979 and 1999 (during which time cumulative risk doubled for both whites and blacks) was borne by those with a high school education or less (Pettit and Western 2004: 162, 164).

31. What this means in everyday life is shown in Goffman's (2009, 2014) account of the strategies and practices of those who are not incarcerated yet are entangled in the criminal justice system in one way or the other and face warrants for their arrest. In the five-block inner-city black Philadelphia neighborhood studied intensively by Goffman—a poor but not hyperpoor neighborhood—a household survey revealed that nearly half of the young male residents "had a warrant issued for their arrest because of either delinquencies with court fines and fees or for failure to appear for a court date within the past three years" (2009: 343).

32. On the difficulty of drawing a sharp distinction between race and ethnicity, see Brubaker 2009: 25–27.

33. From the very large literature, see illustratively Jenkins 1997: chapter 5; Cornell and Hartmann 1998: chapter 6; Burbank and Cooper 2010; and the works cited in Brubaker 2009: 32–33.

34. I discuss religion here since it is both a *component* of ethnicity, a key part of the cultural content of many ethnic identifications, and an *analogue* of ethnicity (in that many forms of religion, like ethnicity, are socially understood as basic sources and forms of social, cultural, and political identification that sort people into distinct, bounded, and largely self-reproducing "communities"). See Chapter 4 of this volume for an extended discussion. A sustained comparison of linguistic and religious pluralism as forms of difference and sources of inequality is found in Brubaker (forthcoming).

35. On moves in liberal states toward a more neutral and even-handed stance toward religion and the limits of such moves, see the discussion in Chapter 3.

36. See, for example, Portes and Zhou 1993: 86, 90. Such strategies of insulation seek to keep children out of certain undesired networks and to embed them in alternative, preferred, more surveyable networks formed by ethnic churches, language schools, camps, and so on. The promotion of more or less arranged marriages with home-country spouses also belongs to such strategies of insulation.

37. Private clubs are a legal gray area. Here too the sphere of the indisputably private has been shrinking. The Supreme Court ruled in two cases from the 1980s that clubs such as the Jaycees and Rotary were too large and effectively public to be able to exclude women by claiming a right of private association. Clubs for women or members of minority groups are in a stronger legal position (Buss 1989).

38. This can lead in certain circumstances to something approximating wholesale categorical exclusion. Bielby and Baron (1986: 760–761), for example, show that extreme levels of occupational sex segregation can be generated by a simple model in which costs of employee turnover are high, employers perceive women as more likely to quit, and information about individual propensity to quit is unavailable.

39. In legal and organizational environments in which hiring, promotion, and firing practices are closely monitored, in which organizations are under pressure to hire or promote minorities or women, and in which the costs of discrimination— or of the appearance of discrimination—can be substantial, the skewing can sometimes favor members of generally disadvantaged categories (Petersen and Saporta 2004: 886).

40. Even when these between-group inequalities are much smaller than within-group inequalities, they may translate into substantial between-group inequalities in representation in particularly desirable or undesirable positions. One reason for this is that even when group-specific distributions (for example, of skills, education, or experience) substantially overlap, there is likely to be much less overlap at the tail ends of the distributions.

41. See, for example, Lareau 2003. On the need for an integrated understanding of the cultural, structural, and social psychological dimensions of unequal environments, with special reference to race, see Emirbayer and Desmond (forthcoming); on the recent renewal of interest in culture on the part of students of poverty, see Small et al. (2010). See also Lamont et al. (2014) for a theorization of the role of cultural processes in the production of inequality.

42. This is a theme developed throughout Bourdieu's oeuvre; among many other discussions, see those in *Pascalian Meditations* (2000: 169ff) and *Masculine Domination* (2001: 22–42). There is a risk, to be sure—of which Bourdieu was well aware—of overemphasizing internalization and its contribution to social and cultural reproduction.

43. For an interesting attempt to bring a psychoanalytically informed extension of Bourdieu's notion of symbolic violence to bear on racial inequality in the United States, see Emirbayer and Desmond forthcoming: chapter 6.

44. On positional inequality—the inequality inscribed in the structure of social positions, irrespective of the characteristics of the persons who occupy them— see Baron and Bielby 1980; Kalleberg and Griffin 1980. On the distinction between positional inequality and status inequality (inequality between kinds of people) in the domain of gender, see Jackson 1998.

45. On the social distribution of honor as an aspect of the distribution of power, the discussion of Weber ([1922] 1978: 926–938) remains foundational.

46. On race, see Emirbayer and Desmond forthcoming: chapter 6.

47. In some contexts, however, categories of personhood are themselves mediated by social position. In much of Latin America, for example, racial or color category membership depends on social position, in accordance with the expression "money whitens."

48. This is an instance of a broader dialectic of internalization and externalization that is a central theme in Bourdieu's work.

49. As I suggested in my discussion of categorically inflected selection processes, there are various intermediate possibilities in which category membership per se matters without being the *only* thing that matters.

50. This is obviously far too sweeping. Given the many relevant axes of categorical difference and the fact that most axes involve multiple socially significant categories and categorical pairs, any hypothesis designed to inform research would have to specify which categorical differences have become less inegalitarian. (On the importance of categorical pairs, even in systems involving multiple categories, see Tilly 1998: 6–7.) In the U.S. context, for example, even as most ethnic and religious categorical differences have become less inegalitarian, the categorical distinction between black and non-black has remained a crucial and refractory focus of inequality. I have discussed some reasons for these differing trajectories. Saperstein and Penner (2012: 676) suggest, in addition, that the patterned microlevel fluidity of racial identification and classification reinforces entrenched black–non-black inequalities "by redefining successful or high-status people as white (or not black) and unsuccessful or low-status people as black (or not white)."

2. The Return of Biology

1. On race and ethnicity as perspectives on and constructions of the world, see Brubaker 2002, 2009; Brubaker et al. 2004. On the multiple meanings of objectivism and subjectivism, see Brubaker 1985. My use of these terms—which

differs from that of Mills (1998) and Kaplan and Winther (2012)—is broadly Bourdieusian in its emphasis on the "objectivity of the subjective" and the resultant facticity, externality, and constraint. Kaplan and Winther treat constructivism as a form of objectivism, whereas I use *constructivism* and *subjectivism* more or less interchangeably.

2. See the classic account of institutionalization in Berger and Luckman 1966.

3. Another influential discussion defines race as "the framework of ranked categories segmenting the human population that was developed by western Europeans following their global expansion beginning in the 1400s" (Sanjek 1996: 1).

4. Objectivist understandings of ethnicity, too, have been in retreat since the seminal work of Barth (1969). But the subjectivist turn has proceeded somewhat differently in the domain of ethnicity. Because objectivist understandings of ethnic groups as entities in the world can be grounded in culture rather than nature, they do not carry the same baggage as objectivist understandings of races. And the question "What is an ethnic group?" continues to be asked. Yet culturalist forms of objectivism were powerfully challenged by Barth. Ethnic boundaries, he argued, do not exist objectively by virtue of shared traits or common culture. Rather, boundaries are the precipitate of practices of classification and categorization, which select certain cultural traits as diacritical and ignore others. One implication of this is that ethnic boundaries can persist even when objective cultural differences diminish or disappear. The critique of objectivist understandings of ethnicity, with antecedents in the characteristically dense and rich pages Max Weber devoted to the subject ([1922] 1978: 385–398), has been developed by Jenkins 1997; Brubaker 2004; Wimmer 2013; and others.

5. By contrast, earlier appeals to biology to validate the claim (in the first UNESCO "Statement on Race" from 1950) that race was less a biological phenomenon than a social myth, or that science had demonstrated the equality of human races, *were* criticized by geneticists: see Provine 1986: 873, 874.

6. See Barkan 1992 for a parallel argument about interwar Britain.

7. "The Race Question," http://unesdoc.unesco.org/images/0012/001282/128291e0 .pdf. As Reardon (2005: 39–43) has observed, the statement did not deny the biological reality of race. But while it noted ways in which race could legitimately be understood as a biological phenomenon, it pointed out that these did not correspond to prevailing folk understandings of race, and it urged that the term *race* be dropped in favor of *ethnic groups*.

8. I draw loosely here on Abbott's (1988) account of the system of professions as an ecology of jurisdictional claims.

9. Biologists were in effect "licensed" to study variation precisely insofar as they were understood as *not* making any claims about race.

10. This is an exaggeration, to be sure. As I discuss in the next section, race remained a key focus of objectivist inquiry in epidemiological and biomedical research.

11. Human Genome Project Information Archive, retrieved November 22, 2012, http://www.ornl.gov/sci/techresources/Human_Genome/project/clinton2 .shtml.

12. This move has been noted by many commentators; see, for example, El-Haj 2007; Koenig et al. 2008; Whitmarsh and Jones 2010; Omi 2010; Bliss 2012.

13. Differences between conventional continental race categories account for between 3 and 10 percent of the total variation, depending on measures and samples (Feldman and Lewontin 2008: 93–95, updating Lewontin's classic [1972] work on this topic).

14. Hochschild et al. 2012 is an important exception.

15. These new NIH and FDA rules were part of a broader institutionalization of race in an inclusionary mode that involved the establishment of offices of women's and minority health in various federal agencies (Epstein 2007: 75, 126–127).

16. As Feldman and Lewontin (2008: 93) point out, however, knowing a person's ancestry "only slightly improves the ability to predict his or her genotype."

17. From another perspective, controlling for covariates can be seen as an inappropriate form of "over-control," in that "race is not confounded by the other variables, [but] is antecedent to them" (Cooper and David 1986: 111; see also Morgenstern 1997: 609).

18. OMB, Revisions to the Standards for the Classification of Federal Data on Race and Ethnicity, http://www.whitehouse.gov/omb/fedreg_1997standards; Kahn 2006: 1966; Lee and Skrentny 2010: 629.

19. Categorical alignment operates on the reception side as well. A survey experiment found that those exposed to a news story reporting a genetic variant more strongly linked to heart attacks in blacks than in whites were more likely to endorse broader views about essential differences between racial groups (Phelan et al. 2013), providing support for Duster's (2003) argument about a spillover of racial objectivism from biomedical to other domains.

20. There is a large literature on BiDil. My account is based primarily on Kahn 2004, 2005, 2013.

21. For a defense of the FDA decision to approve BiDil specifically for African American patients, see Temple and Stockbridge 2007; this defense is itself criticized in Ellison et al. 2008.

22. Since variants negatively influencing drug response (unlike many variants predisposing to disease) would not have been selected against in most environments, such variants may be fairly common. This has led some (Goldstein et al. 2003: 946) to argue that advances in genomics are likely to have a more immediate payoff in pharmacogenetics than in understanding the causes of disease.

23. This individualizing and deracializing outcome would be more likely if the difference in allele frequencies between socially defined racial categories were relatively small. A disease-predisposing genetic variant found in substantially higher frequency among a disadvantaged socially defined racial category, however, would have the potential to stigmatize the entire category, and to stigmatize the disease by associating it with the stigmatized category. As I note in the next section, this potential for stigmatizing an entire category by virtue of its association with a genetic variant linked to an undesirable outcome is even greater in the case of behavioral genetic studies that seek to identify possible genetic factors underlying dispositions or traits linked to behavioral outcomes such as delinquency or crime.

24. Racialization is an instance of what Epstein (2007: chapter 7) calls "niche standardization."

25. On the "politics of the 'meantime,'" see Kahn 2013: chapter 6.

26. To be sure, exaggerated claims about personalized medicine continue to be made, driven by commercial interests; see Nissen 2011; Relman 2012.

27. For a broad account of the development and workings of the UK DNA database, see Williams and Johnson 2008.

28. In *Maryland v. King* (2013), the U.S. Supreme Court ruled that the extraction of DNA from persons arrested though not yet convicted of a crime does not constitute an unreasonable search or seizure under the Fourth Amendment (Wagner 2013).

29. An additional way race is implicated in the forensic use of DNA evidence pertains to the use of DNA evidence in criminal trials (Kahn 2009a, 2009b). When crime scene DNA matches a sample obtained from a suspect, it is necessary to ascertain whether the DNA found at the crime scene might actually belong to someone else. This is theoretically possible since the DNA profiles used to establish matches and construct databases are constructed from a small number of highly variable genetic markers. (Thirteen markers have been used since the late 1990s, with plans to expand to twenty-four). It is therefore necessary to calculate the probability that the match might be a mere coincidence. This is done by calculating the "random match probability"—the probability of finding the same DNA profile in some reference population. Reference populations have traditionally been differentiated by race. This was originally done to ensure fairness in constructing random match probabilities: taking genetically related populations as reference populations favors the defendant, since the odds of finding a match with another person by sheer chance are higher in related subpopulations than in the population at large. However, technical advances in the construction of DNA profiles have made race pragmatically irrelevant; now that random match probabilities are astronomically low (1 in 100 billion, for example), differences between reference populations have ceased to matter. Kahn has therefore argued persuasively that there is no longer any justification for the use of racial categories in constructing random match probabilities and that the continued use of racial categories risks "unfairly prejudicing deliberations through the gratuitous association of race with genetics and violent crime" (2009a: 375).

30. Innocence Project, http://www.innocenceproject.org/.

31. For disparities by race and education in cumulative probabilities of incarceration, see Pettit and Western 2004. On the racial skewing of data in Britain's DNA data bank, see Skinner 2013.

32. Kaye and Smith (2003) argue for a universal DNA database as a way of overcoming the inequalities generated by current racially skewed databases. Since DNA itself is race-blind, they suggest, a universal database would contribute to the partial deracialization of criminal justice.

33. In the United Kingdom, the government's Forensic Science Service has offered an "ethnic inference service" for more than a decade. This service estimates the proportion of an unknown suspect's ancestry attributable to five ethnically defined British populations: White European, Afro-Caribbean, Indian subconti-

nental, Southeast Asian, and Middle Eastern (Williams and Johnson 2008: 69; Koops and Schellekens 2008: 172–173).

34. This is already being done for certain eye and hair colors.

35. Fox (2010) argues that molecular photofitting—which seeks to statistically match the biogeographic ancestry of an unknown suspect against a database of known individuals that includes biogeographic ancestry along with photographs and physical facial measurements in order to generate a range of facial images most likely to approximate that of the suspect (Frudakis 2008)—will work in this deracializing direction. His argument would apply a fortiori to direct forensic DNA phenotyping.

36. To be sure, predicted light skin—like estimates of predominantly European biogeographic ancestry—may in certain contexts help reorient investigations away from marked or minority populations. M'Charek (2008: 400) discusses a sexual assault and murder case in which an analysis suggesting that the perpetrator had predominantly European ancestry deflected the investigation away from the previously suspected residents of a center for asylum seekers in a Dutch village.

37. This is a large subject in its own right, and I can touch on it only briefly here. For a review of behavioral genetic research on antisocial behavior, see Baker et al. 2006. On analytic strategies by which sociology can take account of the "ubiquitous partial heritability" of individual-level outcomes, see Freese 2008. On the potential of behavioral genetic research to stigmatize racial and ethnic minorities in criminal justice contexts, see Rothenberg and Wang 2006. For a Bourdieusian account of the development of the field of behavioral genetics, see Panofsky 2014. For an argument that a recent paradigm shift in genetics has challenged the assumptions underlying the heritability and gene association studies that have been at the core of behavioral genetics, see Charney 2012; see also Charney and English 2012.

38. As ancestry testing has merged with social networking, and as finer-grained DNA testing has converged with nongenetic genealogy, the major companies have been seeking to expand their customer base so as to increase the probability that users will find genetic "matches"—more or less distant relatives—among other users. Pursuit of the self-reinforcing benefits of an expanding network may explain the aggressive pricing practices and the consolidation of the industry in the past few years. (As of late 2013, the prices offered by the major companies—especially for autosomal tests—were substantially lower than those reported by Greely [2008] and Wagner et al. [2012]). Precise figures on the number of those tested are unavailable, but estimates suggest that well over a million people have purchased ancestry tests (Tallbear 2013b:68; Wagner et al. 2012: 586). One leading company alone, 23andMe, claimed to have over 400,000 users in its database (http://www.isogg.org/wiki/Autosomal _DNA_testing_comparison_chart) and lowered the price of its test to $99 in December 2012 in an effort to expand the database to 1 million (http://blog .23andme.com/news/one-million-strong-a-note-from-23andmes-anne -wojcicki/). In the context of preexisting American fascination with genealogy (Bolnick 2003) and favorable public attitudes toward ancestry testing

(endorsed in the 2010 General Social Survey by 61 percent of whites, 64 percent of Hispanics, and 76 percent of blacks [Hochschild and Sen 2012; see also Wagner and Weiss 2012]), the lower prices, more sophisticated tests, and convergence with genealogy and social networking would seem to indicate great potential for further expansion of the market.

39. Since mitochondrial DNA changes much more slowly than Y-chromosome DNA, it is less useful for ancestry testing in historical time frames. Nash notes that this deeply genders the enterprise of genetic genealogy, making "meaningful ancestry profoundly masculine" (2008: 254).

40. A unique event polymorphism is a mutation that is considered overwhelmingly likely to have occurred only once. This uniqueness is what enables the genetic marker to define a unique lineage. All persons with this genetic marker are assumed to have inherited it from a single common ancestor.

41. From the website of the Genographic Project: https://genographic.national-geographic.com/about/, retrieved November 30, 2013. As a public outreach component of its effort to map the genetic diversity of the world—a successor in this respect to the ill-fated Human Genome Diversity Project (Reardon 2005), the Genographic Project invited the public to purchase ancestry testing kits. The project is described for a popular audience by its lead scientist in Wells (2007); for a scholarly account and critique, see Nash 2012.

42. Data for some common haplogroups are reported at Wikipedia, http://en.wikipedia.org/wiki/Y-DNA_haplogroups_by_ethnic_group (retrieved November 10, 2013). See also the (admittedly partly speculative) map of haplogroup distributions circa 1500: http://www.scs.illinois.edu/~mcdonald/WorldHaplogroups Maps.pdf.

43. In theory, each of us has 2^n ancestors n generations back—as many as 1,024 ancestors ten generations back, for example—plus all the intervening ancestors in more recent generations. In fact we don't have anywhere near that many *unique* ancestors. Our ancestral tree is not endlessly ramifying: if it were, the number of ancestors would very quickly exceed the total number of people that have ever lived. The branches of our ancestral tree cross back and intertwine with one another, reflecting greater or lesser degrees of inbreeding. Since first cousins share two grandparents, for example, the child of first cousins has six unique great-grandparents instead of eight. Nonetheless we all have very large numbers of ancestors, and haploid tests necessarily ignore almost all of them. For a broad view of the social reckoning of ancestry, which is always selective and partial, see Zerubavel 2012.

44. Haley's best-selling novel, *Roots: The Saga of an American Family* (1976), based in part on his research into his own family's history, reconstructed a multi-generational family history, beginning with a young Mandinka man living in what is today the Gambia, who was captured and sold into slavery in Virginia in 1767. The novel was also the basis for a sensationally popular television miniseries.

45. African Ancestry, "PatriClan Test Kit" and "MatriClan Test Kit," http://shop.africanancestry.com/PatriClan-Test-Kit-p/pc001.htm; http://shop.africanancestry.com/MatriClan-Test-Kit-p/mc001.htm. The FAQ section is careful to note

various caveats: "There is no test for racial identification. Race is a social construct, not genetically determined. Similarly, ethnicity is more cultural than biological." "Frequently Asked Questions," http://www.africanancestry.com/faq/ (retrieved July 8, 2014).

46. Forms of affiliation with African countries and ethnic groups on the part of African Americans and other Afro-descendant populations are by no means restricted to those who have taken genetic ancestry tests. On the broader phenomenon of African "homecoming" and the ambivalence it often entails, see Schramm 2010.

47. African Ancestry, "PatriClan Test Kit," http://shop.africanancestry.com/Patri Clan-Test-Kit-p/pc001.htm (retrieved July 8, 2014). To reinforce the disclaimer, the following appeared in red italics after an asterisk at the bottom of an earlier version of the same web page, just above where one had to click to buy the test: *"Being African American does not guarantee an African result."* For those seeking African roots, the maternal line is more likely to yield results. The MatriClan test includes a parallel disclaimer, but for women only 8 percent of results do not point to an African ancestor. On the privileging of the maternal line in tests of African ancestry, see also Schramm 2012: 177–178.

48. Y-chromosome DNA tests are also used in various "surname projects" that seek to trace distinctive male lineages. For an account of such projects in the context of the Irish diaspora, see Nash 2008: chapter 7. Such projects, like others that use Y-chromosome and mitochondrial DNA tests, suggest "that a man can have only one genetic ancestry" (260).

49. 23andMe, "Ancestry Composition Basics," https://customercare.23andme .com/entries/22549561-Ancestry-Composition-Basics (retrieved December 6, 2013).

50. Ancestry.com, "Viewing Genetic Ethnicity Results from AncestryDNA," http://help .ancestry.com/app/answers/detail/a_id/5475 (retrieved December 6, 2013).

51. 23andMe, "Reference Populations in Ancestry Composition," https://customer care.23andme.com/entries/22584878-Reference-populations-in-Ancestry-Com position (retrieved December 6, 2013).

52. iGENEA, "Are You a Viking" and "Are You Jewish?", http://www.igenea.com /en/vikings, http://www.igenea.com/en/jews (retrieved December 6, 2013).

53. Research on the social effects of genetic genealogy is just beginning, but it is worth noting that an initial survey of those who had actually taken ancestry tests found that—contrary to media analysis and a survey using vignettes reported by the same authors—tests contributed more to blurring than to sharpening racial boundaries (Hochschild and Sen 2012).

54. This and the following four paragraphs draw primarily on Tallbear 2013b.

55. This can happen as a result of generations of intermarriage between members of different tribes, and between Native Americans and others, both of which are quite common. With every passing generation, a larger fraction of children of intermarried parents cannot meet tribal blood quantum requirements (Tallbear 2013b: 98).

56. For the "racial shifters" discussed by Sturm (2011: 54–57), for example, Cherokeeness offered an enticing alternative to a white identity experienced

as culturally and spiritually "empty." On whiteness as a devalued and even stigmatized identity in certain contexts, see also Storrs 1999; TallBear 2013b: 138–140.

57. Dalit groups in India, for example, have selectively enlisted population genetic studies to revive the old "Aryan migration" or "Aryan invasion" theory, thereby figuring Hindu upper castes as nonindigenous. Hindu nationalists have selectively enlisted other population genetic studies to claim indigeneity for Hindus (which enables them to figure Muslims and Christians as foreign invaders [Egorova 2009; Benjamin 2013]).

58. This account is based on Kent 2013.

59. On the broader phenomenon of the "identity economy," involving multifarious attempts to capitalize on ethnic authenticity, see Comaroff and Comaroff 2009. The genetic evidence mobilized by the Uros was not unambiguous, and subsequent research suggested that some lakeshore residents possessed a genetic profile very similar to that of the Uros. Yet the arguments for genetic distinctiveness seem to have been widely accepted and seem to have strengthened the Uros' claim to a distinctive and ancient ethnic identity.

60. TallBear (2013b: 152) notes that the threat is not only to creation stories but also, and perhaps more important, to constitutive narratives and understandings of peoplehood focused on "pivotal moments in colonial history that reshaped their lands and thus their land-based identities." On competing genomic and indigenous articulations of indigeneity, see also Tallbear 2013a.

61. Like some other far-right parties, the BNP has shifted from an overtly racist position to a "differentialist" stance (Bonifas 2008). This has enabled them to represent the British as an indigenous people in their own ancestral homeland, deserving the same rights and protections as other indigenous peoples. The claim to indigeneity is set forth most fully in the booklet *Four Flags: The Indigenous People of Britain* (Kemp 2010), promoted as "using the very latest genetic research and combining it with the historical record . . . [to prove] conclusively that there is a clearly definable indigenous population in Britain and that they qualify fully for protected status under the United Nations Charter on the Rights of Indigenous Peoples." The word *indigenous* appeared fourteen times in the party's 2010 election manifesto (http://www.general-election-2010.co .uk/2010-general-election-manifestos/BNP-Manifesto-2010.pdf). The roots of the differentialist turn on the right have been explored in a number of publications by Pierre-André Taguieff; see in English Taguieff 2001.

62. This and the follow paragraph are based on Nash 2013; see also Nash 2004, 2008, 2012.

63. As Nash notes, the "project's focus on regional diversity is not incompatible with the theory of the dominance of 'ancient' genes in Britain. For Bodmer [the lead scientist], 'mixture' is relative . . . and Britain is 'actually relatively more homogenous than many other countries'" (2013: 198). Yet the focus on mixedness meant that the project's findings could not be appropriated by an overtly exclusionary ethnonationalist discourse the way other population genetic findings have been.

64. The English text of the open letter is at In Defence of Marxism, http://www .marxist.com/brazil-open-letter-against-race-laws.htm (retrieved December 4, 2013).

65. For a different take on this challenge and how social scientists might respond, see Shiao et al. 2012.

66. Nor does it mean that there are no significant cultural (or genetic) differences between socially defined ethnic categories. For reasons of expository clarity, I focus on race, though the broader argument applies to ethnicity as well.

67. As noted earlier, moreover, the discovery of genetically based differences between socially defined racial categories in disease susceptibility or drug response might even make racial categories *less* rather than more significant in medical practice. Identification of the actual casually significant genetic variants would permit testing patients directly for those variants rather than using socially defined racial categories as a crude proxy.

68. Sensitive to this difference, some biomedical researchers have sought to substitute direct measures of ancestry for racial and ethnic categories. But as Fujimura et al. (2010) show, there is often some slippage between these notions.

69. Socially defined racial and ethnic categories (along with religious and other social categories) are also *causally* related to biogeographic and biogenetic ancestry, insofar as shared understandings about boundaries and belonging, and the practices of social closure that are informed by such understandings, shape patterns of sexual relations. Such shared understandings and practices of social closure can preserve or even augment or create biogenetic differences. But as they change, they can also contribute to the erosion of such differences.

70. The sharpness of categorical boundaries is of course variable. Categories are generally more blurred and ambiguous in everyday life than in administrative practice. And the proliferation of intermediate racial categories in some settings—notably in Latin America—is well known. The increasing use of "mixed race" as a category in the United States and elsewhere, in formal as well as informal settings, is interesting as a kind of performative contradiction that at once denies and reinforces categorical distinctions.

71. The notion of biosocial processes goes back at least to Rabinow (1992). It has come much later to sociology, invested as the discipline has been in defining itself against psychology and biology. But that has begun to change in recent years (Freese 2008; Shiao et al. 2012). For a constructivist analysis of the biosocial processes involved in the geneticization, diagnostic expansion, increasing incidence, and increasing genetic heterogeneity of autism, see Navon and Eyal (2014).

3. Language, Religion, and the Politics of Difference

1. For an alternative perspective on the commonalities of religion and language, see Safran 2008.

2. On language, see, for example, Haugen 1966; on religion, Beyer 2001.

3. For a parallel argument about ethnicity and religion, see Ruane and Todd 2010.

4. To analyze these trajectories is beyond the scope of this chapter. On religion, see, for example, Kaplan 2007; Madeley 2003. On language, see Hobsbawm 1990; Barbour and Carmichael 2000.

5. Whether or not one accepts Chomsky's notion of a universal grammar, language is universal not only in the sense that it is found in all human societies but also in the sense that all humans ordinarily develop proficiency in at least one language. This has no clear analogue in the domain of religion. While everyone may have a capacity for religious experience (depending on how this is defined), it cannot be said that everyone is proficient in at least one religion. Quite apart from explicit irreligiosity or antireligiosity, people differ much more widely in religiosity than in basic "linguosity." Of course people differ substantially in linguistic proficiency or linguistic capital as well, but the differences in religious qualification are much greater and more consequential; they are, among other things, the basis for the opposition between virtuoso and mass religiosity that is central to Weber's sociology of religion (1946: 287).

6. In traditions of virtuoso religiosity, religion may be normatively understood as pervasively relevant to all aspects of life, but that does not make religion a universal medium of social life in the sense that language is.

7. On the broader debate in political theory about the ideal of state neutrality vis-à-vis competing understandings of the good, see Koppelman 2004. Koppelman acknowledges the incoherence of the idea of complete neutrality, yet he affirms the continued relevance and value of neutrality as an ideal.

8. Moves toward neutrality have been driven largely by courts (Koenig forthcoming); and they can be overridden, circumvented, or limited by decidedly less neutral political decisions, as in the political pressures that led to the 2011 reversal of an initial European Court of Human Rights decision banning the crucifix from Italian classrooms (Koenig forthcoming; Joppke 2013), the 2010 French ban on the full-face veil (Joppke and Torpey 2013), or the explicit exemption of Christian symbols in laws designed to bar Muslim teachers from wearing headscarfs in a number of German states (Joppke 2007).

9. See inter alia Casanova 1994; Martin 2005; Taylor 2007; Gorski and Altinordu 2008; Turner 2011; Koenig 2011.

10. This is obviously a gross generalization, and exceptions spring immediately to mind. Still, it and the equally gross generalization in the preceding paragraph hold up reasonably well for the Western world on a time scale of decades and centuries, respectively. But one would need to shift to another level and mode of analysis altogether to account for the varying contexts, contours, and trajectories of conflicts over language and religion in particular places and times.

11. Merle et al. (2010) present their study as a challenge to Fishman, but their finding that only a third of migrants' grandchildren in Basel and Geneva understand or speak the language of their grandparents seems broadly consistent with Fishman.

12. This is not to minimize the thoroughgoing institutionalization of Spanish in the United States, anchored not only in government policies but also, as was already evident to Zolberg and Long (1999: 26), in a substantial media market. Yet, as noted in the text, the process of intergenerational language shift continues among the children and grandchildren of Spanish-speaking immigrants.

13. The literature that points to new or intensified forms of religiosity among some second- or third-generation Muslim immigrants is largely ethnographic (see, for

example, Glynn 2002). Intensified religiosity may be highly visible, but there is no evidence that it is broadly representative. Quantitative studies have reported intergenerational stability in levels of religiosity (Diehl and Koenig 2009, examining Germany), or slight intergenerational declines (Ersanilli and Koopmans 2009, considering Germany, France, and the Netherlands). Kashyap and Lewis (2013), interestingly, find both decreased observance among younger British Muslims and an increased salience of Islam for personal identity.

14. This point was already made by Herberg (1960) and has more recently been emphasized by Warner (1993) and Kurien (1998); but see critically Jeung et al. (2012).

15. In many of these cases, however (in India, Switzerland, Belgium, and Canada, at least with respect to Quebec, for example), linguistic pluralism on the statewide level coincides with linguistic monism—or at least with the strongly institutionalized primacy of a single language—at the level of federal component states or provinces. Linguistic pluralism, in other words, generally exists as a collection of lower-level linguistic monisms. This observation supports the argument of Zolberg and Long that modern states (or at least their component substate polities) tend toward monism in the domain of language. The organization of religious pluralism in liberal states is striking different; it is not territorialized the way linguistic pluralism tends to be.

16. Political theorists are divided about the justice of this sharp difference in the treatment of long-established and recently imported linguistic pluralism; see, for example, Kymlicka 1995; Patten 2006.

17. I borrow the term *deep diversity* from a line of work in political theory (see, for example, Galston 1995) that derives most immediately from Rawls's *Political Liberalism* (1993).

18. Deprivatization and ongoing privatization are not mutually exclusive; given the complexity of the contemporary religious landscape, it is not surprising that both are happening at the same time (Casanova 2009: 29).

19. To underscore the relative normative and cultural "thinness" of language vis-à-vis religion is not to deny that language may carry "thicker" cultural meanings and commitments in some contexts than in others. See Carens (2000: 128–129) and Bauböck (2002: 177–178) on "thin" and "thick" theories of language in relation to cultural commitments.

20. The meanings of and boundaries between "public" and "private," to be sure, are richly ambiguous and chronically contested (Casanova 1994: chapter 2).

4. Religion and Nationalism

1. Indicative of this surge in interest are the collections edited by Hutchison and Lehmann (1994), Van der Veer and Lehmann (1999), Geyer and Lehmann (2004), and Haupt and Langewiesche (2004).

2. Hayes (1926: chapter 4; the quotations are from 95, 104, 124–125). The centrality of this notion for Hayes is suggested by the title of his 1960 book, *Nationalism: A Religion*. In a somewhat more analytical discussion, Smart (1983) specified six dimensions on which nationalism can be compared to religion

(though by "nationalism" he means what he admits might better be called "patriotism," namely "devotion to [one's] own nation-state"). Thus understood, nationalism is weak in doctrine, strong in myth, strong in ethics, intermittent in ritual, strong in experience, and strong in social form.

3. On the uses of religious terms to define civic identities, see Lichterman 2008.

4. The notion of structural pluralism was developed with primary reference to colonial societies, but varying degrees of social segmentation and institutional parallelism can be found elsewhere, the (formerly) "pillarized" society of the Netherlands being a classic example.

5. Other mechanisms may be at work as well, including residential segregation and occupational niches. These are analytically distinct from institutional duplication, though they usually work in tandem.

6. Geertz's seminal essay on politics in postcolonial societies (1963) provided an early argument for treating all such claims together; see also Rothschild (1981: 9) and, more recently, Brubaker (2009). For the limitations of this perspective, see Chapter 3 of the present volume.

7. In addition to claims made on the basis of ethnocultural or ethnoreligious identity, broadly understood, these include claims made in the name of the deaf, understood as a linguistic minority (Plann 1997), or the autistic, as a neurologically based cultural minority (Declaration of the Autistic Community as a Minority Group Deserving of Civil Protections, http://www.petitiononline.com /AFFDec/petition.html; cf. Hacking 2009).

8. For Smith, the myth of ethnic election and divine covenant is constituted by a number of linked ideas, including divine choice, collective sanctification, and conditional privilege (2003: chapter 3, especially 50–51).

9. Smith has consistently distinguished national*ism* as a distinctive ideology and movement from national consciousness or national identity (see, for example, 2003: 268). And he continues to argue that while national identities have deep roots in premodern ethnic and (often) religious identities (Smith 1986; Hastings 1997), nationalism crystallizes as a fully elaborated doctrine only in the late eighteenth century (Smith 2008: x). But he now dates the first nationalist movements to these seventeenth-century cases.

10. See, for example, Gellner (1983: 142), for whom the key elements of Protestantism "foreshadowed an anonymous, individualistic, fairly unstructured mass society, in which relatively equal access to a shared culture prevails, and the culture has its norms publicly accessible in writing, rather than in the keeping of a privileged specialist. Equal access to a scripturalist God paved the way to equal access to high culture. Literacy is no longer a specialism, but a pre-condition of all the specialisms. . . . In such a society, one's prime loyalty is to the medium of our literacy, and to its political protector. The equal access of believers to God eventually becomes equal access of unbelievers to education and culture."

11. For a different perspective on religion and vernacular languages, attributing less importance to Protestantism and more to Christianity per se (which never, unlike Arabic, had a sacred language), see Hastings 1997: 193ff.

12. Smith (1986: 27) has observed that scholars of nationalism have paid too much attention to language and too little to religion. It is ironically partly through

religious developments that vernacular languages acquired the distinctive importance that they would come to have as a key criterion and medium of nationality
in Europe.

13. The Peace of Augsburg codified the territorialization and politicization of religion in the German lands by making the *jus reformandi*—the right to determine the religion of a territory—an attribute of princely sovereignty (Rice
1970: 165). Although the political fragmentation of central Europe meant that
the fusion of culture and polity associated with confessionalization occurred
on lower levels of political space than those later associated with "nations,"
the territorialization and politicization of religion were nonetheless significant in establishing the principle of the congruence of polity and culture and
in providing both a conceptual model of culturally homogeneous political
space and an organizational infrastructure for implementing that model in
practice. Both conceptual model and organizational infrastructure proved to
be transferable to larger scales of political space and to other domains of
culture.

14. Cf. Anderson (1991: 19): "The fall of Latin exemplified a larger process in which
the sacred communities integrated by old sacred languages were gradually frag-
mented, pluralized, and territorialized."

15. The coincidence of religious and ethnic boundaries is suggested by the term
ethnoreligious; there is no corresponding combination term denoting the
intertwining or symbiosis of nation and religion.

5. The "Diaspora" Diaspora

1. Calculated from the ProQuest Dissertations and Theses database.

2. In updating this chapter, originally published in 2005, for the present volume, I
came across an earlier reference to the notion of a "'diaspora' diaspora" that I am
happy to acknowledge here. Henry Goldschmidt introduced a paper prepared
for a 2002 conference by observing that "the term [diaspora] itself has become
somewhat diasporic," spreading out from its original "conceptual and/or historical homeland." He went on to ask, "What exactly do we in the 'Diaspora' diaspora mean by this ostensibly shared term?" Goldschmidt's contribution, cited in
Dufoix (2011a: 15), is available as a working paper (Goldschmidt 2003).

3. The definitive account of the history of the word is found in Dufoix (2011a);
for briefer accounts in English, see Dufoix 2007, 2008.

4. On trading diasporas generally—or what have also been called "middleman
minorities" (Bonacich 1973)—see Fallers 1962; Curtin 1984; Cohen 1997:
83–104. See also Wang (2000) on the overseas Chinese, Winder (1962) on the
Lebanese, Armstrong (1978) on Baltic Germans, and Cohen (1971) on the
Hausa of Nigeria.

5. See, for example, Sheffer 1986, 2003; Angoustures and Pascal 1996; Bhatt and
Mukta 2000. Albanians, Hindu Indians, Irish, Kashmiri, Kurds, Palestinians,
Tamils, and others have been construed as diasporas in this sense.

6. Algerian, Bangladeshi, Filipino, Greek, Haitian, Indian, Italian, Korean, Mexican, Pakistani, Puerto Rican, Polish, Salvadoran, Turkish, Vietnamese, and many

other migrant populations have been conceptualized as diasporas in this sense (Sheffer 2003).

7. For a skeptical discussion of the notion of an Italian diaspora, see Gabaccia 2000: 5–12.

8. I have myself contributed to this form of proliferation, with a paper on "accidental diasporas" (Brubaker 2000). See also Kolstø 1995; Mandel-baum 2000.

9. Vertovec (2000) distances himself from the generalized extension of the term *diaspora* to dispersed adherents of religious faiths. In agreement with Parekh (1993), however, he makes the case for a Hindu diaspora on the grounds that Hinduism, like Judaism and Sikhism, is a special case of a nonproselytizing "ethnic religion." On the Sikh diaspora, see Axel 2001; on the Muslim diaspora, Kastoryano 1999; Saint-Blancat 2002; Werbner 2002.

10. Of these, the academic literature includes articles or books on the Dixie, white, liberal, gay, deaf, queer, and digital diasporas.

11. On the importance of the media for the popularization—and conceptual stretching—of the term, see Tölölyan 1996: 10.

12. The "diaspora" diaspora involves not only a proliferation of putative diasporas and a diffusion of diaspora-talk throughout the academy and into the wider culture and polity but also a proliferation of terms. In addition to the concrete noun, designating a collectivity, there are abstract nouns designating a condition (diasporicity or diasporism), a process (diasporization, de-diasporization, and rediasporization), even a field of inquiry (diasporology or diasporistics). There is an adjective (diasporist) designating a stance or position in a field of debate or struggle and others (diasporic and diasporan) designating an attribute or modality, as in diasporic citizenship, diasporic consciousness, diasporic identity, diasporic imagination, diasporic nationalism, diasporic networks, diasporic culture, diasporic religion, and even the diasporic self (to enumerate only some of the most common conceptual pairings found in recent academic articles). *Diasporist,* it should be noted, can have two quite different meanings. With respect to Jews, and sometimes in other cases (see, for example, Clifford [1994: 321] on the African diaspora), it designates a positive orientation to the diaspora *at the expense of an actual or putative homeland,* a valorization of lateral over centripetal (homeland-oriented) connections, in Clifford's terms. Thus in the Jewish case, diasporist is opposed to Zionist (see, for example, Boyarin and Boyarin 1993), an opposition taken to an extreme in Philip Roth's novel *Operation Shylock.* In many other contexts, however, *diasporist* designates a positive orientation to the diasporic condition (which may include a constitutive commitment to a homeland) in the face of the exclusive claims of the nation-state of residence on loyalty and identity.

13. For sustained discussions of definitional issues, see Safran 1991; Clifford 1994; Tölölyan 1996; Cohen 1997; Sheffer 2003; Dufoix 2008.

14. Safran's passive formulation of this criterion—"they, or their ancestors, have been dispersed"—(1991: 83) does not allow for voluntary dispersion. Cohen (1997) and others see this as too limiting.

15. This point was noted by Cohen, who preserves three homeland-related criteria in his own enumeration of nine "common features of a diaspora" (1997: 23, 26).

16. A further complexity arises in the case of what might be called "second-order diasporas," when more than one potential "homeland" or place of origin is in play. Cohen (1992) has described Caribbeans in North America and Europe as a diaspora of a diaspora. Should a three-stage migration sequence then lead us to speak of a third-order diaspora—a diaspora of a diaspora of a diaspora? And what if the final stage—whether stage two or stage three—leads back to the original homeland? Does this cancel the diasporic condition, or does it complexify it further? What is the homeland, or homelands, of the descendants of German-speaking populations who settled along the Volga as colonists during the eighteenth century, who were deported to Kazakhstan and elsewhere in 1941 after the German invasion of the Soviet Union, and who resettled in Germany as *Aussielder* in the 1990s? What is the homeland, or homelands, of the late Soviet and post-Soviet Jews who resettled en masse in Israel? Of Transylvanian Hungarians who have moved to Hungary? Of Korean Chinese who have settled in South Korea, or Brazilian Japanese who have migrated to Japan? In these and similar cases, the putative coethnics are often marked and sometimes even stigmatized as different, and the putative homeland is often experienced as alien. On ethnic return migration, see Brubaker 1998; Tsuda 2009.

17. On the temporal dimension, see Marienstras 1989: 125; Cohen 1997: 185–186.

18. On methodological nationalism, see Wimmer and Glick Schiller 2003. Although she does not use the term, Soysal (2000) makes a partially similar argument.

19. For related articles about a fundamental shift in perspective, see Glick Schiller et al. 1995; Kearney 1995; Beck 2000.

20. Natan Sznaider, opening remarks to the conference Diaspora Today, Schloss Elmau, Germany, July 17, 2003.

21. For a critique of the view that states have lost their ability to control their borders, see Brubaker 1994; Freeman 1994; and, for a more detailed account, Zolberg 1999. On the mid-nineteenth-century codification of citizenship as a means of controlling migration, see Brubaker 1992: 64ff. On the historical development of passports and related techniques of identification, see Torpey 2000 and the studies collected in Caplan and Torpey 2001.

22. On the nation-state as an idealized conceptual model, see Chapter 6.

23. For a nuanced argument about "cosmopolitics" as a mode of "thinking and feeling beyond the nation" that does not treat the nation-state and cosmopolitanism as antithetical, see Robbins 1998. David Hollinger has also argued eloquently that the "nation" need not be antithetical to cosmopolitan or transnational engagements but can sometimes mediate effectively "between the ethnos and the species" (1998: 87; see also 1995: chapter 6).

24. Among "historical diasporas," the "real numbers" supplied by Sheffer yield 35 million for the Chinese diaspora, 9 million for the Indian diaspora, 8 million for the Jewish and Gypsy diasporas, 5.5 million for the Armenian diaspora, 4 million for the Greek diaspora, 2.5 million for the German diaspora,

and 1 million for the Druze diaspora. Among "modern" diasporas, the African American diaspora numbers 25 million, the Kurdish diaspora 14 million, the Irish diaspora 10 million, the Italian diaspora 8 million, the Hungarian and Polish diasporas 4.5 million each, the Turkish and Iranian diasporas 3.5 million each, the Japanese diaspora 3 million, the Lebanese (Christian) diaspora 2.5 million, and the "Black Atlantic" diaspora 1.5 million. A similar list with numbers is given for thirty "incipient diasporas" (Sheffer 2003: 104–106).

25. For an argument that discussions of identity are similarly bedeviled by a mix of strong and weak definitions, see Brubaker and Cooper 2000.

26. The former possibility has been emphasized by Gilroy (1997: 328) and by Natan Sznaider in his opening remarks to the conference Diaspora Today. The latter possibility has been noted by Anthias 1998: 560, 563, 567.

27. Bhabha's remark, in the context of a discussion of Salman Rushdie's *Satanic Verses,* is quoted in Tambiah 2000: 178.

28. For a very different argument criticizing the use of diaspora as an analytical category in the study of immigration, see Soysal 2000. For an argument about categories of analysis and categories of practice in the study of ethnicity, race, and nation, see Brubaker 2002.

29. Writing on the African diaspora, Patterson and Kelley (2000: 19) observe that "the presumption that black people worldwide share a common culture was not . . . the result of poor scholarship. It responded to a political imperative—one that led to the formation of political and cultural movements premised on international solidarity." They quote Hall's (1990: 224) remark that unitary images of diaspora offered "a way of imposing an imaginary coherence on the experience of dispersal and fragmentation."

30. On the changing historical stances of sending states toward immigrant populations and their descendants, see, for example, R. Smith 2003 (on Mexico, Italy, and Poland), Gabaccia 2000 (on Italy), Itzigsohn 2000 (on the Dominican Republic, Haiti, and El Salvador), and Wang 1993 (on China).

31. There is no reason to expect that people will respond consistently to claims made in their name by political entrepreneurs and organizations in the putative diaspora itself or in the putative homeland. They may well embrace diasporic claims and projects at some moments or in some contexts, yet distance themselves from such claims and projects in other contexts.

6. Migration, Membership, and the Nation-State

1. To be sure, the wide spectrum of polity types found circa 1500—ranging from microprincipalities, city-states, and loose tribal confederations through emerging bureaucratic territorial polities to vast empires—narrowed substantially in succeeding centuries, thanks to the military success of centralizing bureaucratic territorial states (Tilly 1975). Convergence is evident in the tasks undertaken by states (which have everywhere assumed at least nominal responsibility for such matters as education, health, social welfare, dispute resolution, the regulation of economic life, and so on [Meyer 1987]). It is evident in certain aspects of their formal structure (characterized by what Weber [(1922) 1978:

217ff] called legal authority with a bureaucratic administrative staff). And it is evident in fundamental modes of legitimation (which generally appeal in some way to the sovereignty of "the people" or "the nation"). Yet contemporary states remain strikingly unlike in their *nation*-stateness, that is, in the extent to which and manner in which "nation" and "state" are joined. The set of nominal nation-states includes relatively monoethnic states such as Korea and Japan (both of which, however, have growing immigrant populations); states with polyethnic populations arising primarily from large-scale immigration such as Canada, Australia, and many European countries; states throughout the Americas with complex forms of polyethnicity arising from varying mixtures of Afro-descendant, indigenous, and immigrant populations; avowedly binational or multinational states such as Belgium and Spain; and complex multiethnic polities such as India, Russia, Indonesia, China, Lebanon, and Nigeria.

2. The distinction between "models of" and "models for" is borrowed from Geertz 1973: 93.

3. The distinction between categories of analysis and categories of practice is central to the work of Bourdieu (see, for example, Bourdieu 1991). It is roughly similar to the distinction between etic and emic constructs employed in anthropology and to the distinction between analytical and folk categories (Banton 1979).

4. The more recent withdrawal of the state from some modes of social provision in some countries does not represent a fundamental change in this long-term transformation.

5. The distinction between formal and informal belonging applies not only at the level of the nation-state but also at other levels of aggregation and in other sites. Formal membership of a club, church, family, or association does not entail informal acceptance; formal membership may be informally contested or subverted.

6. Chauvin and Garcés-Mascareñas (2012) note that the partial and probationary civic incorporation of undocumented immigrants is not fully captured by the opposition between formal exclusion and informal incorporation; they show that there is a significant formal dimension to their precarious incorporation, made possible by the jurisdictional complexity of the state, which creates contradictions, tensions, and ambiguities within the sphere of formal law and regulation itself.

7. On the difficulties posed by Gellner's functionalist language of "needs," see O'Leary 1998: 51ff.

8. The internal membership politics in these cases does not correspond to a reciprocal external membership politics since these marginalized minority populations do not have an external "homeland" nation-state with which they identify. Membership politics in these configurations, however, is not always devoid of an external reference. Indigenous peoples, for example, have pressed claims in various international forums in recent decades (Tsing 2007), as have Roma (Vermeersch 2005).

9. On the constitutive significance of forgetting (especially of formative moments of violence) in nation-making, see Renan (1882) 1996: 45.

10. Even where self-government is not (or not fully) recognized, it can be claimed and exercised by sub-state polities; see Cornell 2014 on the practice of self-government by indigenous peoples.

11. From a large literature, see, for example, Barry 2006; Fitzgerald 2006; Green and Weil 2007; Dufoix 2011b. On the increasing de facto and de jure tolerance of dual citizenship in Europe, see Faist 2007.

12. The discussion of the German and Korean cases draws on Brubaker and Kim 2011; for other examples, see Joppke 2005.

7. Nationalism, Ethnicity, and Modernity

1. The section heading is borrowed from Wittrock 2000. While acknowledging the multiplicity of institutional forms and cultural programs, Wittrock defends the notion of modernity as a single global condition, though he does so from a perspective different from that developed here.

2. For midcentury modernization theory and convergence arguments, see Parsons 1966; Levy 1966; Inkeles 1998 (a collection of essays written over the course of four decades).

3. On reflexivity see also Beck et al. 1994; for a critique of Beck et al., see Alexander 2006.

4. A similar argument has been made by Schmidt 2010: 514, 530. On the notion of a singular global modernity, see also Dirlik 2003.

5. As others have noted, the critical reaction against modernization theory in the 1970s and 1980s was too sweeping and tended to ignore the considerable sophistication of its leading proponents. See, for example, Alexander 1995; Martinelli 2005; Schmidt 2010.

6. I note in passing the intriguing fact, which is surely no mere coincidence, that three of the major figures in the Anglophone literature on nationalism—Hans Kohn as well as Deutsch and Gellner—were from Prague.

7. It is true that "culture," for Gellner, primarily meant language; despite his long-standing interest in the Muslim world, he gave much less attention to religion.

References

Abbott, Andrew. 1988. *The System of Professions: An Essay on the Division of Expert Labor.* Chicago: University of Chicago Press.

Aburaiya, Issam. 2009. "Islamism, Nationalism, and Western Modernity: The Case of Iran and Palestine." *International Journal of Politics, Culture, and Society* 22(1): 57–68.

Akenson, Donald H. 1992. *God's Peoples: Covenant and Land in South Africa, Israel, and Ulster.* Ithaca, NY: Cornell University Press.

Alba, Richard. 2005. "Bright vs. Blurred Boundaries: Second Generation Assimilation and Exclusion in France, Germany, and the United States." *Ethnic and Racial Studies* 28(1): 20–49.

Alba, Richard, John Logan, Amy Lutz, and Brian Stults. 2002. "Only English by the Third Generation? Loss and Preservation of the Mother Tongue among the Grandchildren of Contemporary Immigrants." *Demography* 39(3): 467–484.

Alba, Richard D., and Victor Nee. 1997. "Rethinking Assimilation Theory for a New Era of Immigration." *International Migration Review* 31(4): 826–874.

———. 2003. *Remaking the American Mainstream: Assimilation and Contemporary Immigration.* Cambridge, MA: Harvard University Press.

Alexander, Jeffrey. 1995. "Modern, Anti, Post and Neo." *New Left Review* 1(210): 63–101.

———. 2006. "Critical Reflections on 'Reflexive Modernization.'" *Theory, Culture & Society* 13: 133–138.

Alpers, Edward A. 2001. "Defining the African Diaspora." Paper presented at the Center for Comparative Social Analysis Workshop, UCLA, October 25.

Anderson, Benedict. 1991. *Imagined Communities: Reflections on the Origin and Spread of Nationalism.* London: Verso.

————. 1998. *The Spectre of Comparisons: Nationalism, Southeast Asia, and the World*. London: Verso.

Anderson, Jon W. 2003. "The Internet and Islam's New Interpreters." Pp. 45–60 in Jon W. Anderson and Dale F. Eickelman, eds., *New Media in the Muslim World*. 2nd ed. Bloomington: Indiana University Press.

Angoustures, A., and V. Pascal. 1996. "Diasporas et financement des conflits." Pp. 495–498 in J. Rufin and J. C. Rufin, eds., *Économie des guerres civiles*. Paris: Hachette.

Anthias, Floya. 1998. "Evaluating 'Diaspora': Beyond Ethnicity?" *Sociology* 32(3): 557–580.

Appadurai, Arjun. 1996. *Modernity at Large: Cultural Dimensions of Globalization*. Minneapolis: University of Minnesota Press.

Arjomand, Said Amir. 1994. "Fundamentalism, Religious Nationalism, or Populism?" *Contemporary Sociology* 23(5): 671–675.

Armstrong, John A. 1976. "Mobilized and Proletarian Diasporas." *American Political Science Review* 70(2): 393–408.

————. 1978. "Mobilized Diaspora in Tsarist Russia: The Case of the Baltic Germans." Pp. 63–104 in Jeremy Azrael, ed., *Soviet Nationality Policies and Practices*. New York: Praeger.

————. 1982. *Nations before Nationalism*. Chapel Hill: University of North Carolina Press.

Asad, Talal. 2003. *Formations of the Secular: Christianity, Islam, Modernity*. Stanford: Stanford University Press.

Ashforth, Blake E., and Glen E. Kreiner. 1999. "'How Can You Do It?' Dirty Work and the Challenge of Constructing a Positive Identity." *Academy of Management Review* 24(3): 413–434.

Axel, Brian K. 2001. *The Nation's Tortured Body*. Durham, NC: Duke University Press.

Bader, Veit. 2007. *Secularism or Democracy: Associational Governance of Religious Diversity*. Amsterdam: Amsterdam University Press.

Bakalian, Anny P. 1993. *Armenian-Americans: From Being to Feeling Armenian*. New Brunswick, NJ: Transaction.

Baker, Keith Michael. 1994. "Enlightenment and the Institution of Society." Pp. 95–120 in W. Melching and W. R. E Velema, eds., *Main Trends in Cultural History: Ten Essays*. Amsterdam: Rodopi.

Baker, Laura A., Serena Bezdjian, and Adrian Raine. 2006. "Behavioral Genetics: The Science of Antisocial Behavior." *Law and Contemporary Problems* 69(1–2): 7–46.

Banton, Michael. 1979. "Analytical and Folk Concepts of Race and Ethnicity." *Ethnic and Racial Studies* 2(2): 127–138.

————. 1998. *Racial Theories*. Cambridge, UK: Cambridge University Press.

Barbour, Stephen, and Cathie Carmichael. 2000. *Language and Nationalism in Europe*. New York: Oxford University Press.

Barkan, Elazar. 1992. *The Retreat of Scientific Racism: Changing Concepts of Race in Britain and the United States between the World Wars*. Cambridge, UK: Cambridge University Press.

Baron, James N., and William T. Bielby. 1980. "Bringing the Firms Back In: Stratification, Segmentation, and the Organization of Work." *American Sociological Review* 45(5): 737–765.

Barry, Kim. 2006. "Home and Away: The Construction of Citizenship in an Emigration Context." *NYU Law Review* 81: 11–59.

Barth, Fredrik. 1969. "Introduction." Pp. 9–38 in Fredrik Barth, ed., *Ethnic Groups and Boundaries: The Social Organization of Culture Difference*. Boston: Little, Brown.

Bauböck, Rainer. 2002. "Cultural Minority Rights in Public Education, Religious and Language Instruction for Immigrant Communities in Western Europe." Pp. 161–189 in Anthony Messina, ed., *West European Immigration and Immigrant Policy in the New Century*. Westport, CT: Greenwood Press.

———. 2003. "Reinventing Urban Citizenship." *Citizenship Studies* 7(2): 139–160.

Baumann, Gerd. 1996. *Contesting Culture: Discourses of Identity in Multi-Ethnic London*. Cambridge, UK: Cambridge University Press.

Beck, Ulrich. 2000. "The Cosmopolitan Perspective: Sociology of the Second Age of Modernity." *British Journal of Sociology* 51(1): 79–105.

Beck, Ulrich, Anthony Giddens, and Scott Lash. 1994. *Reflexive Modernization*. Cambridge, UK: Polity Press.

Bell, David Avrom. 2001. *The Cult of the Nation in France: Inventing Nationalism, 1680–1800*. Cambridge, MA: Harvard University Press.

Bellah, Robert Neelly. 1975. *The Broken Covenant: American Civil Religion in a Time of Trial*. New York: Seabury Press.

Bendix, Reinhard. 1977. *Nation-Building and Citizenship: Studies of Our Changing Social Order*. Berkeley: University of California Press.

Benjamin, Ruha. 2009. "A Lab of Their Own: Genomic Sovereignty as Postcolonial Science Policy." *Policy and Society* 28(4): 341–355.

———. 2013. "Recasting Race, Provincializing Science: Genomic Sovereignty and the Mapping and Marketing of Populations." Paper presented at Reconsidering Race: Cross-Disciplinary and Interdisciplinary Approaches, Texas A&M University, May 3.

Benton, Ted. 1991. "Biology and Social Science: Why the Return of the Repressed Should Be Given a (Cautious) Welcome." *Sociology* 25(1): 1–29.

Berger, Peter L. 1999. "The Desecularization of the World: A Global Overview." Pp. 1–18 in Peter Berger, ed., *The Desecularization of the World: Resurgent Religion and World Politics*. Washington, DC: Ethics and Public Policy Center and W. B. Eerdmans.

Berger, Peter L., and Thomas Luckmann. 1966. *The Social Construction of Reality: A Treatise in the Sociology of Knowledge*. New York: Anchor Books.

Berthier-Foglar, Susanne. 2012. "Human Genomics and the Indigenous." Pp. 3–28 in Susanne Berthier-Foglar, Sheila Collingwood-Whittick, and Sandrine Tolazzi, eds., *Biomapping Indigenous Peoples: Towards an Understanding of the Issues*. Amsterdam: Rodopi.

Berthier-Foglar, Susanne, Sheila Collingwood-Whittick, and Sandrine Tolazzi, eds. 2012. *Biomapping Indigenous Peoples: Towards an Understanding of the Issues*. Amsterdam: Rodopi.

Beyer, Peter. 2001. "What Counts as Religion in Global Society?" Pp. 125–150 in Peter Beyer, ed., *Religion in the Process of Globalization.* Würzburg, Germany: Ergon Verlag.

Bhatt, Chetan, and Parita Mukta. 2000. "Hindutva in the West: Mapping the Antinomies of Diaspora Nationalism." *Ethnic and Racial Studies* 23(3): 407–441.

Bianchi, Suzanne M., John P. Robinson, and Melissa A. Milkie. 2006. *Changing Rhythms of American Family Life.* New York: Russell Sage Foundation.

Bielby, William T., and James N. Baron. 1986. "Men and Women at Work: Sex Segregation and Statistical Discrimination." *American Journal of Sociology* 91(4): 759–799.

Blair-Loy, Mary. 2003. *Competing Devotions: Career and Family among Women Executives.* Cambridge, MA: Harvard University Press.

Blau, Francine D., and Lawrence M. Kahn. 2007. "The Gender Pay Gap: Have Women Gone as Far as They Can?" *Academy of Management Perspectives* 21(1): 7–23.

Blau, Peter Michael. 1977. *Inequality and Heterogeneity: A Primitive Theory of Social Structure.* New York: Free Press.

Bliss, Catherine. 2012. *Race Decoded: The Genomic Fight for Social Justice.* Stanford: Stanford University Press.

Bloch, Maurice. 1996. "Religion and Ritual." Pp. 732–736 in Adam Kuper and Jessica Kuper, eds., *The Social Science Encyclopedia.* London: Routledge.

Bolnick, Deborah A. 2003. "Showing Who They Really Are: Commercial Ventures in Genetic Genealogy." Paper presented at American Anthropological Association Annual Meeting, Chicago, November 22.

———. 2008. "Individual Ancestry Inference and the Reification of Race as a Biological Phenomenon." Pp. 70–88 in Barbara A. Koenig, Sandra Soo-Jin Lee, and Sarah S. Richardson, eds., *Revisiting Race in a Genomic Age.* Rutgers Series in Medical Anthropology. New Brunswick, NJ: Rutgers University Press.

Bonacich, Edna. 1973. "A Theory of Middleman Minorities." *American Sociological Review* 38: 583–594.

Bone, John. 2009. "Beyond Biophobia: A Response to Jackson and Rees," *Sociology* 43(6): 1181–1190.

Bonifas, Gilbert. 2008. "Reconceptualizing Britishness on the Far Right: An Analysis of the British National Party's Identity Magazine." *Cycnos* 25(2). Retrieved November 23, 2013. http://revel.unice.fr/cycnos/index.html?id=6203.

Bourdieu, Pierre. 1974. "Avenir de classe et causalité du probable." *Revue française de sociologie* 15(1): 3–42.

———. 1987. "La Codification." Pp. 94–105 in *Choses dites.* Paris: Editions de Minuit.

———. 1990. *The Logic of Practice.* Stanford: Stanford University Press.

———. 1991. *Language and Symbolic Power.* Cambridge, MA: Harvard University Press.

———. 2000. *Pascalian Meditations.* Stanford: Stanford University Press.

———. 2001. *Masculine Domination.* Stanford: Stanford University Press.

Boyarin, Daniel, and Jonathan Boyarin. 1993. "Diaspora: Generation and the Ground of Jewish Identity." *Critical Inquiry* 19: 693–725.

Braun, Lundy. 2006. "Reifying Human Difference: The Debate on Genetics, Race, and Health." *International Journal of Health Services: Planning, Administration, Evaluation* 36(3): 557–573.

Breuilly, John. 1994. *Nationalism and the State.* 2nd ed. Chicago: University of Chicago Press.

Brodwin, Paul. 2002. "Genetics, Identity, and the Anthropology of Essentialism." *Anthropological Quarterly* 75: 323–330.

Brubaker, Rogers. 1985. "Rethinking Classical Theory: The Sociological Vision of Pierre Bourdieu." *Theory and Society* 14: 745–775.

———. 1989. "Membership without Citizenship: The Economic and Social Rights of Noncitizens." Pp. 145–162 in Rogers Brubaker, ed., *Immigration and the Politics of Citizenship in Europe and North America.* Lanham, MD: German Marshall Fund of the United States and University Press of America.

———. 1990. "Immigration, Citizenship, and the Nation-state in France and Germany." *International Sociology* 5(4): 379–407.

———. 1992. *Citizenship and Nationhood in France and Germany.* Cambridge, MA: Harvard University Press.

———. 1994. "Are Immigration Control Efforts Really Failing?" Pp. 227–231 in Wayne A. Cornelius, Philip L. Martin, and James F. Hollifield, eds., *Controlling Immigration: A Global Perspective.* Stanford: Stanford University Press.

———. 1996. *Nationalism Reframed: Nationhood and the National Question in the New Europe.* Cambridge, UK: Cambridge University Press.

———. 1998. "Migrations of Ethnic Unmixing in the New Europe." *International Migration Review* 32(4): 1047–1065.

———. 2000. "Accidental Diasporas and External 'Homelands' in Central and Eastern Europe: Past and Present." Institute for Advanced Studies, Vienna, Political Science Series no. 71.

———. 2001. "The Return of Assimilation?" *Ethnic and Racial Studies* 24(4): 531–548.

———. 2002. "Ethnicity without Groups." *Archives européenes de sociologie* 43(2): 163–189.

———. 2004. *Ethnicity without Groups.* Cambridge, MA: Harvard University Press.

———. 2009. "Ethnicity, Race, and Nationalism." *Annual Review of Sociology* 35(1): 21–42.

———. 2011a. "Economic Crisis, Nationalism, and Politicized Ethnicity." Pp. 93–108 in Craig Calhoun and Georgi Derluguian, eds., *The Deepening Crisis: Governance Challenges after Neoliberalism.* New York: Social Science Research Council and NYU Press.

———. 2011b. "Nationalizing States Revisited: Projects and Processes of Nationalization in Post-Soviet States." *Ethnic and Racial Studies* 34: 1785–1814.

———. 2012. "Principles of Vision and Division and Cohort Succession: Macrocognitive and Demographic Perspectives on Social Change." Paper presented to Successful Societies Research Program, Canadian Institute for Advanced Research, May 12.

———. 2013. "Categories of analysis and categories of practice: a note on the study of Muslims in European countries of immigration." *Ethnic and Racial Studies* 36: 1–8.

———. 2014. "Beyond Ethnicity." *Ethnic and Racial Studies* 37(5): 804–808.

———. Forthcoming. "Linguistic and Religious Pluralism: Between Difference and Inequality." *Journal of Ethnic and Migration Studies.*

Brubaker, Rogers, and Frederick Cooper. 2000. "Beyond 'Identity.' " *Theory and Society* 29(1): 1–47.

Brubaker, Rogers, Margit Feischmidt, Jon Fox, and Liana Grancea. 2006. *Nationalist Politics and Everyday Ethnicity in a Transylvanian Town.* Princeton, NJ: Princeton University Press.

Brubaker, Rogers, and Jaeeun Kim. 2011. "Transborder Membership Politics in Germany and Korea." *Archives européennes de sociologie/European Journal of Sociology* 52(1): 21–75.

Brubaker, Rogers, Mara Loveman, and Peter Stamatov. 2004. "Ethnicity as Cognition." *Theory and Society* 33(1): 31–64.

Brunham, Liam R., and Michael R. Hayden. 2012. "Whole-Genome Sequencing: The New Standard of Care?" *Science* 336(6085): 1112–1113.

Budig, Michelle J., and Paula England. 2001. "The Wage Penalty for Motherhood." *American Sociological Review* 66(2): 204–225.

Burbank, Jane, and Frederick Cooper. 2010. *Empires in World History: Power and the Politics of Difference.* Princeton, NJ: Princeton University Press.

Bureau of Labor Statistics, Department of Labor. 2012. *Highlights of Women's Earnings in 2011.* Retrieved December 13, 2013. http://www.bls.gov/cps/cps wom2011.pdf.

Burke, Wiley, and Bruce M. Psaty. 2007. "Personalized Medicine in the Era of Genomics." *JAMA: The Journal of the American Medical Association* 298(14): 1682–1684.

Buss, William. 1989. "Discrimination by Private Clubs." *Washington University Law Review* 67(3): 815–853.

Calavita, Kitty. 2000. "The Paradoxes of Race, Class, Identity, and 'Passing': Enforcing the Chinese Exclusion Acts, 1882–1910." *Law & Social Inquiry* 25(1): 1–40.

Calhoun, Craig. 1997. *Nationalism.* Minneapolis: University of Minnesota Press.

Caplan, Jane, and John Torpey, eds. 2001. *Documenting Individual Identity: The Development of State Practices in the Modern World.* Princeton, NJ: Princeton University Press.

Carens, Joseph H. 1987. "Aliens and Citizens: The Case for Open Borders." *Review of Politics* 49(2): 251–273.

———. 2000. *Culture, Citizenship, and Community.* Oxford: Oxford University Press.

Casanova, José. 1994. *Public Religions in the Modern World.* Chicago: University of Chicago Press.

———. 2009. "Religion, Politics and Gender Equality: Public Religions Revisited." Pp. 2–33 in *A Debate on the Public Role of Religion and Its Social and Gender Implications*. Gender and Development Programme Paper 5. Geneva: United Nations Research Institute for Social Development.

Caspi, Avshalom, et al. 2002. "Role of Genotype in the Cycle of Violence in Maltreated Children." *Science* 297(5582): 851–854.

Castles, Stephen, and Mark J. Miller. 1998. *The Age of Migration: International Population Movements in the Modern World*. 2nd ed. New York: Guilford Press.

Cesari, Jocelyne. 2002. "Islam in France: The Shaping of a Religious Minority." Pp. 36–51 in Yvonne Haddad-Yazbek, ed., *Muslims in the West, from Sojourners to Citizens*. New York: Oxford University Press.

Charles, Maria, and Karen Bradley. 2009. "Indulging Our Gendered Selves? Sex Segregation by Field of Study in 44 Countries." *American Journal of Sociology* 114(4): 924–976.

Charles, Maria, and David B. Grusky. 2004. *Occupational Ghettos: The Worldwide Segregation of Women and Men*. Stanford: Stanford University Press.

Charney, Evan. 2012. "Behavior Genetics and Postgenomics." *Behavioral and Brain Sciences* 35(5): 331–358.

Charney, Evan, and William English. 2012. "Candidate Genes and Political Behavior." *American Political Science Review* 106(1): 1–34.

Chatterjee, Partha. 1986. *Nationalist Thought and the Colonial World: A Derivative Discourse?* London: Zed Books.

Chauvin, Sébastien, and Blanca Garcés-Mascareñas. 2012. "Beyond Informal Citizenship: The New Moral Economy of Migrant Illegality." *International Political Sociology* 6(3): 241–259.

Clifford, James. 1994. "Diasporas." *Cultural Anthropology* 9(3): 302–338.

Cohen, Abner. 1971. "Cultural Strategies in the Organization of Trading Diasporas." Pp. 266–284 in Claude Meillassoux, ed., *The Development of Indigenous Trade and Markets*. London: Oxford University Press.

Cohen, Robin. 1992. "The Diaspora of a Diaspora: The Case of the Caribbean." *Social Science Information* 31(1): 159–169.

———. 1997. *Global Diasporas: An Introduction*. Seattle: University of Washington Press.

———. 2009. "Solid, Ductile and Liquid: Changing Notions of Homeland and Home in Diaspora Studies." Pp. 117–133 in Eliezer Ben Rafael and Yitzak Sternberg, eds., *Transnationalism: Diasporas and the Advent of a New (Dis)order*. Boston: Brill.

Collingwood-Whittick. 2012. "Indigenous Opposition to Genetics." Pp. 295–328 in Susanne Berthier-Foglar, Sheila Collingwood-Whittick, and Sandrine Tolazzi, eds., *Biomapping Indigenous Peoples: Towards an Understanding of the Issues*. Amsterdam: Rodopi.

Comaroff, John L., and Jean Comaroff. 2009. *Ethnicity, Inc*. Chicago: University of Chicago Press.

Condit, Celeste Michelle. 1999. *The Meanings of the Gene: Public Debates about Human Heredity*. Madison: University of Wisconsin Press.

Connor, Walker. 1986. "The Impact of Homelands upon Diasporas." Pp. 16–46 in Gabriel Sheffer, ed., *Modern Diasporas in International Politics.* London: Croom Helm.

Cooper, R., and R. David. 1986. "The Biological Concept of Race and Its Application to Public Health and Epidemiology." *Journal of Health Politics, Policy and Law* 11(1): 97–116.

Cornell, Stephen. 1996. "The Variable Ties That Bind: Content and Circumstance in Ethnic Processes." *Ethnic and Racial Studies* 19(2): 265–289.

Cornell, Stephen. "Processes of Native Nationhood: The Indigenous Politics of Self-Government." 2014. Paper presented at Workshop on "Ethnocultural Diversity, Religious Freedom and Forms of Claims-Making," Center for American Political Studies, Harvard University, March 28.

Cornell, Stephen E., and Douglas Hartmann. 1998. *Ethnicity and Race: Making Identities in a Changing World.* Thousand Oaks, CA: Pine Forge Press.

Curtin, Philip D. 1984. *Cross-Cultural Trade in World History.* Cambridge, UK: Cambridge University Press.

D'Andrade, Roy G. 1995. *The Development of Cognitive Anthropology.* Cambridge, UK: Cambridge University Press.

Dao, James. 2011. "In California, Indian Tribes With Casino Money Cast Off Members." *New York Times,* December 12. Retrieved January 2, 2012. http://www.nytimes.com/2011/12/13/us/california-indian-tribes-eject-thousands-of-members.html.

Davis, Dena S. 2004. "Genetic Research and Communal Narratives." *Hastings Center Report* 34(4): 40–49.

Degler, Carl N. 1991. *In Search of Human Nature: The Decline and Revival of Darwinism in American Social Thought.* New York: Oxford University Press.

Deutsch, Karl. 1953. *Nationalism and Social Communication: An Inquiry into the Foundations of Nationality.* Cambridge, MA: Technology Press of the Massachusetts Institute of Technology and Wiley.

Diehl, Claudia, and Matthias Koenig. 2009. "Religiosität türkischer Migranten im Generationenverlauf: Ein Befund und einige Erklärungsversuche." *Zeitschrift für Soziologie* 38(4): 300–319.

DiMaggio, Paul. 1997. "Culture and Cognition." *Annual Review of Sociology* 23(1): 263–287.

DiMaggio, Paul, and Filiz Garip. 2012. "Network Effects and Social Inequality." *Annual Review of Sociology* 38(1): 93–118.

Dirlik, Arif. 2003. "Global Modernity? Modernity in an Age of Global Capitalism." *European Journal of Social Theory* 6(3): 275–292.

Douglas, Mary. 1994. *Purity and Danger: An Analysis of the Concepts of Pollution and Taboo.* New York: Routledge.

Drew, Shirley K., Melanie Mills, and Bob M. Gassaway. 2007. *Dirty Work: The Social Construction of Taint.* Waco, TX: Baylor University Press.

Duderija, Adis. 2007. "Literature Review: Identity Construction in the Context of Being a Minority Immigrant Religion: The Case of Western-Born Muslims." *Immigrants & Minorities* 25(2): 141–162.

Dufoix, Stéphane. 2007. "Diasporas." Pp. 311–316 in Roland Robertson and Jan Aart Scholte, eds., *Encyclopedia of Globalization,* vol. 1. New York: Routledge.

———. 2008. *Diasporas.* Berkeley: University of California Press.

———. 2011a. *La dispersion: Une histoire des usages du mot diaspora.* Paris: Éditions Amsterdam.

———. 2011b. "From Nationals Abroad to 'Diaspora': The Rise and Progress of Extra-Territorial and Over-State Nations." *Diaspora Studies* 4(1): 1–20.

Dunn, L. C., and Theodosius Dobzhansky. 1952. *Heredity, Race, and Society.* New York: Penguin.

Durkheim, Emile. 1995. *The Elementary Forms of Religious Life.* New York: Free Press.

Duster, Troy. 2003. *Backdoor to Eugenics.* 2nd ed. New York: Routledge.

Eckstein, Susan, and Thanh-Nghi Nguyen. 2011. "The Making and Transnationalization of an Ethnic Niche: Vietnamese Manicurists." *International Migration Review* 45(3): 639–674.

Edwards, Brent H. 2001. "The Uses of *Diaspora.*" *Social Text* 19(1): 45–73.

Egorova, Yulia. 2009. "De/geneticizing Caste: Population Genetic Research in South Asia." *Science as Culture* 18(4): 417–434.

———. 2010. "Castes of Genes? Representing Human Genetic Diversity in India." *Life Sciences, Society and Policy* 6(3): 32.

Eisenstadt, S. N. 2000. "Multiple Modernities." *Daedalus* 129(1): 1–29.

El-Haj, Nadia. 2007. "The Genetic Reinscription of Race." *Annual Review of Anthropology* 36: 283–300.

Ellison, George T. H., et al. 2008. "Flaws in the U.S. Food and Drug Administration's Rationale for Supporting the Development and Approval of BiDil as a Treatment for Heart Failure Only in Black Patients." *Journal of Law, Medicine & Ethics* 36(3): 449–457.

Emirbayer, Mustafa, and Matthew Desmond. Forthcoming. *The Racial Order.* Chicago: University of Chicago Press.

Emirbayer, Mustafa, and Jeff Goodwin. 1994. "Network Analysis, Culture, and the Problem of Agency." *American Journal of Sociology* 99(6): 1411–1454.

England, Paula. 1992. "From Status Attainment to Segregation and Devaluation." *Contemporary Sociology* 21(5): 643–647.

England, Paula, George Farkas, Barbara Stanek Kilbourne, and Thomas Dou. 1988. "Explaining Occupational Sex Segregation and Wages: Findings from a Model with Fixed Effects." *American Sociological Review* 53(4): 544–558.

England, Paula, Joan Hermsen, and David A. Cotter. 2000. "The Devaluation of Women's Work: A Comment on Tam." *American Journal of Sociology* 105(6): 1741–1751.

Epstein, Steven. 2007. *Inclusion: The Politics of Difference in Medical Research.* Chicago: University of Chicago Press.

Ersanilli, Evelyn, and Ruud Koopmans. 2009. "Ethnic Retention and Host Culture Adoption among Turkish Immigrants in Germany, France and the Netherlands:

A Controlled Comparison." Working Paper, Social Science Research Center, Berlin.

Faist, Thomas, ed. 2007. *Dual Citizenship in Europe: From Nationhood to Societal Integration.* Aldershot, UK: Ashgate.

Fallers, Lloyd A. 1962. "Comments on 'The Lebanese in West Africa.'" *Comparative Studies in Society and History* 4(3): 334–336.

Falzon, Mark-Anthony. 2003. "'Bombay, Our Cultural Heart': Rethinking the Relation between Homeland and Diaspora." *Ethnic and Racial Studies* 26(4): 662–683.

Favell, Adrian. 2001. "Migration, Mobility and Globaloney: Metaphors and Rhetoric in the Sociology of Globalization." *Global Networks* 1(4): 389–398.

Federal Bureau of Investigation. 2013. "CODIS—NDIS Statistics." Retrieved October 18, 2013. http://www.fbi.gov/about-us/lab/biometric-analysis/codis/ndis-statistics.

Feldman, Marcus W., and Richard C. Lewontin. 2008. "Race, Ancestry, and Medicine." Pp. 89–101 in Barbara A. Koenig, Sandra Soo-Jin Lee, and Sarah S. Richardson, eds., *Revisiting Race in a Genomic Age.* New Brunswick, NJ: Rutgers University Press.

Fishman, Joshua. 1966. "Language Maintenance in a Supra-ethnic Age: Summary and Conclusions." Pp. 392–411 in Joshua Fishman et al., *Language Loyalty in the United States.* The Hague: Mouton, 1966.

Fiske, Susan T. 1998. "Stereotyping, Prejudice and Discrimination." Pp. 357–411 in D. T. Gilbert, S. T. Fiske, and G. Lindzey, eds., *Handbook of Social Psychology,* 4th ed., vol. 2. New York: McGraw-Hill.

Fitzgerald, David. 2006. "Rethinking Emigrant Citizenship." *New York University Law Review* 81(1): 90–116.

———. 2009. *A Nation of Emigrants: How Mexico Manages Its Migration.* Berkeley: University of California Press.

Fligstein, Neil. 2008. *Euroclash: The EU, European Identity, and the Future of Europe.* New York: Oxford University Press.

Fortier, Anne-Marie. 2012. "Genetic Indigenisation in 'The People of the British Isles.'" *Science as Culture* 21(2): 153–175.

Foucault, Michel. 1984. "Le pouvoir, comment s'exerce-t-il?" Pp. 308–321 in Hubert Dreyfus and Paul Rabinow, eds., *Michel Foucault, un parcours philosophique: Au-delà de l'objectivité et de la subjectivité.* Paris: Gallimard.

Fox, Dov. 2010. "The Second Generation of Racial Profiling." *American Journal of Criminal Law* 38: 49.

Fraser, Nancy. 1995. "From Redistribution to Recognition? Dilemmas of Justice in a 'Post-Socialist' Age." *New Left Review* 1(212): 68–93.

Freeman, Gary P. 1994. "Can Liberal States Control Unwanted Migration?" *Annals of the American Academy of Political and Social Science* 534: 17–30.

Freese, Jeremy. 2008. "Genetics and the Social Science Explanation of Individual Outcomes." *American Journal of Sociology* 114(S1): S1–S35.

Freese, Jeremy, Jui-Chung Allen Li, and Lisa D. Wade. 2003. "The Potential Relevances of Biology to Social Inquiry." *Annual Review of Sociology* 29: 233–256.

Friedland, Roger. 2002. "Money, Sex, and God: The Erotic Logic of Religious Nationalism." *Sociological Theory* 20(3): 381–425.

Frudakis, Tony Nick. 2008. *Molecular Photofitting: Predicting Ancestry and Phenotype Using DNA.* Amsterdam: Elsevier and Academic Press.

Fujimura, Joan H., Troy Duster, and Ramya Rajagopalan. 2008. "Introduction: Race, Genetics, and Disease Questions of Evidence, Matters of Consequence." *Social Studies of Science* 38(5): 643–656.

Fujimura, Joan H., Ramya Rajagopalan, Pilar N. Ossorio, and Kjell A. Doksum. 2010. "Race and Ancestry: Operationalizing Population in Human Genetic Variation Studies." Pp. 169–183 in I. Whitmarsh and D. S. Jones, eds., *What's the Use of Race? Modern Governance and the Biology of Difference.* Cambridge, MA: MIT Press.

Fukase-Indergaard, Fumiko, and Michael Indergaard. 2008. "Religious Nationalism and the Making of the Modern Japanese State." *Theory and Society* 37(4): 343–374.

Fukuyama, Francis. 1992. *The End of History and the Last Man.* New York: Free Press.

Fullwiley, Duana. 2008. "The Biologistical Construction of Race 'Admixture' Technology and the New Genetic Medicine." *Social Studies of Science* 38(5): 695–735.

Gabaccia, Donna R. 2000. *Italy's Many Diasporas.* London: UCL Press.

Gal, Susan. 1989. "Language and Political Economy." *Annual Review of Anthropology* 18: 345–367.

Galston, William A. 1995. "Two Concepts of Liberalism." *Ethics* 105(3): 516–534.

Gannett, Lisa. 2001. "Racism and Human Genome Diversity Research: The Ethical Limits of 'Population Thinking.' " *Philosophy of Science* 68(3): S479–S492.

———. 2004. "The Biological Reification of Race." *British Journal for the Philosophy of Science* 55(2): 323–345.

Gans, Herbert J. 1979. "Symbolic Ethnicity: The Future of Ethnic Groups and Cultures in America." *Ethnic and Racial Studies* 2(1): 1–20.

———. 1994. "Symbolic Ethnicity and Symbolic Religiosity: Towards a Comparison of Ethnic and Religious Acculturation." *Ethnic and Racial Studies* 17(4): 577–592.

Gauchet, Marcel. 1997. *The Disenchantment of the World: A Political History of Religion.* Princeton, NJ: Princeton University Press.

Geertz, Clifford. 1963. "The Integrative Revolution: Primordial Sentiments and Politics in the New States." Pp. 105–157 in Clifford Geertz, ed., *Old Societies and New States: The Quest for Modernity in Asia and Africa.* New York: Free Press.

———. 1973. *The Interpretation of Cultures.* New York: Basic Books.

Gellner, Ernest. (1964) 1974. "Nationalism." Pp. 147–178 in *Thought and Change.* Chicago: University of Chicago Press.

———. 1983. *Nations and Nationalism.* Ithaca, NY: Cornell University Press.

———. 1994. *Encounters with Nationalism.* Oxford: Blackwell.

————. 1997. "Reply to Critics." *New Left Review* 1(221): 81–118.

German Islam Conference. 2009. "Interim Résumé by the Working Groups and the Round Table." Paper for the Fourth Plenary Session of the German Islam Conference, Berlin, June 25. Retrieved April 5, 2012. http://www.deutsche-islam -konferenz.de/SharedDocs/Anlagen/DIK/EN/Downloads/Plenum/DIK-viertes -Plenum-en.pdf?__blob=publicationFile

Geyer, Michael, and Hartmut Lehmann, eds. 2004. *Religion und Nation, Nation und Religion*. Göttingen: Wallstein Verlag.

Gilroy, Paul. 1997. "Diaspora and the Detours of Identity." Pp. 299–343 in Kathryn Woodward, ed., *Identity and Difference*. London: Sage Publications and Open University.

————. 2000. *Against Race: Imagining Political Culture beyond the Color Line*. Cambridge, MA: Belknap Press of Harvard University Press.

Ginsburg, Geoffrey S., and Huntington F. Willard. 2009. "Genomic and Personalized Medicine: Foundations and Applications." *Translational Research* 154(6): 277–287.

Gissis, Snait B. 2008. "When Is 'Race' a Race? 1946–2003." *Studies in History and Philosophy of Biological and Biomedical Sciences* 39(4): 437–450.

Glazer, Nathan, and Daniel Patrick Moynihan. 1963. *Beyond the Melting Pot: The Negroes, Puerto Ricans, Jews, Italians, and Irish of New York City*. Cambridge, MA: MIT Press.

Gleason, Philip. 1983. "Identifying Identity: A Semantic History." *Journal of American History* 69(4): 910–931.

Glick Schiller, Nina, Linda Basch, and Cristina Szanton Blanc. 1995. "From Immigrant to Transmigrant: Theorizing Transnational Migration." *Anthropological Quarterly* 68: 43–63.

Glynn, Sarah. 2002. "Bengali Muslims: The New East End Radicals?" *Ethnic and Racial Studies* 25(6): 969–988.

Godechot, Olivier. 2007. *Working Rich: Salaires, bonus et appropriation du profit dans l'industrie financière*. Paris: La Découverte.

Goffman, Alice. 2009. "On the Run: Wanted Men in a Philadelphia Ghetto." *American Sociological Review* 74(3): 339–357.

————. 2014. *On the Run: Fugitive Life in an American City*. Chicago: University of Chicago Press.

Goffman, Erving. 1956. "The Nature of Deference and Demeanor." *American Anthropologist* 58(3): 473–502.

Golbeck, Natasha, and Wendy Roth. 2012. "Aboriginal Claims: DNA Ancestry Testing and Changing Concepts of Indigeneity." Pp. 415–432 in Susanne Berthier-Foglar, Sheila Collingwood-Whittick, and Sandrine Tolazzi, eds., *Biomapping Indigenous Peoples: Towards an Understanding of the Issues*. Amsterdam and New York: Rodopi.

Goldschmidt, Henry. 2003. "Jews and Others in Brooklyn and Its Diaspora: Constructing an Unlikely Homeland in a Diasporic World." Proceedings of the symposium Diaspora: Movement, Memory, Politics and Identity, Columbia International Affairs Online Working Papers. Retrieved January 30, 2014. http://www.ciaonet.org/wps/goho1/goho1.pdf.

Goldstein, David B., Sarah K. Tate, and Sanjay M. Sisodiya. 2003. "Pharmacogenetics Goes Genomic." *Nature Reviews Genetics* 4(12): 937–947.

Goldthorpe, J. H., and K. Hope. 1972. "Occupational Grading and Occupational Prestige." *Social Science Information* 11(5): 17–73.

Gorski, Philip S. 2000a. "Historicizing the Secularization Debate: Church, State, and Society in Late Medieval and Early Modern Europe, ca. 1300 to 1700." *American Sociological Review* 65(1): 138–167.

———. 2000b. "The Mosaic Moment: An Early Modernist Critique of Modernist Theories of Nationalism." *American Journal of Sociology* 105(5): 1428–1468.

———. 2003. *The Disciplinary Revolution: Calvinism and the Rise of the State in Early Modern Europe.* Chicago: University of Chicago Press.

Gorski, Philip S., and Ates Altinordu. 2008. "After Secularization?" *Annual Review of Sociology* 34: 55–85.

Gravlee, Clarence C. 2009. "How Race Becomes Biology: Embodiment of Social Inequality." *American Journal of Physical Anthropology* 139: 47–57.

Greely, Henry T. 2008. "Genetic Genealogy: Genetics Meets the Marketplace." Pp. 215–252 in Barbara A. Koenig, Sandra Soo-Jin Lee, and Sarah S. Richardson, eds., *Revisiting Race in a Genomic Age.* Rutgers Series in Medical Anthropology. New Brunswick, NJ: Rutgers University Press.

Green, Nancy L., and Francois Weil, eds. 2007. *Citizenship and Those Who Leave: The Politics of Emigration and Expatriation.* Urbana: University of Illinois Press.

Greenawalt, Kent. 2006. *Religion and the Constitution.* Vol. 1: *Free Exercise and Fairness.* Princeton, NJ: Princeton University Press.

Greenfeld, Liah. 1992. *Nationalism: Five Roads to Modernity.* Cambridge, MA: Harvard University Press.

Grusky, David B. 2012. "What to Do about Inequality." *Boston Review,* March 1. Retrieved January 2, 2014. http://www.bostonreview.net/grusky-forum-inequality.

Habermas, Jürgen. 2008. "Notes on Post-Secular Society." *New Perspectives Quarterly* 25(4): 17–29.

Hacker, Jacob S., and Paul Pierson. 2010. *Winner-Take-All Politics: How Washington Made the Rich Richer—and Turned Its Back on the Middle Class.* New York: Simon and Schuster.

Hacking, Ian. 2005. "Why Race Still Matters." *Daedalus* 134: 102–116.

———. 2006. "Genetics, Biosocial Groups and the Future of Identity." *Daedalus* 135(4): 81–95.

———. 2009. "Humans, Aliens and Autism." *Daedalus* 138(3): 44–59.

Hall, Stuart. 1990. "Cultural Identity and Diaspora." Pp. 222–237 in Jonathan Rutherford, ed., *Identity: Community, Culture, Difference.* London: Lawrence & Wishart.

Handley, Lori J. Lawson, Andrea Manica, Jérôme Goudet, and François Balloux. 2007. "Going the Distance: Human Population Genetics in a Clinal World." *Trends in Genetics* 23(9): 432–439.

Harmon, Amy. 2006. "Seeking Ancestry in DNA Ties Uncovered by Tests." *New York Times,* April 12. Retrieved November 25, 2013. http://www.nytimes.com/2006/04/12/us/12genes.html.

Hastings, Adrian. 1997. *The Construction of Nationhood: Ethnicity, Religion, and Nationalism*. Cambridge, UK: Cambridge University Press.

Haugen, Einar. 1966. "Dialect, Language, Nation." *American Anthropologist* 68(4): 922–935.

Haupt, Heinz Gerhard, and Dieter Langewiesche, eds. 2004. *Nation und Religion in Europa*. Frankfurt: Campus.

Hayes, Carlton J. H. 1926. *Essays on Nationalism*. New York: Macmillan.

Hechter, Michael. 2000. *Containing Nationalism*. Oxford: Oxford University Press.

Hegewisch, Ariane, et al. 2010. "Separate and Not Equal? Gender Segregation in the Labor Market and the Gender Wage Gap." Institution for Women's Policy Research Briefing Paper, IWPR C377. Retrieved July 24, 2013. http://www.iwpr.org/publications/pubs/separate-and-not-equal-gender-segregation-in-the-labor-market-and-the-gender-wage-gap.

Held, David, Anthony McGrew, David Goldblatt, and Jonathan Perraton. 1999. *Global Transformations: Politics, Economics, and Culture*. Stanford: Stanford University Press.

Herberg, Will. 1960. *Protestant, Catholic, Jew: An Essay in American Religious Sociology*. Garden City, NY: Anchor Books.

Hiers, Wesley. 2013. "American Ethnocracy: Origins and Development of Legal Racial Exclusion in Comparative Perspective, 1600s to 1900s." PhD dissertation, University of California, Los Angeles.

Hill, Christopher. 1993. *The English Bible and the Seventeenth-Century Revolution*. London: Allen Lane.

Hirschl, Ran, and Ayelet Shachar. 2009. "The New Wall of Separation: Permitting Diversity, Restricting Competition." *Cardozo Law Review* 30: 2535–2560.

Hirschman, Charles. 2004. "The Role of Religion in the Origins and Adaptations of Immigrant Groups in the United States." *International Migration Review* 38(3): 1206–1233.

Hirschman, Elizabeth C., and Donald Panther-Yates. 2008. "Peering Inward for Ethnic Identity: Consumer Interpretation of DNA Test Results." *Identity: An International Journal of Theory and Research* 8: 47–66.

Hirst, Paul, and Grahame Thompson. 1999. *Globalization in Question*. 2nd ed. Cambridge, UK: Polity Press.

Hobsbawm, Eric J. 1990. *Nations and Nationalism since 1780*. Cambridge, UK: Cambridge University Press.

Hochschild, Jennifer L., and Maya Sen. 2012. "Sharpening or Blurring: The Impact of Genomic Ancestry Testing on Americans' Racial Identity." Working Paper, Harvard University and University of Rochester. Retrieved November 9, 2013. http://papers.ssrn.com/sol3/papers.cfm?abstract_id=1917384.

Hochschild, Jennifer L., Vesla M. Weaver, and Traci R. Burch. 2012. *Creating a New Racial Order: How Immigration, Multiracialism, Genomics, and the Young Can Remake Race in America*. Princeton, NJ: Princeton University Press.

Hollinger, David A. 1995. *Postethnic America: Beyond Multiculturalism*. New York: Basic Books.

————. 1998. "Nationalism, Cosmopolitanism, and the United States." Pp. 85–89 in Noah M. J. Pickus, ed., *Immigration and Citizenship in the Twenty-First Century*. Lanham, MD: Rowman and Littlefield.

Horowitz, Donald L. 1985. *Ethnic Groups in Conflict*. Berkeley: University of California Press.

Hughes, Everett C. 1958. *Men and Their Work*. Glencoe, IL: Free Press.

Huizinga, David, et al. 2006. "Childhood Maltreatment, Subsequent Antisocial Behavior, and the Role of Monoamine Oxidase A Genotype." *Biological Psychiatry* 60(7): 677–683.

Huntington, Samuel P. 2004. "The Hispanic Challenge." *Foreign Policy* (141): 30–45.

Hurenkamp, Menno, Evelien Tonkens, and Jan Willem Duyvendak. 2012. *Crafting Citizenship: Negotiating Tensions in Modern Society*. New York: Macmillan.

Hutchison, William R., and Hartmut Lehmann, eds. 1994. *Many Are Chosen: Divine Election and Western Nationalisms*. Minneapolis: Fortress Press.

Hyman, Steven E. 2009. "How Adversity Gets under the Skin." *Nature Neuroscience* 12(3): 241–243.

Inkeles, Alex. 1998. *One World Emerging? Convergence and Divergence in Industrial Societies*. Boulder, CO: Westview Press.

International Organization for Migration. 2013. "World Migration Report 2013." Geneva: International Organization for Migration. http://publications.iom.int/bookstore/free/WMR2013_EN.pdf.

Itzigsohn, Jose. 2000. "Immigration and the Boundaries of Citizenship: The Institutions of Immigrants' Political Transnationalism." *Immigration and the Boundaries of Citizenship* 34(4): 1126–1154.

Jackson, Robert Max. 1998. *Destined for Equality: The Inevitable Rise of Women's Status*. Cambridge, MA: Harvard University Press.

Jenkins, Richard. 1996. *Social Identity*. London: Routledge.

————. 1997. *Rethinking Ethnicity: Arguments and Explorations*. London: Sage.

Jenkins, Stephen P., and John Micklewright. 2007. *New Directions in the Analysis of Inequality and Poverty*. Rochester, NY: Social Science Research Network. Retrieved January 2, 2014. http://papers.ssrn.com/sol3/papers.cfm?abstract_id=995502.

Jeung, Russell, Carolyn Chen, and Jerry Z. Park. 2012. "Introduction: Religious, Racial, and Ethnic Identities of the New Second Generation." Pp. 1–22 in *Sustaining Faith Traditions: Race, Ethnicity, and Religion among the Latino and Asian American Second Generation*, edited by Carolyn Chen and Russell Jeung. New York and London: NYU Press.

Joppke, Christian. 2003. "Citizenship between De- and Re-ethnicization." *European Journal of Sociology* 44(3): 429–458.

————. 2004. "The Retreat of Multiculturalism in the Liberal State: Theory and Policy." *British Journal of Sociology* 55(2): 237–257.

————. 2005. *Selecting by Origin: Ethnic Migration in the Liberal State*. Cambridge, MA: Harvard University Press.

———. 2007. "State Neutrality and Islamic Headscarf Laws in France and Germany." *Theory and Society* 36(4): 313–342.

———. 2009. *Veil: Mirror of Identity.* Cambridge, UK: Polity Press.

———. 2013. "Double Standards? Veils and Crucifixes in the European Legal Order." *European Journal of Sociology / Archives Européennes de Sociologie* 54(1): 97–123.

Joppke, Christian, and John Torpey. 2013. *Legal Integration of Islam: A Transatlantic Comparison.* Cambridge, MA: Harvard University Press.

Jordan, Miriam. 2008. "Refugee Program Halted as DNA Tests Show Fraud." *Wall Street Journal,* August 20. Retrieved November 5, 2012. http://online.wsj.com /article/SB121919647430755373.html?mod=googlenews_wsj.

Juergensmeyer, Mark. 1993. *The New Cold War? Religious Nationalism Confronts the Secular State.* Berkeley: University of California Press.

Kahn, Jonathan. 2004. "How a Drug Becomes 'Ethnic': Law, Commerce, and the Production of Racial Categories in Medicine." *Yale Journal of Health Policy, Law, and Ethics* 4(1): 1–46.

———. 2005. "From Disparity to Difference: How Race-Specific Medicines May Undermine Policies to Address Inequalities in Health Care." *Southern California Interdisciplinary Law Journal* 15: 105.

———. 2006. "Genes, Race, and Population: Avoiding a Collision of Categories." *American Journal of Public Health* 96(11): 1965–1970.

———. 2009a. "Race, Genes, and Justice: A Call to Reform the Presentation of Forensic DNA Evidence in Criminal Trials." *Brooklyn Law Review* 74(2): 325–375.

———. 2009b. "Race No Longer Relevant in DNA Trial Evidence." *Criminal Justice* 24: 39–41.

———. 2013. *Race in a Bottle: The Story of BiDil and Racialized Medicine in a Post-Genomic Age.* New York: Columbia University Press.

Kalinowski, S. T. 2011. "The Computer Program STRUCTURE Does Not Reliably Identify the Main Genetic Clusters within Species: Simulations and Implications for Human Population Structure." *Heredity* 106(4): 625–632.

Kalleberg, Arne L., and Larry J. Griffin. 1980. "Class, Occupation, and Inequality in Job Rewards." *American Journal of Sociology* 85(4): 731–768.

Kapferer, Bruce. 1988. *Legends of People, Myths of State: Violence, Intolerance, and Political Culture in Sri Lanka and Australia.* Washington, DC: Smithsonian Institution Press.

Kaplan, Benjamin J. 2007. *Divided by Faith: Religious Conflict and the Practice of Toleration in Early Modern Europe.* Cambridge, MA: Harvard University Press.

Kaplan, Jonathan Michael, and Rasmus Grønfeldt Winther. 2012. "Prisoners of Abstraction? The Theory and Measure of Genetic Variation, and the Very Concept of 'Race.'" *Biological Theory* 1–12.

Karabel, Jerome. 2005. *The Chosen: The Hidden History of Admission and Exclusion at Harvard, Yale, and Princeton.* Boston: Houghton Mifflin.

Kashyap, Ridhi, and Valerie A. Lewis. 2013. "British Muslim Youth and Religious Fundamentalism: A Quantitative Investigation." *Ethnic and Racial Studies* 36: 2117–2140.

Kastoryano, Riva. 1999. "Muslim Diaspora(s) in Western Europe." *South Atlantic Quarterly* 98(1–2): 191–202.

Kaufman, Jay S., and Richard S. Cooper. 2001. "Commentary: Considerations for Use of Racial/Ethnic Classification in Etiologic Research." *American Journal of Epidemiology* 154(4): 291–298.

Kaufman, Jay S., Richard S. Cooper, and Daniel L. McGee. 1997. "Socioeconomic Status and Health in Blacks and Whites: The Problem of Residual Confounding and the Resiliency of Race." *Epidemiology* 8(6): 621–628.

Kaye, D. H., and Michael E. Smith. 2003. "DNA Identification Databases: Legality, Legitimacy, and the Case for Population-Wide Coverage." *Wisconsin Law Review* 413.

Kearney, Michael. 1991. "Borders and Boundaries of State and Self at the End of Empire." *Journal of Historical Sociology* 4(1): 52–74.

———. 1995. "The Local and the Global: The Anthropology of Globalization and Transnationalism." *Annual Review of Anthropology* 24: 547–565.

Kemp, Arthur. 2010. *Four Flags: The Indigenous People of Britain.* Deeside, UK: Excalibur Books.

Kent, Michael. 2013. "The Importance of Being Uros: Indigenous Identity Politics in the Genomic Age." *Social Studies of Science* 43(4): 534–556.

Kim-Cohen, J., et al. 2006. "MAOA, Maltreatment, and Gene–Environment Interaction Predicting Children's Mental Health: New Evidence and a Meta-Analysis." *Molecular Psychiatry* 11(10): 903–913.

Kimmelman, Jonathan. 2000. "Risking Ethical Insolvency: A Survey of Trends in Criminal DNA Databanking." *Journal of Law, Medicine & Ethics* 28(3): 209–221.

King, Charles, and Neil J. Melvin. 1998. *Nations Abroad: Diaspora Politics and International Relations in the Former Soviet Union.* Boulder, CO: Westview Press.

King, Charles, and Neil J. Melvin. 1999. "Diaspora Politics." *International Security* 24(3): 108–124.

Koenig, Barbara A., Sandra Soo-Jin Lee, and Sarah S. Richardson. 2008. "Introduction: Race and Genetics in a Genomic Age." Pp. 1–20 in Barbara A. Koenig, Sandra Soo-Jin Lee, and Sarah S. Richardson, eds., *Revisiting Race in a Genomic Age.* New Brunswick, NJ: Rutgers University Press.

Koenig, Matthias. 2008. "Institutional Change in the World Polity: International Human Rights and the Construction of Collective Identities." *International Sociology* 23(1): 95–114.

———. 2010. "Gerichte als Arenen religiöser Anerkennungskämpfe." Pp. 144–164 in Astrid Reuter and Hans G. Kippenberg, eds., *Religionskonflikte im Verfassungsstaat.* Göttingen: Vandenhoeck & Ruprecht.

———. 2011. "Jenseits des Säkularisierungsparadigmas." *Kölner Zeitschrift für Soziologie une Sozialpsychologie* 63(4): 649–674.

———. Forthcoming. "Governance of Religious Diversity at European Court of Human Rights." In Jane Bolden and Will Kymlicka, eds., *International Approaches to the Governance of Ethnic Diversity.* Oxford: Oxford University Press.

Kohn, Hans. 1940. "The Genesis and Character of English Nationalism." *Journal of the History of Ideas* 1(1): 69–94.

Kolstø, Paul. 1995. *Russians in the Former Soviet Republics*. London: Hurst.

Koops, Bert-Jaap, and Maurice Schellekens. 2008. "Forensic DNA Phenotyping: Regulatory Issues." *Columbia Science and Technology Law Review* 9: 158–202.

Koppelman, Andrew. 2004. "The Fluidity of Neutrality." *Review of Politics* 66(4): 633–648.

Korzeniewicz, Roberto Patricio and Timothy Patrick Moran. 2009. *Unveiling Inequality: A World-Historical Perspective*. New York: Russell Sage Foundation.

Kraft, Peter, and David J. Hunter. 2009. "Genetic Risk Prediction—Are We There Yet?" *New England Journal of Medicine* 360(17): 1701–1703.

Kristof, Nicholas. 2003. "Is Race Real?" *New York Times,* July 11. Retrieved October 30, 2013. http://www.nytimes.com/2003/07/11/opinion/is-race-real .html.

Kurien, Prema. 1998. "Becoming American by Becoming Hindu: Indian Americans Take Their Place at the Multicultural Table." Pp. 37–71 in Stephen R. Warner and Judith G. Wittner, eds., *Gatherings in Diaspora*. Philadelphia: Temple University Press.

Kymlicka, Will. 1995. *Multicultural Citizenship: A Liberal Theory of Minority Rights*. Oxford: Oxford University Press.

Laitin, David D. 1995. "Marginality: A Microperspective." *Rationality and Society* 7(1): 31–57.

Lamont, Michèle. 2009. "Responses to Racism, Health, and Social Inclusion as a Dimension of Successful Societies." Pp. 151–168 in Peter A. Hall and Michèle Lamont, eds., *Successful Societies: How Institutions and Culture Affect Health*. New York: Cambridge University Press.

Lamont, Michèle, Stefan Beljean, and Matthew Clair. 2014. "What Is Missing? Cultural Processes and Causal Pathways to Inequality." *Socio-Economic Review* 12: 573–608.

Lamont, Michèle, and Nissim Mizrachi. 2012. "Ordinary People Doing Extraordinary Things: Responses to Stigmatization in Comparative Perspective." *Ethnic and Racial Studies* 35(3): 365–381.

Landa, Janet T. 1981. "A Theory of the Ethnically Homogeneous Middleman Group: An Institutional Alternative to Contract Law." *Journal of Legal Studies* 10(2): 349–362.

Lapidus, Ira M. 2001. "Between Universalism and Particularism: The Historical Bases of Muslim Communal, National, and Global Identities." *Global Networks: A Journal of Transnational Affairs* 1(1): 37–55.

Lareau, Annette. 2003. *Unequal Childhoods: Class, Race, and Family Life*. Berkeley: University of California Press.

Larsen, Christian Albrekt. 2011. "Ethnic Heterogeneity and Public Support for Welfare: Is the American Experience Replicated in Britain, Sweden and Denmark?" *Scandinavian Political Studies* 34(4): 332–353.

Laurence, Jonathan. 2012. *The Emancipation of Europe's Muslims.* Princeton, NJ: Princeton University Press.

Lea, Rod, and Geoffrey Chambers. 2007. "Monoamine Oxidase, Addiction, and the 'Warrior' Gene Hypothesis." *New Zealand Medical Journal* 120(1250). Retrieved November 3, 2013. http://journal.nzma.org.nz/journal/120-1250/2441/.

Lee, Catherine, and John Skrentny. 2010. "Race Categorization and the Regulation of Business and Science." *Law & Society Review* 44: 617–650.

Lee, Sandra Soo-Jin, Joanna Mountain, and Barbara A. Koenig. 2001. "The Meanings of Race in the New Genomics: Implications for Health Disparities Research" *Yale Journal of Health Policy, Law, and Ethics* 1: 33–75.

Lehmann, Hartmut. 1982. "Pietism and Nationalism: The Relationship between Protestant Revivalism and National Renewal in Nineteenth-Century Germany." *Church History* 51(1): 39–53.

Leustean, Lucian N. 2008. "Orthodoxy and Political Myths in Balkan National Identities." *National Identities* 10(4): 421.

Levy, Marion. 1966. *Modernization and the Structure of Society.* Princeton, NJ: Princeton University Press.

Lewontin, Richard D. 1972. "The Apportionment of Human Diversity." Evolutionary Biology 6: 381–398.

Li, Chumei. 2011. "Personalized Medicine—The Promised Land: Are We There Yet?" *Clinical Genetics* 79(5): 403–412.

Lichterman, Paul. 2008. "Religion and the Construction of Civic Identity." *American Sociological Review* 73(1): 83–104.

Lie, John. 1995. "From International Migration to Transnational Diaspora." *Contemporary Sociology* 24(4): 303–306.

Lin, Ken-Hou, and Donald Tomaskovic-Devey. 2013. "Financialization and U.S. Income Inequality, 1970–2008." *American Journal of Sociology* 118(5): 1284–1329.

Livingstone, Frank B. 1962. "On the Non-existence of Human Races." *Current Anthropology* 3(3): 279–281.

Logan, John, and Brian Stults. 2011. "The Persistence of Segregation in the Metropolis: New Findings from the 2010 Census." Census Brief prepared for Project US2010. Retrieved August 3, 2013. http://www.s4.brown.edu/us2010.

Lovell, Terry. 2000. "Thinking Feminism with and against Bourdieu." *Feminist Theory* 1(1): 11–32.

Loveman, Mara. 2005. "The Modern State and the Primitive Accumulation of Symbolic Power." *American Journal of Sociology* 110: 1651–1683.

Luhmann, Niklas. 1977. "Differentiation of Society." *Canadian Journal of Sociology / Cahiers canadiens de sociologie* 2(1): 29–53.

Lynch, Michael. 2008. *Truth Machine: The Contentious History of DNA Fingerprinting.* Chicago: University of Chicago Press.

Madeley, John. 2003. "A Framework for the Comparative Analysis of Church-State Relations in Europe." *West European Politics* 26(1): 23–50.

Mandelbaum, Michael, ed. 2000. *The New European Diasporas: National Minorities and Conflict in Eastern Europe*. New York: Council on Foreign Relations Press.

Mann, Michael. 1997. "Has Globalization Ended the Rise and Rise of the Nation-State?" *Review of International Political Economy* 4(3): 472–496.

———. 1999. "The History of All Previous Society Is the History of Durable Dichotomies." *Contemporary Sociology* 28(1): 29–30.

———. 2005. *The Dark Side of Democracy: Explaining Ethnic Cleansing*. Cambridge, UK: Cambridge University Press.

Marienstras, Richard. 1989. "On the Notion of Diaspora." Pp. 119–125 in Gérard Chaliand, ed., *Minority Peoples in the Age of Nation-States*. London: Pluto.

Marsh, Robert. 2008. "Convergence in Relation to Level of Societal Development." *Sociological Quarterly* 49: 797–824.

Marshall, Thomas H. 1950. *Citizenship and Social Class, and Other Essays*. Cambridge, UK: Cambridge University Press.

Martin, David. 2005. *On Secularization: Towards a Revised General Theory*. Ashgate, UK: Aldershot.

Martinelli, Alberto. 2005. *Global Modernization: Rethinking the Project of Modernity*. London: Sage.

Massey, Douglas S. 2002. "A Brief History of Human Society: The Origin and Role of Emotion in Social Life. 2001 Presidential Address." *American Sociological Review* 67(1): 1–29.

———. 2007. *Categorically Unequal: The American Stratification System*. New York: Russell Sage Foundation.

Massey, Douglas S., and Nancy A. Denton. 1993. *American Apartheid: Segregation and the Making of the Underclass*. Cambridge, MA: Harvard University Press.

Mauer, Marc. 2006. *Race to Incarcerate.*, 2nd ed. New York: New Press.

May, Stephen. 2001. *Language and Minority Rights: Ethnicity, Nationalism, and the Politics of Language*. New York: Longman.

Mayr, Ernst. 1970. *Populations, Species, and Evolution*. Cambridge, MA: Harvard University Press.

_____. 1982. *The Growth of Biological Thought*. Cambridge, MA: Belknap.

M'charek, Amade. 2008. "Contrasts and Comparisons: Three Practices of Forensic Investigation." *Comparative Sociology* 7(3): 387–412.

McPherson, Miller, Lynn Smith-Lovin, and James M. Cook. 2001. "Birds of a Feather: Homophily in Social Networks." *Annual Review of Sociology* 27(1): 415–444.

Meloni, Maurizio. 2014. "Biology without Biologism: Social Theory in a Postgenomic Age." *Sociology* 48(4): 731–746.

Merle, Maud, Marinette Matthey, Cristina Bonsignori, and Rosita Fibbi. 2010. "De la langue d'origine à la langue héritée: Le cas des familles espagnoles à Bâle et à Genéve." *Travaux neuchâtelois de linguistique*, no. 52: 9–28.

Meyer, John. 1987. "The World Polity and the Authority of the Nation-State." Pp. 41–70 in George M. Thomas, John W. Meyer, and Francisco O. Ramirez, eds.,

Institutional Structure: Constituting State, Society, and the Individual. Newbury Park, CA: Sage.

Milanovic, Branko. 2014. "The Return of 'Patrimonial Capitalism': Review of Thomas Piketty's *Capital in the Twenty-First Century.*" *Journal of Economic Literature* 52(2): 519–34.

Mills, Charles W. 1998 "'But What Are You Really?' The Metaphysics of Race." Pp. 41–66 in *Blackness Visible: Essays on Philosophy and Race.* Ithaca, NY: Cornell University Press.

Morawska, Ewa. 2001. "Immigrants, Transnationalism, and Ethnicization: A Comparison of This Great Wave and the Last." Pp. 175–212 in Gary Gerstle and John Mollenkopf, eds., *E Pluribus Unum? Contemporary and Historical Perspectives on Immigrant Political Incorporation.* New York: Russell Sage.

Morgenstern, Hal. 1997. "Defining and Explaining Race Effects." *Epidemiology* 8(6): 609–611.

Morning, Ann. 2011. *The Nature of Race: How Scientists Think and Teach about Human Difference.* Berkeley: University of California Press.

Nash, Catherine. 2004. "Genetic Kinship." *Cultural Studies* 18: 1–33.

———. 2008. *Of Irish Descent: Origin Stories, Genealogy, and the Politics of Belonging.* Syracuse, NY: Syracuse University Press.

———. 2012. "Genetics, Race, and Relatedness: Human Mobility and Human Diversity in the Genographic Project." *Annals of the Association of American Geographers* 102(3): 667–684.

———. 2013. "Genome Geographies: Mapping National Ancestry and Diversity in Human Population Genetics." *Transactions of the Institute of British Geographers* 38(2): 193–206.

National DNA Strategy Board. N.d. "National DNA Database Annual Report, 2011–12." Retrieved October 18, 2013. https://www.gov.uk/government/uploads/system/uploads/attachment_data/file/200407/NDNAD_Annual_Report_2011-12.pdf.

Nature Genetics. 2000. "Editorial: Census, Race and Science." *Nature Genetics* 24: 97–98.

———. 2001. "Genes, Drugs and Race." *Nature Genetics* 29: 239–240.

Navon, Daniel, and Gil Eyal. 2014. "Looping Genomes: Diagnostic Expansion and the Genetic Makeup of the Autism Population." Unpublished manuscript.

Neckerman, Kathryn M., and Florencia Torche. 2007. "Inequality: Causes and Consequences." *Annual Review of Sociology* 33(1): 335–357.

Nelson, Alondra. 2008a. "Bio Science: Genetic Genealogy Testing and the Pursuit of African Ancestry." *Social Studies of Science* 38(5): 759–783.

———. 2008b. "The Factness of Diaspora: The Social Sources of Genetic Genealogy." Pp. 253–270 in Barbara A. Koenig, Sandra Soo-Jin Lee, and Sarah S. Richardson, eds., *Revisiting Race in a Genomic Age.* Rutgers Series in Medical Anthropology. New Brunswick, NJ: Rutgers University Press.

Newsome, Melba. 2007. "A New DNA Test Can ID a Suspect's Race, But Police Won't Touch It." *Wired, December 20.* Retrieved October 21, 2013. http://archive.wired.com/politics/law/magazine/16-01/ps_dna.

Ng, Pauline C., Q. Zhao, S. Levy, R. L. Strausberg, and J. C. Venter. 2008. "Individual Genomes Instead of Race for Personalized Medicine." *Clinical Pharmacology and Therapeutics* 84(3): 306–309.

Nissen, Steven. 2011. "Pharmacogenomics and Clopidogrel: Irrational Exuberance?" *JAMA: The Journal of the American Medical Association* 306(24): 2727–2728.

Noah, Timothy. 2012. *The Great Divergence: America's Growing Inequality Crisis and What We Can Do about It.* New York: Bloomsbury.

Noiriel, Gérard. 1997. "Représentation nationale et catégories sociales: L'exemple des réfugiés politiques." *Genèses*, no. 26: 25–54.

Novas, Carlos, and Nikolas Rose. 2000. "Genetic Risk and the Birth of the Somatic Individual." *Economy and Society* 29(4): 485–513.

O'Leary, Brendan. 1998. "Ernest Gellner's Diagnoses of Nationalism: A Critical Overview, or, What Is Living and What Is Dead in Ernest Gellner's Philosophy of Nationalism?" Pp. 40–88 in John A. Hall, ed., *The State of the Nation: Ernest Gellner and the Theory of Nationalism.* Cambridge, UK: Cambridge University Press.

Omi, Michael. 2010. "'Slippin' into Darkness': The (Re)Biologization of Race." *Journal of Asian American Studies* 13(3): 343–358.

Omi, Michael, and Howard Winant. 1994. *Racial Formation in the United States: From the 1960s to the 1990s.* New York: Routledge.

Orfield, Gary, and Chungmei Lee. 2006. *Racial Transformation and the Changing Nature of Segregation.* Cambridge, MA: Civil Rights Project at Harvard University.

Ossorio, Pilar N. 2006. "About Face: Forensic Genetic Testing for Race and Visible Traits." *Journal of Law, Medicine & Ethics* 34(2): 277–292.

Ossorio, Pilar, and Troy Duster. 2005. "Race and Genetics: Controversies in Biomedical, Behavioral, and Forensic Sciences." *American Psychologist* 60(1): 115–128.

Pager, Devah. 2008. *Marked: Race, Crime, and Finding Work in an Era of Mass Incarceration.* Chicago: University of Chicago Press.

Pager, Devah, and Hana Shepherd. 2008. "The Sociology of Discrimination: Racial Discrimination in Employment, Housing, Credit, and Consumer Markets." *Annual Review of Sociology* 34(1): 181–209.

Pálsson, Gisli. 2008. "Genomic Anthropology: Coming in from the Cold?" *Current Anthropology* 49: 545–568.

Panofsky, Aaron. 2014. *Misbehaving Science: Controversy and the Development of Behavior Genetics.* Chicago: University of Chicago Press.

Parekh, Bhikhu. 1993. "Some Reflections on the Indian Diaspora." *Journal of Contemporary Thought* 3: 105–151.

———. 2000. *Rethinking Multiculturalism: Cultural Diversity and Political Theory.* Cambridge, MA: Harvard University Press.

Parsons, Talcott. 1965. "Full Citizenship for the Negro American? A Sociological Problem." Pp. 709–754 in Talcott Parsons and Kenneth B. Clark, eds., *The Negro American.* Boston: Houghton Mifflin.

———. 1966. *The Evolution of Societies.* Englewood Cliffs, NJ: Prentice-Hall.

Patten, Alan. 2006. "Who Should Have Official Language Rights?" *Supreme Court Law Review* 31(2): 101–115.

Patten, Alan, and Will Kymlicka. 2003. "Introduction: Language Rights and Political Theory. Contexts, Issues, and Approaches." Pp. 1–51 in Will Kymlicka and Alan Patten, eds., *Language Rights and Political Theory*. Oxford: Oxford University Press.

Patterson, Tiffany R., and Robin D. G. Kelley. 2000. "Unfinished Migrations: Reflections on the African Diaspora and the Making of the Modern World." *African Studies Review* 43(1): 11–45.

Pearson, Helen. 2006. "Human Genome More Variable than Previously Thought." *Nature News*, November 22. Retrieved April 22, 2014. http://www.nature.com/news/2006/061120/full/news061120-9.html.

Pelham, Nicolas, and Max Rodenbeck. 2009. "Which Way for Hamas?" *New York Review*, November 5.

Personalized Medicine Coalition. 2014. "The Case for Personalized Medicine." Retrieved July 7, 2014. http://www.personalizedmedicinecoalition.org/Userfiles/PMC-Corporate/file/pmc_the_case_for_personalized_medicine.pdf.

Petersen, Trond. 2006. "Motive and Cognition: Conscious and Unconscious Processes in Employment Discrimination." Pp. 225–248 in Jon Elster et al., eds., *Understanding Choice, Explaining Behaviour: Essays in Honour of Ole-Jørgen Skog*. Oslo: Oslo Academic Press.

Petersen, Trond, and Laurie A. Morgan. 1995. "Separate and Unequal: Occupation-Establishment Sex Segregation and the Gender Wage Gap." *American Journal of Sociology* 101(2): 329–365.

Petersen, Trond, and Ishak Saporta. 2004. "The Opportunity Structure for Discrimination." *American Journal of Sociology* 109(4): 852–901.

Pettigrew, Thomas F. 1979. "Racial Change and Social Policy." *Annals of the American Academy of Political and Social Science* 441: 114–131.

Pettit, Becky. 2012. *Invisible Men: Mass Incarceration and the Myth of Black Progress*. New York: Russell Sage Foundation.

Pettit, Becky, and Bruce Western. 2004. "Mass Imprisonment and the Life Course: Race and Class Inequality in U.S. Incarceration." *American Sociological Review* 69(2): 151–169.

Pew Hispanic Center. 2006. "Modes of Entry for the Unauthorized Migrant Population." May 22. Retrieved December 15, 2013. http://pewhispanic.org/files/factsheets/19.pdf.

Phelan, Jo C., Bruce G. Link, and Naumi M. Feldman. 2013. "The Genomic Revolution and Beliefs about Essential Racial Differences: A Backdoor to Eugenics?" *American Sociological Review* 78(2): 167–191.

Piketty, Thomas. 2014. *Capital in the Twenty-First Century*. Cambridge, MA: Belknap Press of Harvard University Press.

Plann, Susan. 1997. *A Silent Minority: Deaf Education in Spain, 1550–1835*. Berkeley: University of California Press.

Portes, Alejandro, and Min Zhou. 1993. "The New Second Generation: Segmented Assimilation and Its Variants." *Annals of the American Academy of Political and Social Science* 530(1): 74–96.

Pritchett, Lant. 2006. *Let Their People Come: Breaking the Gridlock on Global Labor Mobility.* Washington, DC: Center for Global Development. Available at http://www.cgdev.org/publication/9781933286105-let-their-people-come-breaking-gridlock-global-labor-mobility.

Proctor, Robert. 1988. "From Anthropologie to Rassenkunde in the German Anthropological Tradition." Pp. 138–179 in George Stocking, ed., *Bones, Bodies, and Behavior.* Madison: University of Wisconsin Press.

Provine, William B. 1986. "Geneticists and Race." *American Zoologist* 26(3): 857–888.

Rabinow, Paul. 1992. "Artificiality and Enlightenment: From Sociobiology to Biosociality." Pp. 234–252 in Jonathan Crary and Sanford Kwinter, eds., *Incorporations.* New York: Bradbury Tamblyn and Boorne.

Rawls, John. 1993. *Political Liberalism.* New York: Columbia University Press.

Reardon, Jenny. 2005. *Race to the Finish: Identity and Governance in an Age of Genomics.* Princeton, NJ: Princeton University Press.

Reich, Rob. 2002. *Bridging Liberalism and Multiculturalism in American Education.* Chicago: University of Chicago Press.

Relman, Arnold. 2012. "A Coming Medical Revolution?" *New York Review of Books,* October 25.

Renan, Ernest. (1882) 1996. "What Is a Nation?" Pp. 42–55 in Geoff Eley and Ronald Grigor Suny, eds., *Becoming National.* New York: Oxford University Press.

Reskin, Barbara F. 2000. "The Proximate Causes of Employment Discrimination." *Contemporary Sociology* 29(2): 319–328.

Rice, Eugene F. 1970. *The Foundations of Early Modern Europe, 1460–1559.* New York: Norton.

Ridgeway, Cecilia L. 2011. *Framed by Gender: How Gender Inequality Persists in the Modern World.* New York: Oxford University Press.

Risch, Neil, Esteban Burchard, Elad Ziv, and Hua Tang. 2002. "Categorization of Humans in Biomedical Research: Genes, Race, and Disease." *Genome Biology* 3(7): 1–12.

Robbins, Bruce. 1998. "Introduction Part I: Actually Existing Cosmopolitanism." Pp. 1–19 in Pheng Cheah and Bruce Robbins, eds., *Cosmopolitics: Thinking and Feeling beyond the Nation.* Minneapolis: University of Minnesota Press.

Roberts, Dorothy. 2011. "Collateral Consequences, Genetic Surveillance and the New Biopolitics of Race." *Howard Law Journal* 54: 567–586.

Rose, Nikolas. 2013. "The Human Sciences in a Biological Age." *Theory, Culture & Society* 30(1): 3–34.

Rosenberg, Noah A., et al. 2005. "Clines, Clusters, and the Effect of Study Design on the Inference of Human Population Structure." *PLoS Genetics* 1(6): e70.

Rothenberg, Karen, and Alice Wang. 2006. "The Scarlet Gene: Behavioral Genetics, Criminal Law, and Racial and Ethnic Stigma." *Law and Contemporary Problems* 69(1): 343–366.

Rothschild, Joseph. 1981. *Ethnopolitics, a Conceptual Framework.* New York: Columbia University Press.

Roy, Oliver. 2004. *Globalized Islam: The Search for a New Ummah*. New York: Columbia University Press.

Royal, Charmaine D., et al. 2010. "Inferring Genetic Ancestry: Opportunities, Challenges, and Implications." *American Journal of Human Genetics* 86(5): 661–673.

Ruane, Joseph, and Jennifer Todd. 2010. "Ethnicity and Religion: Redefining the Research Agenda." *Ethnopolitics* 9(1): 1–8.

Saez, Emmanuel. 2013. "Striking It Richer: The Evolution of Top Incomes in the United States (Updated with 2012 Preliminary Estimates)." Retrieved July 3, 2014. eml.berkeley.edu/~saez/saez-UStopincomes-2012.pdf.

Safran, William. 1991. "Diasporas in Modern Societies: Myths of Homeland and Return." *Diaspora* 1(1): 83–99.

———. 2008. "Language, Ethnicity and Religion: A Complex and Persistent Linkage." *Nations and Nationalism* 14(1): 171–190.

Saint-Blancat, C. 2002. "Islam in Diaspora: Between Reterritorialization and Extraterritoriality." *International Journal of Urban and Regional Research* 26(1): 138–151.

Sampson, Robert J., Patrick Sharkey, and Stephen W. Raudenbush. 2008. "Durable Effects of Concentrated Disadvantage on Verbal Ability among African-American Children." *Proceedings of the National Academy of Sciences* 105(3): 845–852.

Sanjek, Roger. 1996. "The Enduring Inequalities of Race." Pp. 1–17 in Steven Gregory and Roger Sanjek, eds., *Race*. New Brunswick, NJ: Rutgers University Press.

Sankar, Pamela. 2010. "Forensic DNA Prototyping: Reinforcing Race in Law Enforcement." Pp. 49–61 in I. Whitmarsh and D. S. Jones, eds., *What's the Use of Race? Modern Governance and the Biology of Difference*. Cambridge, MA: MIT Press.

Santos, Ricardo Ventura, and Marcos Chor Maio. 2004. "Race, Genomics, Identities and Politics in Contemporary Brazil." *Critique of Anthropology* 24(4): 347–378.

Santos, Ricardo Ventura, et al. 2009. "Color, Race, and Genomic Ancestry in Brazil: Dialogues between Anthropology and Genetics." *Current Anthropology* 50: 787–819.

Saperstein, Aliya, and Andrew M. Penner. 2012. "Racial Fluidity and Inequality in the United States." *American Journal of Sociology* 118(3): 676–727.

Sartori, Giovanni. 1970. "Concept Misformation in Comparative Politics." *American Political Science Review* 64(4): 1033–1053.

Saunders, Robert A. 2008. "The Ummah as Nation: A Reappraisal in the Wake of the Cartoons Affair." *Nations and Nationalism* 14(2): 303–321.

Schama, Simon. 1988. *The Embarrassment of Riches: An Interpretation of Dutch Culture in the Golden Age*. Berkeley: University of California Press.

Schmidt, Volker H. 2010. "Modernity and Diversity: Reflections on the Controversy between Modernization Theory and Multiple Modernists." *Social Science Information* 49(4): 511–538.

————. 2011. "How Unique Is East Asian Modernity?" *Asian Journal of Social Science* 39(3): 304–331.

————. 2013. "Gradual and Categorical Inequalities." Pp. 239–257 in Said Arjomand and Elisa Reis, eds., *Worlds of Difference*. London: Sage.

Schramm, Katharina. 2010. *African Homecoming: Pan-African Ideology and Contested Heritage*. Walnut Creek, CA: Left Coast Press.

————. 2012. "Genomics En Route: Ancestry, Heritage, and the Politics of Identity across the Black Atlantic." Pp. 167–192 in David Skinner, Richard Rottenburg, and Katharina Schramm, eds., *Identity Politics and the New Genetics: Re/Creating Categories of Difference and Belonging*. New York: Berghahn Books.

Schramm, Katharina, David Skinner, and Richard Rottenburg, eds. 2012. *Identity Politics and the New Genetics: Re/Creating Categories of Difference and Belonging*. New York: Berghahn Books.

Schulze Wessel, Martin, ed. 2006. *Nationalisierung der Religion und Sakralisierung der Nation im östlichen Europa*. Stuttgart: F. Steiner Verlag.

Schwartz, Robert S. 2001. "Racial Profiling in Medical Research." *New England Journal of Medicine* 344(18): 1392–1393.

Schwartz-Marín, Ernesto, and Irma Silva-Zolezzi. 2010. "'The Map of the Mexican's Genome': Overlapping National Identity, and Population Genomics." *Identity in the Information Society* 3(3): 489–514.

Science. 2011. "Around the World." *Science* 332(6037): 1488. http://www.sciencemag.org/content/332/6037/1488.2.full.pdf.

Serre, David, and Svante Pääbo. 2004. "Evidence for Gradients of Human Genetic Diversity within and among Continents." *Genome Research* 14(9): 1679–1685.

Shachar, Ayelet. 2009. *The Birthright Lottery: Citizenship and Global Inequality*. Cambridge, MA: Harvard University Press.

Sharkey, Patrick. 2013. *Stuck in Place: Urban Neighborhoods and the End of Progress toward Racial Equality*. Chicago: University of Chicago Press.

Sheffer, Gabriel. 1986. "A New Field of Study: Modern Diasporas in International Politics." Pp. 1–15 in Gabriel Sheffer, ed., *Modern Diasporas in International Politics*. London: Croom Helm.

————. 2003. *Diaspora Politics: At Home Abroad*. Cambridge, UK: Cambridge University Press.

Shepperson, George. 1966. "The African Diaspora—or the African Abroad." *African Forum* 1(2): 76–93.

Shiao, Jiannbin Lee, Thomas Bode, Amber Beyer, and Daniel Selvig. 2012. "The Genomic Challenge to the Social Construction of Race." *Sociological Theory* 30(2): 67–88.

Shields, Alexandra E., et al. 2005. "The Use of Race Variables in Genetic Studies of Complex Traits and the Goal of Reducing Health Disparities: A Transdisciplinary Perspective." *American Psychologist* 60(1): 77–103.

Shields, William and William Thompson. 2003. "Racial Identification." Paper presented at Forensic Bioinformatics Second Annual Conference, Dayton, OH,

August 29–30. Retrieved October 22, 2013. http://bioforensics.com/conference/Racial%20Identification/.

Shils, Edward. 1968. "Deference." Pp. 104–132 in John Archer Jackson, ed., *Social Stratification*. Cambridge, UK: Cambridge University Press.

Skinner, David. 2006. "Racialized Futures: Biologism and the Changing Politics of Identity." *Social Studies of Science* 36(3): 459–488.

———. 2013. "'The NDNAD Has No Ability in Itself to Be Discriminatory': Ethnicity and the Governance of the UK National DNA Database." *Sociology* 47(5): 976–992.

Skrentny, John David. 2002. *The Minority Rights Revolution*. Cambridge, MA: Belknap Press of Harvard University Press.

Small, Mario L., David J. Harding, and Michele. Lamont. 2010. "Reconsidering Culture and Poverty." *Annals of the American Academy of Political and Social Science* 629(1): 6–27.

Smart, Ninian. 1983. "Religion, Myth and Nationalism." Pp. 15–28 in Peter H. Merkl and Ninian Smart, eds., *Religion and Politics in the Modern World*. New York: New York University Press.

Smith, Anthony D. 1983. *Theories of Nationalism*. 2nd ed. New York: Holmes & Meier.

———. 1986. *The Ethnic Origins of Nations*. Oxford: Basil Blackwell.

———. 1991. *National Identity*. London: Penguin.

———. 2003. *Chosen Peoples*. Oxford: Oxford University Press.

———. 2008. *The Cultural Foundations of Nations: Hierarchy, Covenant and Republic*. Malden, MA: Blackwell.

Smith, Robert C. 2003. "Diasporic Memberships in Historical Perspective: Comparative Insights from the Mexican, Italian, and Polish Cases." *International Migration Review* 37(3): 724–759.

Snow, David A., and Richard Machalek. 1984. "The Sociology of Conversion." *Annual Review of Sociology* 167–190.

Snyder, Karrie Ann, and Adam Isaiah Green. 2008. "Revisiting the Glass Escalator: The Case of Gender Segregation in a Female Dominated Occupation." *Social Problems* 55(2): 271–299.

Sökefeld, Martin. 2006. "Mobilizing in Transnational Space: A Social Movement Approach to the Formation of Diaspora." *Global Networks* 6(3): 265–284.

Soysal, Yasemin. 1994. *Limits of Citizenship: Migrants and Postnational Membership in Europe*. Chicago: University of Chicago Press.

———. 2000. "Citizenship and Identity: Living in Diasporas in Post-War Europe?" *Ethnic and Racial Studies* 23(1): 1–15.

Spohn, Willfried. 2001. "Eisenstadt on Civilizations and Multiple Modernity." *European Journal of Social Theory* 4(4): 499–508.

———. 2003. "Multiple Modernity, Nationalism and Religion: A Global Perspective." *Current Sociology* 51: 265–286.

Stephanson, Anders. 1995. *Manifest Destiny: American Expansionism and the Empire of Right*. New York: Hill and Wang.

Stiglitz, Joseph E. 2012. *The Price of Inequality: How Today's Divided Society Endangers Our Future.* New York: Norton.

Stolzenberg, Nomi Maya. 1993. "'He Drew a Circle That Shut Me Out': Assimilation, Indoctrination, and the Paradox of Liberal Education." *Harvard Law Review* 106: 581–667.

Storrs, Debbie. 1999. "Whiteness as Stigma: Essentialist Identity Work by Mixed-Race Women." *Symbolic Interaction* 22(3): 187–212.

Sturm, Circe. 2011. *Becoming Indian: The Struggle over Cherokee Identity in the Twenty-First Century.* Santa Fe, NM: School for Advanced Research Press.

Taguieff, Pierre-André. 2001. *The Force of Prejudice: On Racism and Its Doubles.* Minneapolis: University of Minnesota Press.

Taitz, J., J. E. M. Weekers, and D. T. Mosca. 2002. "The Last Resort: Exploring the Use of DNA Testing for Family Reunification." *Health and Human Rights* 6(1): 20.

TallBear, Kimberly. 2013a. "Genomic Articulations of Indigeneity." *Social Studies of Science* 43(4): 509–533.

———. 2013b. *Native American DNA: Tribal Belonging and the False Promise of Genetic Science.* Minneapolis: University of Minnesota Press.

Tam, Tony. 1997. "Sex Segregation and Occupational Gender Inequality in the United States: Devaluation or Specialized Training?" *American Journal of Sociology* 102(6): 1652–1692.

———. 2000. "Occupational Wage Inequality and Devaluation: A Cautionary Tale of Measurement Error." *American Journal of Sociology* 105(6): 1752–1760.

Tambiah, Stanley J. 2000. "Transitional Movements, Diaspora, and Multiple Modernities." *Daedalus* 129(1): 163–194.

Tate, Sarah K., and David B Goldstein. 2004. "Will Tomorrow's Medicines Work for Everyone?" *Nature Genetics* 36(11 Suppl): S34–42.

Taylor, Charles. 2007. *A Secular Age.* Cambridge, MA: Harvard University Press.

Temple, Robert, and Norman L Stockbridge. 2007. "BiDil for Heart Failure in Black Patients: The U.S. Food and Drug Administration Perspective." *Annals of Internal Medicine* 146(1): 57–62.

Thernstrom, Stephan. 1983. "Ethnic Pluralism: The U.S. Model." Pp. 247–254 in C. Fried, ed., *Minorities: Community and Identity, Life Sciences Research Reports.* Heidelberg: Springer Berlin.

Thompson, William C. 2008. "The Potential for Error in Forensic DNA Testing." *Genewatch* 21(3–4): 5–8.

Tilly, Charles. 1975. "Reflections on the History of European State-Making." Pp. 3–83 in Charles Tilly, ed., *The Formation of National States in Western Europe.* Princeton, NJ: Princeton University Press.

———. 1984. *Big Structures, Large Processes, Huge Comparisons.* New York: Russell Sage Foundation.

———. 1996. "The State of Nationalism." *Critical Review: A Journal of Politics and Society* 10(2): 299.

———. 1998. *Durable Inequality.* Berkeley: University of California Press.

Tölölyan, Khachig. 1991. "The Nation-State and Its Others: In Lieu of a Preface." *Diaspora* 1(1): 3–7.

————. 1996. "Rethinking Diaspora(s): Stateless Power in the Transnational Moment." *Diaspora* 5(1): 3–36.

Tomaskovic-Devey, Donald. 1993. "The Gender and Race Composition of Jobs and the Male/Female, White/Black Pay Gaps." *Social Forces* 72(1): 45–76.

Torpey, John. 2000. *The Invention of the Passport: Surveillance, Citizenship and the State.* Cambridge, UK: Cambridge University Press.

————. 2010. "A (Post-)Secular Age?" *Social Research* 77(1): 269–296.

Travis, John. 2009. "Scientists Decry Isotope, DNA Testing of 'Nationality.'" *Science* 326(5949): 30–31.

Triadafilopoulos, Phil, and Thomas Faist. 2006. "Beyond Nationhood: Citizenship Politics in Germany since Unification." Paper prepared for 2006 Meeting of the Canadian Political Science Association. http://www.cpsa-acsp.ca/papers-2006/Faist-Triadafilopoulos.pdf.

Triadafilopoulos, Triadafilos. 2011. "Illiberal Means to Liberal Ends? Understanding Recent Immigrant Integration Policies in Europe." *Journal of Ethnic and Migration Studies* 37(6): 861–880.

Tsing, Anna. 2007. "Indigenous Voice." Pp. 33–67 in Marisol de la Cadena and Orin Starn, eds., *Indigenous Experience Today.* New York: Berg.

Tsuda, Takeyuki, ed. 2009. *Diasporic Homecomings: Ethnic Return Migration in Comparative Perspective.* Stanford: Stanford University Press.

Turner, Bryan S. 2011. *Religion and Modern Society.* New York: Cambridge University Press.

Tutton, Richard, Christine Hauskeller, and Steve Sturdy. 2014. "Suspect Technologies: Forensic Testing of Asylum Seekers at the UK Border." *Ethnic and Racial Studies* 37(5): 738–752.

Tuveson, Ernest Lee. 1968. *Redeemer Nation: The Idea of America's Millennial Role.* Chicago: University of Chicago Press.

Van den Berghe, Pierre L. 1967. *Race and Racism: A Comparative Perspective.* New York: Wiley.

Van der Veer, Peter. 1994. *Religious Nationalism: Hindus and Muslims in India.* Berkeley: University of California Press.

Van der Veer, Peter, and Hartmut Lehmann, eds. 1999. *Nation and Religion: Perspectives on Europe and Asia.* Princeton, NJ: Princeton University Press.

Van Parijs, Philippe. 2009. "Grab a Territory! How Equal Linguistic Dignity Can Be Reconciled with English Dominance in the European Union." Pp. 155–172 in Johanne Poirier, John Erik Fossum, and Paul Magnette, eds., *Ties That Bind: Accommodating Diversity in Canada and the European Union.* Bern: Peter Lang.

Veltman, Calvin. 1983. *Language Shift in the United States.* Berlin: Walter de Gruyter.

Vermeersch, Peter. 2005. "Does European Integration Expand Political Opportunities for Ethnic Mobilization?" Paper presented at the 46th Annual Convention of the International Studies Association, March 5, Honolulu. ISA Annual Meeting Paper Archive.

Vertovec, Steven. 2000. *The Hindu Diaspora: Comparative Patterns.* London: Routledge.

Wacquant, Loïc. 2007. "Territorial Stigmatization in the Age of Advanced Marginality." *Thesis Eleven* 91(1): 66–77.

———. 2008. *Urban Outcasts: A Comparative Sociology of Advanced Marginality.* Cambridge, UK: Polity Press.

———. 2010. "Class, Race and Hyperincarceration in Revanchist America." *Daedalus* 139(3): 74–90.

———. 2013. "Symbolic Power and Group-Making: On Pierre Bourdieu's Reframing of Class." *Journal of Classical Sociology* 13(2): 274–291.

Wagner, J. K., and K. M. Weiss. 2012. "Attitudes on DNA Ancestry Tests." *Human Genetics* 1–16.

Wagner, Jennifer K. 2013. "DNA Fingerprinting as Routine Arrest Booking Procedure Upheld as Anticipated." *Genomics Law Report*, June 10. Retrieved December 6, 2013. http://www.genomicslawreport.com/index.php/2013/06/10/dna-fingerprinting-as-routine-arrest-booking-procedure-upheld-as-anticipated/.

Wagner, Jennifer K., Jill D. Cooper, Rene Sterling, and Charmaine D. Royal. 2012. "Tilting at Windmills No Longer: A Data-Driven Discussion of DTC DNA Ancestry Tests." *Genetics in Medicine* 14(6): 586–593.

Waldinger, Roger. 1997. "Black/Immigrant Competition Re-assessed: New Evidence from Los Angeles." *Sociological Perspectives* 40(3): 365–386.

———. 2008. "Foreword." Pp. xi–xvi in Stéphane Dufoix, *Diasporas.* Berkeley: University of California Press.

Waldinger, Roger, and David Fitzgerald. 2004. "Transnationalism in Question." *American Journal of Sociology* 109(5): 1177–1195.

Walzer, Michael. 1983. *Spheres of Justice.* New York: Basic Books.

Wang, Gungwu. 1993. "Greater China and the Chinese Overseas." *China Quarterly* 136: 926–948.

———. 2000. *The Chinese Overseas: From Earthbound China to the Quest for Autonomy.* Cambridge, MA: Harvard University Press.

Warner, Stephen R. 1993. "Work in Progress: Toward a New Paradigm for the Sociological Study of Religion in the United States." *American Journal of Sociology* 98(5): 1044–1093.

Warren, Carrol A. B. 1980. "Destigmatization of Identity: From Deviant to Charismatic." *Qualitative Sociology* 3(1): 59–72.

Weber, Max. (1922) 1978. *Economy and Society.* Edited by Guenther Roth and Claus Wittich. 2 vols. Berkeley: University of California Press.

———. 1946. *From Max Weber: Essays in Sociology.* Translated and edited by Hans. H. Gerth and Charles W. Mills. New York: Oxford University Press.

———. 1958. *The Protestant Ethic and the Spirit of Capitalism.* New York: Scribner.

Weeden, Kim A., and David B. Grusky. 2012. "The Three Worlds of Inequality." *American Journal of Sociology* 117(6): 1723–1785.

Wells, Spencer. 2007. *Deep Ancestry: Inside the Genographic Project.* Washington, DC: National Geographic Society.

Werbner, Pnina. 2002. *Imagined Diasporas among Manchester Muslims.* Oxford: James Currey.

Western, Bruce. 2006. *Punishment and Inequality in America.* New York: Russell Sage.

Whitmarsh, Ian, and David S. Jones. 2010. "Governance and the Uses of Race." Pp. 1–23 in I. Whitmarsh and D. S. Jones, eds., *What's the Use of Race? Modern Governance and the Biology of Difference.* Cambridge, MA: MIT Press.

Wilkinson, Richard G., and Kate E. Pickett. 2009. "Income Inequality and Social Dysfunction." *Annual Review of Sociology* 35(1): 493–511.

Williams, Robin, and Paul Johnson. 2008. *Genetic Policing: The Use of DNA in Criminal Investigations.* Cullompton, UK: Willan.

Wilson, William J. 1987. *The Truly Disadvantaged: The Inner City, the Underclass, and Public Policy.* Chicago: University of Chicago Press.

Wimmer, Andreas. 2002. *Nationalist Exclusion and Ethnic Conflict: Shadows of Modernity.* Cambridge, UK: Cambridge University Press.

———. 2013. *Ethnic Boundary Making: Institutions, Power, Networks.* New York: Oxford University Press.

Wimmer, Andreas, and Nina Glick Schiller. 2003. "Methodological Nationalism, the Social Sciences, and the Study of Migration: An Essay in Historical Epistemology." *International Migration Review* 37(3): 576–610.

Winders, R. Bayly. 1962. "The Lebanese in West Africa." *Comparative Studies in Society and History* 4(3): 296–333.

Winker, M. A. 2004. "Measuring Race and Ethnicity: Why and How?" *Journal of the American Medical Association* 292(13): 1612–1614.

Wittrock, Bjorn. 2000. "Modernity: One, None, or Many? European Origins and Modernity as Global Condition." *Daedalus* 129(1): 31–60.

Wolff, Megan J. 2006. "The Myth of the Actuary: Life Insurance and Frederick L. Hoffman's Race Traits and Tendencies of the American Negro." *Public Health Reports* 121(1): 84–91.

Yang, Fenggang, and Helen Rose Ebaugh. 2001. "Transformations in New Immigrant Religions and Their Global Implications." *American Sociological Review* 66(2): 269–288.

Yong, Ed. 2010. "Dangerous DNA: The Truth about the Warrior Gene." *New Scientist,* April 12. Retrieved November 2, 2013. http://www.newscientist.com/article/mg20627557.300-dangerous-dna-the-truth-about-the-warrior-gene.html

Yudell, Michael. 2008. "Making Race: Biology and the Evolution of the Race Concept in 20th Century American Thought." PhD dissertation, Columbia University.

Zerubavel, Eviatar. 2012. *Ancestors and Relatives: Genealogy, Identity and Community.* Oxford: Oxford University Press.

Zolberg, Aristide. 1999. "Matters of State: Theorizing Immigration Policy." Pp. 71–93 in Charles Hirschman, Philip Kastinitz, and Josh DeWind, eds., *The Handbook of International Migration: The American Experience.* New York: Russell Sage Foundation.

Zolberg, Aristide R., and Litt Woon Long. 1999. "Why Islam Is Like Spanish: Cultural Incorporation in Europe and the United States." *Politics and Society* 27(1): 5–38.

Zubrzycki, Geneviève. 2006. *The Crosses of Auschwitz: Nationalism and Religion in Post-Communist Poland.* Chicago: University of Chicago Press.

Index